MIGRATION
RESHAPING HUMAN HISTORY

Bimalendu Bhattacharya

CONCEPT PUBLISHING COMPANY PVT. LTD.
NEW DELHI - 110 059

ISBN: 978-93-5594-175-6

First Published 2023

Published and Printed by

Concept Since 1974

Concept Publishing Company Pvt. Ltd.
A/15-16, Commercial Block, Mohan Garden
New Delhi-110059 (India)
T: +91-11-41101460
E: publishing@conceptpub.com, W: www.conceptpub.com

Cataloging in Publication--Courtesy: D.K. Agencies (P) Ltd. <docinfo@dkagencies.com>

Bhattacharya, Bimalendu, 1931- **author.**
Migration reshaping human history / Bimalendu Bhattacharya.
pages cm
Includes bibliographical references and index.
ISBN 9789355941756

1. Emigration and immigration--History. 2. India--Emigration and immigration--History.
I. Title.

LCC JV6021.B43 2023 | DDC 304.809 23

MIGRATION
RESHAPING HUMAN HISTORY

About the Author

Professor Bimalendu Bhattacharya, completed his BA and Master's in Geography from Presidency College and the University of Calcutta, before conducting his research at the London School of Economics as a Commonwealth Scholar. He has consistently pursued a career in teaching and research, having taught at many of India's premier institutions like Gauhati University (Assam), Indian Institute of Technology (Kharagpur), Presidency College, Calcutta (now University) and the University of North Bengal where he was instrumental in founding India's first Department of Geography and Applied Geography, was a Senior Professor, Head of Department and Dean of the Faculty of Science. Prof. Bhattacharya is an established Geography scholar and his publications include *Samaj Bigyaniyo Bhugol* (Social Geography in Bengali) co-authored with his late wife, Prof. Anima Bhattacharya. He is the author of *Urban Development in India Since Prehistoric Times* (1979; Revd. Edn. 2006), *Sikkim: Land and People* (1997), *Geography of a Himalayan Kingdom* (with Anima Bhattacharya and Neil Fraser, 2001), *Urbanisation, Urban Sustainability and the Future of Cities* (2010), *Geography of Deprivation: An Unfair World* (2014), *Global Urban Process: Growth of Towns and Cities* (2017), *Food: The Growing Challenge for Human Survival* (2020). His book, entitled *Agricultural Practices Sustaining Mankind* is in press.

Dedication

To Rupsha, Christoph
and
Louie

home permanently – a sprawling building which he built after the previous one was accidently gutted, – and all land and other property – with nothing else but the clothes we wore (carrying no gold or valuables for our secure passage) was a risky crossing across a border which we had not desired or dreamt.

But before my father moved with his family on the Partition of Indian Subcontinent in August 1947, I, personally, had moved to Calcutta (now Kolkata) to study in Presidency College, the pride of undivided Bengal, if not the whole undivided India, as it was considered the best seat of learning, and I was admitted a year before the of the vivisection of country had taken place. In fact, I attended classes for four days in August 1946, just before the 'Great Calcutta Killing' (communal riots) took place as a preamble to force India's partition on a communal basis. It was declared as a pre-warning to communal division by the Muslim League, then in power in undivided Bengal Province and there is no actual record about how many people on both sides of the religious demarcation – Hindus and Muslims – were brutally killed on a day declared holiday by the sitting-government, or how many women were raped, and houses burnt and looted in a 'free for all' game.

As an eyewitness, I can never forget the unspeakable brutality that unfolded on the streets as we watched the horrifying events from the balcony of our hostel where I was a boarder, beholding innocent people getting butchered by people on a simple issue of not belonging to the same religion.

I happened to stay on in Calcutta (Kolkata) from then onwards and my father with the rest of our family, lived in different places in India till retirement (and long after that). My father never agreed to declare himself or any of his family members as 'refugees' in spite of the fact that he could have had a number of benefits from the government by having a refugee status. He remained extremely stern about his status and hated the term 'refugee' as he declared – 'I was born an Indian, and I will die an Indian'. And so he did, as we, all his children have done.

Truly speaking, I feel hugely proud of my father for his unflinching loyalty to his country and his immense strength in declaring that he was a son of the Indian soil and not a 'migrant', in spite of the hardship we faced all through our lives in not having any personal property, and in my case, not even a house to call my own until my retirement. In fact, as I look back, it has taken four generations, starting from my parents, for our descendants to finally find a real foothold in the country of my father, and subsequently, what has become, our choice.

Preface

I am not a Migrant

International migration has been taking place for thousands of years. It is often self-motivated, intended for better prospects, or may be because of persecution, forcing people to seek a more peaceful life elsewhere, sometimes risking becoming as 'victims of trafficking', a situation which especially affects women and children. However, many who do not face such dire conditions, may not be migrants even though they do not live in the place of their birth. In fact, few people stay where they were born, but they cannot be designated as migrants on the background or circumstances of these individuals.

In my case, for example, the reasons that apply to many others for living elsewhere and make them migrants, do not describe my situation; so I am not a migrant in the typical sense of the term, because of the choices that have been made by me to pursue my interests and fulfil my dreams of a better life. The reasons that make me a non-migrant are simple enough.

In August 1947, the Indian subcontinent (as popularly called then) was divided into three segments consisting of independent (of British rule) West Pakistan and East Pakistan with independent (of British rule) India in the middle, keeping the two parts of Pakistan at a distance from each other with an intervening continuous landmass of 3600 miles. My father, being in government service in undivided India was, like many others in a similar position, asked for his 'option' to choose where to live and his option was for India (independent), resulting in his movement from then – East Pakistan, an integral part of Pakistan to India, where he obtained a new posting and shifted there with his family. East Pakistan is now Bangladesh, becoming an independent nation in 1971, and thus ceasing any political connection with Pakistan. In my candid opinion, this movement, involving his whole family, including myself, leaving his rural

However, looking back to the time before India was partitioned, from my conversations with family members I have gathered that our family was, perhaps, a migrant family, moving from their permanent home in Bhatpara, a part of West Bengal, as they were lured by an offer of a huge landed property as a *Jagirdar* or owner of a vast landed property where they prospered till the *Jagir* (land ownership) was confiscated by Warren Hastings, the then Governor of Bengal Presidency on flimsy grounds. Right now there are no supporting documents to support these events, as all records were gutted when the main house got burnt down in what remains a hazy past. Later, our surname also changed from the original Ghoshal to Bhatta+Acharya (Bhattacharya) at some time because our forefathers gradually turned to learning, and some of them, made a reputation as respected scholars. Since written documents have been destroyed by a fire, I can say that my status of being a non-migrant cannot be challenged.

Bimalendu Bhattacharya

Acknowledgements

I take it as my primary duty to acknowledge my immeasurable debt to my son-in-law, Neil Fraser, an Oxford scholar in Economics with a long teaching background in Edinburgh University for editing my writing with meticulous care bringing it to its present shape. Next, I owe great debt to my daughter, Dr. (Professor) Bashabi Fraser, CBE, who, in spite of having been teaching English Literature all her life, has retained a wide-ranging interest in issues relevant to life, such as the causes leading to the peril the Earth faces now with the worsening environmental situation. She has always been a serious reader of my work and her comments and advice have strengthened my arguments. At the same time, I will be failing in my responsibility if I do not mention the inspiration and help in understanding many of the moral issues connected with the planet's health status which I have gained in my debates with my granddaughter, Dr. Rupsha Fraser, a scientist lately engaged in an international project probing into effects as well as progress of the current pandemic, in an honorary capacity beside her own research and teaching responsibilities.

I am immensely grateful to the great scholars who have worked earlier in relevant fields, providing me their insight into many of the problems related to my work on migration. They have informed this study and are listed in the references.

I owe a tremendous debt to Dr. Saptarshi Mallick who has helped with the copy editing and formatting of this book with his meticulous dedication.

Further I am greatly indebted to Jayne Richards for taking a interest in the subject and the responsibility of typing up my hand-written manuscript making it ready for the press.

Bimalendu Bhattacharya

Contents

	Preface	**vii**
	Acknowledgements	**x**
	List of Tables	**xiii**
1.	**Introduction**	**1**
	I. Human and Non-Human Migration	1
	II. Scope for Mass Migration: New Migration Paths	5
	III. Migration Involving Africa	7
2.	**Themes of the Book**	**15**
	I. Human Migration More a Necessity than an Impulse	15
	II. A Brief History of Migration	20
	III. International Migration as Global Force of Development – Skills and Remittances	29
	IV. Migrants and Ethnicity	29
	V. Recent Growing International Migration	31
	VI. Source of Immigration	36
	VII. Ethnic Minority and Social Problems	38
3.	**An Analysis of Recent Migration**	**44**
	I. International Migration and the Current Trends	44
	II. Migration Flows and Migration Paths	45
	III. An Analysis of Migrants	48
4.	**Migration Leading to Slavery: Its Changing Phases**	**64**
	I. The Earliest Phase	64
	II. Slavery in the Medieval Period	67
	III. Slave Trade During the Modern Period	68

IV. Indentured Labour: Another Instance of International Mass-Migration 80
V. Cultural Impact of Indentured Labour 94

5. Theories of Migration and Development, with Special Reference to India **105**
I. Theories of International Migration and Development 105
II. International Migration in the Context of Indian Experience 121

6. Migration by Refugees **129**
I. Refugees: Victims of Political Unrest 129
II. Lack of Mutual Understanding between Host Countries and Refugees 137
III. The Plight of Bengali Hindu Refugees from East Pakistan for the Andamans, Dandakaranya and other Places 145

Appendix I **165**
Appendix II **169**
Bibliography **178**
Index **180**

List of Tables

2.1. EU + Asylum Decisions on First Instance by Applicant's Countries 27
2.2. US Population by Race and Hispanic Origin, 2000 Census 39
3.1. International Migrants, 1970-2015 45
3.2. Movement of Migrants along different Pathways According to Different Sources 47
3.3. Proportion of Female Migrants as per cent of the Total Female Migrants in Corridors of Flow 48
3.4. Migrant Workers, by Sex and Income-Level of Destination Countries, 2013 50
3.5. Ten Top Countries as Beneficiaries from Migrants' Remittances (2000-2015) 51
4.1. Indentured Indian Migration to the Caribbean 81
4.2. Daily Wages in North, Middle and South India 82
4.3. Average Annual Production of Sugar in British Colonies 84
4.4. Estimated Average in Principal Crops for Selected Years in Trinidad 86
4.5. Sugar Exports and Values, Trinidad 1831 to 1907 87
4.6. Average Annual Sugar Production in Britain's Four Most Important Sugar Colonies 88
4.7. Suicide Among Fiji Indians in the Indentured Period 90
4.8. Overseas Population in the UK, 2019 101
4.9. Total Number of International Migrants (i.e. Foreign-born Residents) in Selected Countries as per cent of Total Population 101
5.1. Immigrants as per cent of the Total Population of Western European Countries (1950-1975) 111
5.2. World Stock of Migrants, 1960-2010 115
5.3. Net Migration from Europe to America 1500-1760, by Country of Origin 116

5.4 Slaves Transported to the Americas and Europe by Destination, 1450-1870 117
6.1 Arrivals and Fatalities in the Mediterranean Sea, 2014-2017 135
6.2 Reasons Why Refugees Fled from East Bengal (East Pakistan) 1946-1970 146
6.3 Refugees in West Bengal in and outside Government Camps and Colonies (1958) 149
6.4 Statement Showing the Number of East Pakistan Displaced Persons Resettled Outside West Bengal 157

1
Introduction

Perhaps, 'bipedalism' may have taken the most important role in the evolution of human life resulting from supernovae-activities having taken place some 8 to 2.6 million years ago. According to authors recently reporting in the *Journal of Geology* of the University of Chicago about such supernovae-activities, they note that the most recent one happened 2.6 million years ago at the beginning of the Ice Age, causing a 150-fold increase in ionisation which led to increases in lightning strikes with simultaneous drop in CO_2 causing atmospheric cooling, no doubt, but the greater frequency of lightning strikes, almost 50-fold, caused devastating forest fires, particularly in East Africa, and changed the eco-system, from forests to grasslands. Such drastic change in ecosystems by the incidence of wildfires and consequent destruction of tree-cover is taken to be the reason making humans biped, so that with enhanced vision they had a greater scope of escaping predators and thus multiply in number and ultimately migrate to more inviting situations for survival.[1]

The most important consequence of bipedalism lies in the fact that it was the root of human spatial movement, initiating the earliest instances of migration, setting in mobility till today, though factors causing such movements are much more complex.

I. Human and Non-Human Migration

It is interesting to observe that apart from humans there are quite a number of non-humans who migrate on a large scale. But the fundamental difference between human and non-human migrations is that while there is no specific time, direction, or duration in human migration, it is seasonal or periodic in the case of non-humans. For example, non-humans have been migrating from time immemorial, taking different directions spurred by various reasons and generally not coming back to the place of origin. It is never time bound except being mostly seasonal, as for example, work sought by agricultural labour, which should not be considered as migration in the true sense of the term, as seasonal migrants usually return to the place of origin wherefrom they came after a season is over. In contrast, however, the migratory paths for most of the non-humans, such as birds, fish, tortoise, and the like, are generally annual, characterised by seasons, routes, or some other factors, making them more seasonal than otherwise.

Besides, the most characteristic of human migration is that the reasons for triggering human exodus from one to another location have varied over time and space, making it more complex than factors like trade, war, drastic changes in geographical setting such as environmental factors like protracted drought, or expanding desert as in Africa, Asia, and Australia.

> 'For at least 3000 years the widening deserts of Central Asia have witnessed genuine tribal migrations. Archaeological evidence indicates prehistoric movements to China, to Europe and the Fertile Crescent. Central Asian people are usual nomads. When desert expanded, these tent dwellers were organised to move as units with their herds and beasts of burden ... (These) tribes repeatedly invaded China as early as the 3rd century B.C. ... (which) stimulated the Chinese to build the Great Wall ... In the 5th century A.D., the Hüna (white Huns) invaded India via the passes of the Hindukush'.[2]

However, such tribal migration no longer takes place in the modern period, but is replaced by migration mostly by individuals though evidence of mass migration is ample, generated by factors like war, famines, as well as political factors like changes in geographical boundaries such as the emergence of new countries following the Second World War (1939-1945) changing the political map, largely of Europe, and partly of Africa, besides the emergence of new political entities in the Indian Subcontinent like, India, Pakistan and Bangladesh.

Going further into human migration over time and space induced mostly by humans themselves, migration of non-humans such as fish, tortoise, birds, reptiles, and some microorganisms like plankton is fundamentally different from human migration apart from largely being self-induced, or dependent indirectly on factors resulting from human actions adverse to life setting off mass migrations in search of safer locations, as has happened in recent years, people in millions originating from turbulent Middle East Countries as well as some strife-torn African countries seeking rehabilitation (still continuing at the time of writing this book) in European countries, risking life in travelling across the Mediterranean Sea, many of them losing life in such dangerous efforts.

This, however, is not the case for non-humans which takes place all the time irrespective of the changing human-world. One of the non-human migrations is characterised by Lunar migration in which the cycle of the moon is taken as a guiding factor in which for many of the organisms there is a correlation between their reproductive cycle and the moon-cycle. This is very much pronounced in a fish called 'smelt' or 'grunior' in California where during the full moon between March and July when tides run very high at night, these fish in thousands 'ride on to the beach' where the females burrowing into the sand discharge eggs which hatch two weeks later during the dark of the moon, and the young ones are 'washed back to the sea'. In comparison however, seasonal migration among animals, is a much more common feature. Change in temperature is a big factor, taking place at the beginning of the dry season in tropical and sub-tropical areas in response to temperature.

Migration of animals, such as fish, lobsters, crabs, prawns, and squids, includes change in their locations vertically, rising to surface water in summer but going down into deeper waters in winter, and many fish move from deep to shallow water for breeding. Similarly, seasonal migratory movement takes place with large animals like caribou and reindeer in search of food. Migratory birds, involving seasonal movements over large distances, in some cases across continents, have often roused the sentiments of poets and writers recording their movements. This happens in Asia, Europe, North America as well as South America and Africa. In India, there are many such instances where large flocks of birds come every year during winter and settle down on large water bodies where they breed and return to their places of origin, in Siberia in some instances, at the onset of summer. Besides, another type of migration is also a characteristic feature of some animal life, known as 'cycle migration'[3], the most illustrious example of which is offered by salmon fish, the young ones hatching in small fresh water streams go down into the ocean and stay there from one to three years and return as adults to the rivers where they spawned before to lay their eggs and die, travelling often 800 to 900 miles in their venture. Just the reverse takes place with the eels which when young hatch in the deeper water in mid-Atlantic and the females, according to this source, 'ascend freshwater streams' spending many years there and finally 'return to their birthplace for spawning'.

On the whole, human migration differs very largely from that of animal migration, the former by and large dominated by the quest for fresh pastures for accommodating the multiplying numbers or goaded by various other reasons and not controlled by any intention of returning to the places from where they came. This obviously makes a fundamental difference between human and non-human migration where the former is free of any obligation of returning to the places of origin while the latter seems to be tied up with a habit of going back to where they came from, thus keeping the migratory zone often quite limited in distance or defined. Besides, another very distinctive characteristic of animal migration is, it is tied up with procreation in many cases as well as often defined by a particular duration. Contrastingly, human migration is usually free of any duration-factors, not controlled by any factor like phases of moon or sun's position, is often dominated by an element of adventurism resulting from a desire of taking risk and hardships, rather, characterised by a veiled intention of exploration, making it completely different from animal migration. Thus, human migration is a chosen course of action often remaining under its control while animal-migration is a feature of their lifestyle.

Perhaps, the distinctive line between human and animal migration may be characterised as aggressive for the former but non-aggressive for the latter as the major identifying difference between them. Besides, human migration has no permanent direction of movement. It moves in any direction as demanded by the situation whereas animal migration is a defined process, taking place in same geographical or natural settings, confined (often) within a limited area, without contesting with natural limits. It is, in effect, more for maintaining preservation of the procreational process than otherwise having no clash with nature's systems. In sharp contrast, human migration is often more of a destructive nature exemplified by burning and slashing forests, clearing fields, reclaiming waterbodies, damming up rivers etc., in other words removing all so-called impediments on its way of preferred destination, ignoring natural processes, and caring least for what is obtainable as nature's bounty, thus destroying biodiversity. As pointed out by V. Gordon Childe (2003), the most evolutionary achievement of early man in getting free of environmental bondages was control of fire, achieved, presumably sometimes quite early in Pleistocene times which made it easier to reclaim land from forests, grasslands etc., and thus quickening the process of the destruction of biodiversity to the gravest peril to humankind in future.

In other words, human migration taking place, perhaps, not more than 2.6 million years ago at the most generous guess, has played a destructive role to natural process which created proper habitats for different life-systems, ultimately making the earth less and less liveable. For example, what we face today in the form of global warming and its associated catastrophes severely threatening human existence in the long run, is the creation of man and his uncompromising lust for living today regardless of what may happen tomorrow. Besides, another great shortcoming of man, in general, persisting even today is the feeling of being the superior sex to take all responsibilities themselves relegating insignificant tasks to the other sex – the females – when the latter are already burdened with responsibilities like bearing children, rearing them, cooking, and feeding the family, sewing, and mending – an endless unproductive chore. These are real handicaps, no doubt, but man could easily share many of those responsibilities, barring reproduction, and thus free half of human talent used for much more creative activities as has already been amply demonstrated in millions of instances. Looking at the general attitude of womenfolk there is no doubt that the fast destruction of biodiversity on which hinges the worsening climate change, would have been much slower had women been given a better role in controlling human activities. The time-long prejudice about women's ability should be entirely discouraged to save mankind from the superiority-complex of the menfolk to avoid impending peril which will not spare them either.*

II. Scope for Mass Migration: New Migration Paths

Until the beginning of the seventeenth century apart from conjectures there was no concrete evidence of mass migration. By this time, the writings of Ptolemy, Marco Polo and others ignited a great urge for finding a new route to India travelling west for trade which took a deep root among some Europeans, and the pioneer in this was Christopher Columbus and with the King and Queen of Spain providing the necessary funds, he proceeded on his voyage but going West returned after reaching Cuba, the Caribbean and the Central America in altogether five voyages made between 1492 and 1504 to die with an unshaken belief that those were the Oriental lands. But when Spain tried to establish its claim to the newly discovered lands, Portugal protested on the basis of its new findings off the African Coast and ultimately on the intervention of the Pope sought by both countries, a line was drawn from,

> 'Pole to Pole 370 leagues west of the Cape Verde Islands Spain was to have all non-Christian lands west of the line, and Portugal everything to the east of the line.'[5]

Meanwhile, the Spanish explorers had explored the Caribbean mainland extending their quest from Central America to the 'shoulder' of Brazil by 1500 while Portuguese navigator Vasco da Gama exploring India returned in 1499 carrying a huge cargo of spices making the trip round the southern coast of Africa. Following this there were more voyages from Portugal with another to India, and one to Brazil by Amerigo Vespucci in traversing South America, from Brazil to Patagonia establishing claim for Portugal to them in 1501 with Spain conquering Cuba, Jamaica and Puerto Rico proceeding further to Panama by 1513. But realising their mistake that America was not the Orient, they later focused more on South America in establishing a claim to its untold resources, destroyed the Inca Empire to take possession of Peru by 1536 and compelled the subjugation of the Chilean empire by 1584. In eastern South America they had established the city of Buenos Aires in 1536. On the other hand, both French and Dutch forces prevented the Portuguese gaining more foothold beyond Brazil until the 17th century.

Against this backdrop, the efforts of both English and French had been rather sluggish for a long time, the first ever from the English taking place sometime before 1497 when Bristol Merchants sent an expedition to New Found Land (then known as Brazil) to which John Cabot, an Italian employed by Henry the VII in Britain, was sent, and his son later visiting the place and discovered the Hudson Strait and Hudson Bay further inland in 1509, but Henry VIII succeeding to British throne following Henry the VII's death, lost interest in such expeditions and hence the initiative for further exploration of North America (particularly) shifted to the French who explored the coast lying between Florida to South Carolina still looking for a 'desired strait' through North America giving access to Asia. Another explorer, Verrazano 'went from the Carolina's to Nova Scotia', becoming the first European to visit New York while Jacques Cartier, another French explorer went by the St. Lawrence to Montreal in Canada.

English interest in North America was renewed during the reign of Elizabeth I (1558-1603), making herself a 'formidable sea rival of Spain', the English efforts being directed to lands further north 'out of Spanish reach', discovering Greenland, Labrador, and Baffin Island. However, the French interest renewed in exploring North America further in the early 17th century, Samuel de Champlain, the greatest of French explorers, founded Quebec in the North in 1608, explored Lake Huron and by the time of his death in 1635, the entire Great Lake system was known though there is no clear evidence who discovered the Niagara Falls. It may be interesting to observe in this connection, 'French missionaries, mostly Jesuits', joining in these explorations travelling all over the vast country going down the Mississippi to Arkansas in 1673.

Now we can turn to Russian ventures, who took deep interest in pushing across Siberia to the Pacific Coast during the 17th century and took the challenge of further quest to determine the area where Asia met

America, taking this venture from Okhotsk already established in 1638. Though the first attempt was aborted, the next one joined by the Russian Academy of Sciences finally marking a voyage undertaken by Bering and Chirikov separately in 1741, in which it was established that Bering reached the Alaskan mainland 'while the two expeditions together revealed the great north-west shoulder of America'.

The exploration of Canada at this time drew great attention and for this purpose a company called the 'Hudson Bay Company' was established and among all Anglo-Canadian explorers, the Scotsman, Alexander Mackenzie was the best, working for a small free-lance trading group engaged in search of fur provided by local natives and markets to sell.

The interests of different nations, particularly Britain, France and Spain led ultimately to the conflict of possession of chunks of this vast, empty country (America) which ultimately turned into a conflict between Britain and 13 of America's independent colonies, later known as New Hampshire, Massachusetts, Rhode Island, Connecticut, New York, New Jersey, Pennsylvania, Delaware, Maryland, Virginia, North Carolina, South Carolina, and Georgia. Beginning near Boston in Massachusetts in 1775, the American War of Independence ended in 1783 with the declaration of Independence on July 4, 1776, making the thirteen colonies the independent United States of America.

Such a development, stopping overseas control from Britain, gave the USA competitive opportunities for development where people from their own countries, like Britain, France, Germany, or Russia could play a role according to local demand as interests which naturally involved migration from those countries.

III. Migration Involving Africa

The most important fact about Africa, where bipedalism is presumed to have taken place and may thus be called the earliest human cradle, had suffered long as no other continent did from the curse of colonisation in spite of the fact that it gave birth to one of the most advanced urban civilisations (Egyptian) long before the rise of Indian Urban Civilisation (around 2500 B.C.), coming next to the earliest of all – the Mesopotamian Civilisation (around 3500 B.C.) in Tigris-Euphrates Valleys.

The history of Africa is much more complicated than any other because of its varied geographical setting. Without going into details, we can take up the period since then when political as well as human history of the continent came to be deeply affected making migration forcible. To understand this, one needs to go back to a time, around the late 14th century when the threat from the Mongols to China was ultimately cut off and the growing anarchy in Central Asia made it necessary for the Europeans to find new ways to reach the Orient. Prince Henry the Navigator of Portugal (1394-1460) encouraged explorers to move along the forbidding coast of West Africa and thus the mouth of the River Congo was discovered, and Portugal succeeded in making diplomatic relations with the Kingdom of Congo. By 1498, the Cape of Good Hope had been rounded by ships giving direct access to India while bases had been established by the Portuguese on the east coast of Africa and some adventurous ones made their way up to the Zambezi River establishing cordial relationships with local Kings/Tribal Chiefs. Meanwhile, Portuguese missionaries introducing Christianity among local people explored Ethiopia and discovered the source of the Blue Nile in 1613. However, it was West Africa which attracted most of the Europeans in the 16th and 17th centuries, who remained close to the coast and forts giving protection when slaves, gold and ivory were supplied by the tribal people. The first systematic exploration of the interior started in 1788, discovering the Niger flowing eastward through a wide delta. The Sahara was traversed by a British team in 1822 who discovered Lake Chad. They also explored Nigeria at this time visiting Kano.

The exploration of the interior of the continent by European explorers continued ceaselessly resulting in the tracing of the source of the Blue Nile from Lake Tana in 1770 reaffirming the finding made by the Portuguese 150 years before, discovering Lake Tanganyika in 1858, and Lake Victoria as the source of Nile, while the real intention behind these efforts was colonisation, giving unresistant opportunity for trading in valuable minerals in which Africa is extremely rich, and above all slaves with their increasing demand in, especially, North America getting slowly populated with people migrating from countries like Britain, France, Germany, Ireland and Italy, to name a few, requiring labour for hard work, especially in agriculture as well as domestic services. This constant supply of slaves, was largely possible through internal feuds in different African countries and the absence of power to resist without arms. The colonising countries were all Europeans and, as shown in Tables 1.1 to 1.4 (Appendix I), apart from the Union of South Africa, which was British, all others – European powers – continued their hold for a long period till Independence earned following the Second World War (1939-1945).

While Liberia appears to be the only country in the continent to have remained independent since 1847, colonisation in Africa had been one of the most aggressive factors controlling the activities of the countries involved. As Tables 1.1 to 1.4 (Appendix I) show, giving a picture of the period from 1900 to 1970, though colonisation had started much earlier in many cases, at the opening of the twentieth century Britain's share was far greater than any other country, all of them being European, the former having colonised altogether 16 countries, some of them quite large in size, such as Nigeria, Egypt, Uganda, Kenya etc., followed by France having its sway over 9 countries. In contrast, Germany, Portugal, Spain, and Italy played a much modest role. The situation remained nearly the same (Table 1.2) twenty years after in 1920, when Britain, as before, maintained control in determining the activities of almost 16 countries, large and small, followed by France, as before, exercising power on 9 countries while Portugal, Spain and Italy had much less. The situation did not alter much, even two years after the cessation of the Second World War. For instance, even in 1947, Britain held its power in about 16 countries followed closely by France, still then controlling power in 12 countries followed by Portugal, Spain, and Italy (Appendix I, Table 1.3). The picture, however, underwent a visible change by 1970, including two remarkable departures, one of them being Britain which had completely disappeared from the scene while France had vividly shrunk, remaining concentrated in an Island group besides two tiny specs of land in Somaliland while Portugal was still maintaining its hold in Angola and Mozambique, presenting a remarkable case when almost the entire continent had shaken off the political subjugation of the European colonisers.

In seeking for actual reasons for colonisation to continue in a large part of Africa for such a long time one cannot avoid the fact that Africa's internal political strife arising from various tribal chiefs' mistrust of its own people often made way for foreign intervention. Sometimes, even local military rulers paved the way for foreign interference. In this connection, one may consider the fact the Africans had very rich traditions of economic activities, almost ninety per cent of people remaining engaged in agriculture as their basic source of survival and having thus developed a rich tradition in the production of a great variety of crops.

Lying between Asia and the New World (even before the New World representing North and South Americas attracted migrants, or colonisers mostly from Europe) Africa remained attractive in the eyes of traders from Asia. It was a cordial relationship, in general, though Arab traders later on turned it sour in forcing needy Africans into slavery, especially meant for the Americas on lucrative terms in which the colonisers to the New World undoubtedly took part in giving rise to enforced one-way migration of people who though economically poor were culturally very advanced. Developing different types of songs, dances and musical instruments, their contribution reverberates even today in some of the most popular music. Besides, the continent is very rich in its mineral resources, having, as estimated over half of the world's bauxite, phosphate and manganese, and an extensive reserve of iron ore, besides gold and diamonds while more were to come out through further explorations.

As a matter of fact, all these were not known to the European colonisers then and their interest was mostly confined, till around the 16th and 17th centuries, to settling down at trading posts where they could barter with products including slaves from the interior, and their first move for systematic exploration of the interior came from,

> 'the African Association of British Scientists in 1788 under its auspices a number of explorers were sent to West Africa to explore the Niger River.'[6]

All these activities invariably expanded the scope for slave trade in the long run which turned out to be the major commodity in the unfair trade relationship built up between colonisers and the native countries involved. Before going into the various facets of this relationship we may take stock of the changing situation in another part of the world where colonisers took an entirely different role giving migration a new character with settling down in uninhabited regions left uncharted for a long time. Here the continent involved was Australia presenting a case like North America with a major difference between the two being that while in North America settlers came from different European countries to grab the vast stretches of land pushing away the few natives, or even killing indigenous populations in their urge to establish their own settlements, migration to Australia involved only British people, giving it altogether a different character in the future development of the continent.

Lying very close to south-eastern Asia, parts of Australia were known to some Asians for a long time, but its uninviting terrain never interested them for settlement and until 1700s, large scale immigration of Europeans did not take place. Extensive explorations of the continent by the Dutch ultimately led to the establishment of the first British settlement of Sydney in 1788 located on the fertile east coast leading to the emergence of habitation along the temperate-zone coastline as well as in Tasmania. Meanwhile, increasing supplies of wool from the growing flocks of sheep in Australia made a larger impact on British industry at home though the total number of populations settled amounted to about 1,50,000 even after 50 years of occupation, but rose to 4,00,000 getting a sudden spurt with the discovery of gold in 1851. This further added to the development of agriculture and pastoral activities along with the rudiments of industrial activities established since then made Australia self-sufficient in steel production by 1920 followed by the development of heavy industries following the Second World War.

> However, it is highly interesting to observe that, 'the first settlers, who arrived in New South Wales beginning in 1788 were chiefly convicts, military personnel, or government officials'.[7]

Convicts made the major source of population or immigrants till 1830 after which free immigrants along with natural increase gradually represented the major constituents of the population. Between 1946 and 1965, Australia received 23,56,569 permanent new arrivals; immigration gain was approximately 2 million – the largest 20-year increase from immigrants on record.[8] Referring to the same source, it can further be established that by 1933, the Australian people were 'essentially' dependents of British immigrants originating from Britain and Ireland consisting of people primarily from lower middle and working classes with sprinkling of immigrants from Germany, Scandinavia, Greece, Poland, Yugoslavia, and Italy. However, economic recession in the early 1930s brought about a 'cessation' of immigration and slump in birth rate. According to the1961 census, 55.6 per cent of the population resided in the 6 state capitals, 26.4 per cent in other urban centres, leaving only 17.8 per cent living in rural areas and the remaining 0.2 per cent being migratory.[9] However, a partial relaxation of the traditional immigration policy barring non-Europeans from entry into Australia partially paved the way for Asian immigrants.

Brief references to cases made above makes it necessary to define the actual meaning of migration, whether wilful/intentional or forced, involving movement from one 'country place or locality to another'.[10] However, the simple, almost unromantic explanation does not reveal the meaning in the drastic change that took place since mid-sixteenth century when migration no longer remained a voluntary process but turned in many cases into a forcible one involving capture of innocent people applying force to making them slaves or indentured labour of which the former-slaves from Africa – studied in detail gives real shudder down the spines of modern readers.

Many of the European colonial countries played an active role in enjoying the financial bounties of the slave trade, but Britain's role in this most heinous game surpasses that of all others, and started earliest from 1562 when the first 'cargo' of five hundred slaves from west Africa was transported to the Americas, 'a venture (which) so impressed Queen

Elizabeth I (that) she funded a return trip – every British monarch to George III gave his or her direct support to the trans-Atlantic slave trade'.[11]

> "The relationship between the monarchy and slavery was formalised in 1672 with King Charles II's establishment of Britain's 'slave trading – the Royal African Company'. It's no exaggeration to say that the wealth of the Royal Family, much like the wealth of the nation itself, was built on the back of slavery and related trade, investment and industry".[12]

Repeating Afua Hirsch (2018), it is further interesting to note that:

> "Within fifty years, Britain became the leading slave nation in the world, the foremost supplier of slaves for the rest of Europe, and the financial heart of the triangular slave trade. Of the 12 million slaves abducted from Africa, a conservative estimate – 40 per cent was transported on British ships. An estimated 15 per cent died on the notorious Middle passage, and millions ended up in Spanish and Portuguese colonies – four million in Brazil alone. But well over one million were put to work, and often to death, in British colonies. Britain had more profits from its slave-trading investments and extracted more wealth from the Caribbean than any other European slave-trading nation".[13]

Another side of the forcible migration is represented by indentured labour used by colonial countries among which Britain also took the leading role between 1834 and 1920, providing another glaring example of dehumanised form of migration and combined with slavery, played a significant role in affecting the composition of population in the countries involved. In this perspective, it is interesting to observe that sugar – growing in popularity for drinks like coffee, tea, chocolate, and rum – was in great demand, the consumption increasing fourfold between 1660 and 1700, and twenty times between 1663 and 1775.[14]

Thus, between 1834 and 1920, indentured labour migration took place in ever-growing numbers to British Colonies spreading from Jamaica, British Guiana, Trinidad, Mauritius, Fiji, Malaya, Queensland in Australia for the production of cane sugar to fulfil the requirement of Britain. More details in this respect will be discussed later. It may, however, be mentioned in this connection that 1.3 million Indians were taken to the sugar plantations in British colonies for replacing slaves which also will be discussed in greater details in a following chapter.[15]

No account of migration will be a complete appraisal without taking into consideration the migration of fortune-seekers from Europe to the two Americas, the most unwelcome or rather forced mass-migration induced by the political division of the Indian subcontinent, the talent migration of the modern days, and the most recent, but still continuing movement of people, branded as refugees arriving from some Sub-Saharan countries like Somalia, Eritrea, Nigeria, or from war-torn Syria and Iraq, or from Afghanistan and Pakistan displaced by politically violent movements, seeking asylum in European countries. 'More than 1.5 million persons came to Europe in 2015 looking for protection, two-thirds of them to Germany'.[16]

Internal migration, taking place all the time within a country such as India, has a great socio-economic role in shaping up regional variations in the countries involved, and hence is of significance in defining the destiny of a country.

Before concluding, one feels any account on migration cannot be complete without reference to the most gruesome case of migration involving the case of the most frightening and horrific death of 39 people, all Chinese or Vietnamese in origin very recently reported (29.10.2019) as meeting violent death trapped in refrigerated truck bringing them from Northern Ireland *via* Holyhead to Essex near London. It points to the most inhuman angle of migration amounting to 'mass murder'.

> According to the International Organisation for Migration missing migrants project, 'more than 4000 people have died or have gone missing on migratory routes around the world for each of the last five years. In 2000, 58 Chinese people were found dead in Dover in a truck … died of suffocation after the container's only air vent had been closed to lessen the chance of detection. In 2014, 35 men, women and children were discovered near to death in a container at Tilbury (England)'.[17]

NOTES

*Das, Subrata. *Desh* (a fortnightly Bengali magazine). Kolkata. 17 March, 2019, p. 65.

In another essay written by Rupali Ganguli mentions few more lady scientists who were not given Nobel Prize though beneficiaries later gave the credit for work done much earlier by those lady scientists. Noted in same issue of magazine as noted above.

'The extreme degree of masculine priority is very much evident among man-scientists and even when the women scientists proved superior in many cases got cruelly deprived of their due recognition. At least two cases may be cited here about this. For example, Susan Jocelin Bel Burnel's discovery published in 'Nature' in June 1968 of 'Pulsar' on her own was omitted from the award of Nobel Prize for this discovery which went to two of her teachers under whom she was employed but the former teachers not having any direct role in the discovery. Her comments made much later about scientific bodies, including Nobel Committee maintaining a kind of allergy in giving due recognition to women. Jocelin made this comment:

'While filling up any form one has to tick off one of the two boxes specifying one's gender. Have you ever noticed which gender comes first? The day when this order will become alphabetical, you can start thinking that our world has started to change. Not before that.'

1. Ananthanaryanan, S. *The Statesman*. Kolkata, 5 June, 2019.
2. *The Encyclopaedia Americana*. New York: Americana Corporation, Vol. 19, p. 48.
3. *Ibid.*, p. 50.
4. *The Encyclopaedia Americana*. New York: Americana Corporation, Vol. 1, p. 62.
5. *Ibid.*, p. 317.
6. *Ibid.*
7. *The Encyclopaedia Americana*. New York: Americana Corporation, Vol. 2, p. 707.
8. *Ibid.*
9. *Ibid.*, p. 709.
10. Webster's *Seventh New Collegiate Dictionary*. Calcutta: Scientific Book Agency, 1971, p. 537.
    Little, W., Fowler, H.W., and Coulson, J. *The Shorter Oxford Dictionary of Historical Principles*. Rev. and Ed. C.T. Onions. Calcutta: Oxford Clarendon Press for the Standard Literature Company Private Ltd. 3rd ed., 1959-1961, Vol. 1, p. 1249.
11. Hirsch, Afua. *Brit(ish), On Race, Identity and Belonging*. London: Vintage, 2018, p. 51.
12. *Ibid.*
13. *Ibid.*, p. 54.
14. *Ibid.*, p. 52.
15. Gubili, Krishna. *Viriah*. India and Singapore: Notion Press, 2018, Cover Page.
16. Pries, Ludger. *Refugees, Civil Society, and the State: European Experiences and Global Challenge*. UK, USA: Edward Elgar Publishing, 2018, p. 3.
17. Editorial Column and News Item, *The Statesman*. Kolkata, 28 October, 2019.

2
Themes of the Book

I. Human Migration More a Necessity than an Impulse

While bipedalism, mentioned in the Introduction, may be the most important step in human-evolutional history, setting him free from his original place of birth (east-African rift valley) and look for new destinations, making it the first step initiating the process of migration which from then onwards came to be the most defining characteristic of the human race. In spite of lack of concrete evidence in our hand, it is not difficult to imagine that the earliest people, slowly multiplying in number resulting from larger supply of food in new habitats settled down temporarily, as long as compelled to seek fresh, newer locations offering greater possibilities of survival as foragers, moved incessantly over millions of years, becoming globe-trotters left with a choice of permanent settlement – which did not happen till they started the process of food production, or in other words, agriculture.

But however, adapted to their natural environment, the ancestors of present-day human beings were not the same as we are, the *Homo sapiens*, appearing during the Pleistocene period, physically weaker than earlier or older species of human races, such as Neanderthals or Pithecanthropus (Java man) and Sinanthropes (Peking man). For better clarification it can be said that, about 1,40,000 years ago, towards the close of middle Pleistocene times, a race called Neanderthal inhabited Europe, a distinct species of humanity,

> 'specialised and adapted for living under Arctic conditions and the species became extinct when conditions passed away'.[1]

According to the latest investigations, the Neanderthal stood upright. They were technically advanced than their predecessors, contributed to human culture, possessed specialised implements, such as spearheads, distinctive tools for scraping and chopping made out of flakes. Their bodies were better equipped than the *Homo sapiens* for fighting,[2] but for *Homo sapiens* the:

> 'Compensation for this relatively poor bodily endowment has been the possession of an extensive and delicate nervous system. These permit a great variety of accurately controlled movements being adjusted exactly to the impulses received by keen organs of sense. It is only so that man has been enabled to make himself protections against climate and weather, arms and weapons of attack and defence'.[3]

Going into the evolution of the present human race it is necessary to focus in greater details about the past with emphasis on racial interactions. For instance, humans evolved in the East African rift valley some time about 2.5 million years back and some of these archaic men and women left their homeland about 2 million years ago and settled in the vast areas of North Africa, Europe, and Asia. Since they had to cope with widely differing climatic as well as environmental situations, the races gradually evolved into different types in adjustment, thus giving rise to distinct types, such as Neanderthals in cold climates of Europe and Western Asia; *Homo erectus* in the eastern regions of Asia; *Homo soloensis* in the tropics, They comprised,

> 'at least six different species of man'[4]

including the *Homo sapiens* of whom we are direct descendants, and being the only human species around for the last 10,000 years while during the span of 2 million or so years to this period all other human species became extinct. We will come back later to the factors contributing to the unique resistance of the *Homo sapiens* as against the extinction of all other human races.

According to Harari (2011), *Homo sapiens* first evolved as a distinct species of this chain of different human species sometime 'by 1,50,000 years ago in East Africa', and in around 70,000 years ago, they spread into the Arabian Peninsula from where they further 'overran the entire Eurasian landmass' which was already settled 'by other human' races. But all of them became extinct in the long run whenever they came into direct contact with the *Homo sapiens*, the last human species.*

Harari (2011) maintains that:

> 'beginning about 70,000 years ago, *Homo sapiens* started doing very special things. Around that date Sapiens bands left Africa for a second time. This time they drove the Neanderthals and other human species not only from the Middle East, but from the face of the earth. Within a remarkably short period, Sapiens reached Europe, and East Asia. About 45,000 years ago, they somehow crossed the open sea and landed in Australia – a continent hitherto untouched by humans. The period from 70,000 years ago to about 30,000 years ago witnessed the invention of boats, oil lamps, bows, and arrows and needles (essential for sewing warm clothing). The first objects that can reliably be called art date from this date … as does the first clear evidence of religion, commerce and social stratification'.[5]

However, all the human species, irrespective of their locations subsisted as hunters and gatherers, depending directly on nature or the surrounding environment, foraging both vegetation as well as non-vegetation (wild animals) food in raw form as long as fire was not discovered as a tool for cooking raw food.** Occasional use of fire started as early as 8,00,000 years ago evidences indicate, '*Homo erectus*, Neanderthals and the forefathers of the *Homo sapiens* started daily use of fire which in the long run turned into the most important medium for cooking raw food, such as 'wheat, rice, and potatoes' as well as animals, killing 'germs and parasites' infesting food till then, making it much more palatable, hygienic, easy to digest and cutting down the time needed for chewing hitherto raw food, and thus making life healthier no doubt, besides,

> 'cooking inadvertently opened the way to the jumbo brains of Neanderthals and Sapiens'.[6]

In their last movement, the *Homo sapiens* foragers arrived in the Americas some time 'in or around 14,000 B.C.' crossing the land-bridge connecting north-eastern Siberia with north-western Alaska and by then they have already been used to living in arctic conditions of northern Siberia attracted by vast resources of big game, such as mammoths providing a 'vast quantity of juicy meat, tasty fat with warm fur and valuable ivory'.[7] The global warming following the melting of ice of the last Ice Age made it possible for these foragers to travel further inland into the new continents of North and South Americas, and their descendants gradually spread and settled in the 'thick forests of the eastern United States, the swamps of the Mississippi Delta, the deserts of Mexico and the steaming jungles of Central America'. By 10,000 B.C., *Homo sapiens* had completed their footfalls down to the Southern tip of South America, meanwhile covering the thick jungles of the Amazon and spreading into the Andes.

As usual, the march of *Homo sapiens* left distinct 'trail of victims', in the continents where:

> 'within 2,000 years of the Sapiens arrival, most of these unique species were gone. According to current estimates within that short interval, North America lost thirty-four out of its fifty-seven species of large mammals. South America lost fifty out of sixty. The sabre-tooth cats, after flourishing for more than 30 million years, disappeared, and so did the giant ground sloths, the over-sized lions, native American horses, native American camels, the giant rodents, and the mammoths. Thousands of species of smaller mammals, reptiles, birds and even insects and parasites became extinct'.[8]

Quite assuredly, the intimate connection between the arrival of *Homo sapiens* and the gradual extinction of local species, representing one of the 'biggest and swiftest ecological disasters to befall the animal kingdom; cannot be ignored, affecting most severely the large, furry animals like the mammoths, resulting in the disappearance of large terrestrial mammals almost by a half at the time of agricultural revolution. This is very much evident in recent times in Madagascar where the 'elephant birds and the giant lemurs', the globe's largest primates along with 'other large animals suddenly vanished about 1500 years ago', exactly timing with the arrival of the 'first humans'.

Homo sapiens originating from East Africa spread into the Middle East, to Europe and Asia and then to Australia and the two Americas and thus presenting the first, the earliest set of international migration paths. They were still foragers feeding themselves with gathering and hunting till it changed about 10,000 years ago, when they started spending all their time,

> 'manipulating the lives of a few animals and plant species'[9]

providing them with 'more fruit, grain and meat' and thus invoking a 'revolution in human life, called the Agricultural Revolution, considered to be the most important episode in entire human history till then to be succeeded by an Industrial Revolution taking place later. However, the agricultural revolution was not a space- or time-specific process, in other words, it did not take place at one particular time or in one particular place (space). Rather, it had more been of sporadic nature in its development, such as:

> 'The transition to agriculture began around 9000 – 8500 B.C., in the hill country of South-Eastern Turkey, Western Iran and the Levant (modern Syria and Lebanon). It began slowly and in a restricted geographical area. Wheat and goats were domesticated by approximately 9000 B.C.; peas and lentils around 8000 B.C.; olive trees by 5000 B.C.; horse by 4000 B.C.; and grapevine by 3500 B.C. Some animals and plants such as camels and cashew nuts, were domesticated even later, but by 3500 B.C. the main wave of domestication was over'.[10]

However, as pointed out by Harari (2011) it was an independent process, not one of importing an idea but many locations developed around this time, such as domestication of maize and beans in Central America; potatoes and llamas in South America; rice, millet, and pigs in China; pumpkins in North America; sugarcane and bananas in New Guinea; and millet, rice, sorghum and wheat in Africa.

The impact of the Agricultural Revolution assumed almost a threatening level when, according to Harari (2011), we look at the worldwide spread of some man-made products, one of them being wheat which today covers 'about 2.5 million square kilometres of global surface' while ten thousand years ago:

> 'not more than a few million sheep, cattle, goats, boars and chicken lived in restricted Afro-Asian niches. Today the world contains about a billion sheep, a billion pigs, more than a billion cattle, and more than 25 million chickens'.[11]

However, it is evident that *Homo sapiens* was very well equipped for this change (perhaps also much more cunning than other human races) succeeding in annihilating all the other races besides taking a predator's role to many of the existing large animals posing threat to their food-stock and making its role uncontested in the living world. We are not sure if as its progeny we are expected to learn any lesson about preservation/ cooperation than tussle with natural phenomena to sustain a more peaceful existence.

II. A Brief History of Migration

The sustaining cultures of the past have been divided by archaeologists into the Stone Age – old and new, the Bronze Age and Iron Age. The old Stone Age (Palaeolithic) is defined by,

> 'living entirely on hunting, fishing and gathering wild berries, roots, slugs, and shellfish'.[12]

Obviously, provision of food made by nature restricted the number of people to survive unlike that in the New Stone Age (Neolithic) when,

> 'men control their own food-supply by cultivating plants and breeding animals'[13] resulting in multiplication of numbers.

The Bronze Age is characterised by specialist industries and the beginning of trade, both requiring workers engaged in such activities and thus withdrawing from activities related to the production of food which made it necessary to produce more foodstuffs to support those activities. Diversification of activities eventually gave rise to a section of population which needed to be fed for their services by the society while others engaged in producing food for the entire community. Ultimately, this transformed some of the settlements into urban settlements where food producing, that is agricultural activities, lost their prominence to non-agricultural activities and feeding people dependent more on food imported from outside along with imports of raw materials, such as metals or mined products to sustain the growing industries and tradeable products. This ultimately initiated the *second revolution* in human activities, the *first-one* set by the beginning of agriculture prior to this, mentioned earlier, exerting a profound effect on the multiplication of our species.

The spectacular effect of the use of working implements using bronze during the Neolithic period, replacing implements of stone developed during the 'Stone Age' had a revolutionary effect on human activities dealing with agriculture as well as other life-supporting activities, and may be considered as the greatest scientific achievements of this time differentiating Old Stone Age (Palaeolithic) from the New Stone Age (Neolithic), which makes an important watershed in human history, ultimately releasing man from the direct control of nature in supplying food and thus putting some check on migration in relentless search for newer locations. Thus, not only man came to be more settled in preferrable locations, but at the same time it heralded perhaps one of the greatest achievements of human history which is the emergence of urban centres where man equipped with talents gave rise to an increasing variety of activities enriching societies in proper exploitation of human brain. In other words, it set the stage for ushering in the most important stage of human development coterminous with human civilization.

This got greater impetus during the 'Iron Age' in Europe as well as in tropical countries where the environment was more suitable for iron's wider availability than bronze. Smelted economically, less expensive than bronze tools, and being tougher, iron tools came to be more useful in tilling soils, clearing land for agriculture as well as cutting forests, besides making better implements for war.[14]

Thus, 'Bronze Age' and 'Iron Age' together made a clear watershed between them, while the 'New Stone Age' (Neolithic) made greater transition in their cultural impact on human history, termed by V. Gordon Childe (2003) as the *Second Revolution* in their economic impact as it happened again much later during the 'Industrial Revolution' in Britain in the eighteenth century.

However explained, one cannot give up the idea that migration had remained as an essential part of life associated with people of these pre-historic dates as innumerable instances of people of different origin have been found settled at places far away from their places of origin. In many cases, they have been proved to be connected with trade, but there are many instances of travellers who took it in their stride as love for travelling, such as Marco Polo, Ibn Battuta and such like who cite similar instances besides Indian and Arabian traders settling down at different places far beyond their places of origin out of their own volition.

Nevertheless, international migration makes an extremely interesting story which, as mentioned earlier, originating from the Rift Valley of Africa some time between about 1.5 million and 5000 B.C. (involving *Homo erectus* and *Homo sapiens*).

> 'Spreading initially into Europe and later into other continents. In the ancient world, Greek colonisation and Roman expansion depended on migration, and outside Europe significant movements were also associated with the Mesopotamian, Inca, Indus, and Zhoa empires. Other significant migrations in early history include that of Vikings and of Crusaders to the Holy Land'.[15]

Besides, there has been large scale migration for all mercantile powers, such as Britain, the Dutch, Spain and France particularly encouraging settlement of their nationals including 'peasants, dissident soldiers, convicts' (as in Australia), and orphans in their colonies continuing until it was resisted by the anti-colonial movements taking place towards the end of the nineteenth century. But one of the most important patterns of migration was represented by the flow of Europeans to North America continuing from the 1850s to the Great Depression of the 1930s. The stagnant, repressive economies of Northern, Southern and Eastern Europe encouraged people to take an active role in the development of the North American economy particularly the part represented by present-day America, and the magnitude of this huge flow of people may be ascertained from the fact that,

> 'Some 12 million of these migrants landed at Ellis Island in New York harbour for immigration inspections'.[16]

Hence, international migration in the modern period is directly the product of European colonisation, giving rise to various types of outward movement of people.

> 'One was the large outward movement from Europe, first to Africa and Asia, then to the Americas, and later to Oceania. Europeans migrated, either permanently or temporarily, as sailors, soldiers, farmers, traders, priests, and administrators. Some of them had already migrated within Europe ... around half the soldiers and sailors of the Dutch East India Company in the seventeenth and eighteenth centuries were not Dutch, but 'transmigrants', mainly from poor areas of Germany'.[17]

One of the major aspects of labour migration during the late seventeenth to mid-nineteenth century constituted slavery utilised for commodity production in the plantations and mines of the New World. The slaves, belonging to both sexes, were engaged in the production of sugar, tobacco, coffee, cotton and gold, and countries like Britain and France took the leading role followed by Spain, Portugal, and the Netherlands in this exploitative process.

> 'By 1770 there were nearly 2.5 million slaves in the Americas producing a third of the total value of European commerce. The slave system was organised in the notorious 'triangular trade' ships laden with manufactured goods, such as guns or household implements, sailed from ports such as Bristol, Liverpool, Bordeaux, and Le Havre, to the coast of West Africa. There Africans were either forcibly abducted or were

> purchased from local chiefs or traders in return for the goods. Then the ships sailed to the Caribbean or the Coasts of North or South America, where the slaves were sold for cash. This was used to purchase the products of the plantations which were then brought back for sale in Europe'.[18]

The size and glaring cruelty of the slave trade, discussed in greater detail in a following chapter, is shown in the fact that, by 1850, a total of 15 million slaves had been taken to the Americas where the women as well as men were put to hard labour in the mines, plantations and households, often coming to be the victims of sexual exploitation by the owners, and the children born of such contacts remained as the personal property of the owners to be used as they wished, till slavery was abolished in 1834 in British colonies, in 1863 in Dutch colonies, in 1865 in the Southern States of the United States. The economic significance of the slave trade is clearly shown in the growth of the number of slaves which doubled in the Americas between 1800 and 1860 from 3 to 6 million with 'corresponding growth pattern in plantation agriculture in the South-Western USA, Cuba and Brazil'.[19]

The most inhuman, shameless practice of exploiting slaves taking a very important role, particularly in the extension of plantation agriculture producing consumable goods for the consumption of European markets, was gradually replaced by another process of human exploitation in the form of indentured labour, recruited often by applying force, such as from the Indian Subcontinent as the British colonial authorities did for working in the 'sugar plantations of Trinidad, British Guiana, and the Caribbean countries'. In addition, indentured labour sourced from other countries like China and Japan as well had been employed to work in plantations, mines as well as railway construction in Malaya, and about a million recruited from Japan were employed in Hawaii, the USA, Brazil, and Peru. The system involving 12 to 37 million workers between 1834 and 1941, were used in 40 countries by all the major colonial powers as they were comparatively cheaper than slave labour, and many of them later settled permanently in these places, such as in East Africa, Mauritius, the Caribbean, Fiji and elsewhere taking up land and business[20] and contributing to the population-mix through intermarriage.

Castle and Miller (2003), focusing on migration to North America and Australia taking place before 1914, find an interesting relationship between industrial development in home countries and movement of workers to America and Australia. For instance, the peak period of British migration to America was during the industrial revolution when between 1800 and

1860 'migrants representing 66 per cent of the total to the USA came from Britain and another 22 per cent from Germany'. In all, 40 million Europeans went overseas as permanent migrants settling down in North and South America and Australia. Between 1850 and 1914, the majority of those migrants came from Ireland, Italy, Spain, and Eastern Europe.

After the Second World War (1939-45), the second phase of major migration took place to satisfy the labour requirements for post war reconstruction in Europe, North America, and Australia. A large contingent of Turkish labour arrived for this purpose concentrated mainly in Germany, while labour from North African countries came to France and Belgium. During this period, about one million Britons migrated to Australia for permanent settlement.[21] This is also the period of decolonisation, many countries particularly in Asia and Africa getting rid of colonial rule earned independence, giving rise to mass migration as a consequence, the largest of which involving a few million took place in Indian Subcontinent migrating both ways from and to India and newly formed Pakistan, both preceeded and succeeded by mass-killings, rapes, and molestation of helpless women, providing one of the worst cases of inhuman barbarism.

Flow of labour migration to Europe came to a halt by the 1970s, and in the early 1990s in the USA, though the 'brain-drain', particularly directed to the USA and some European countries gathered momentum in later years, especially from middle-economy countries like India, Pakistan, Bangladesh, and Sri Lanka to avail of better working opportunities particularly in the USA tagged with higher salaries offered to talented, highly skilled persons.

The concept of migration has broadened further in the recent years, affecting some specific parts of the world. For example, refugees, or asylum seekers comprise another set of migrants. The 1951 United Nations Convention defining the status of refugees accepted someone as a refugee,

> 'who owing to a well-founded fear of being persecuted for reasons of race, religion, nationality, membership of a particular social group or political opinion, is outside the country of his nationality'.[22]

The implementation of this idea was felt very urgent after the cessation of the Second World War with urgent concern for the rehabilitation of people who fled Nazi persecution in Germany and occupied Europe. Later, by 1960s, the result of decolonisation generated in some African countries civil wars arising out of tribal contests when many refugees in order to avoid internal conflicts in their country of origin preferred settling down in neighbouring countries. The focus later shifted to South and Southeast Asia involving Bangladesh gaining independence in 1971, and the war in Vietnam turned many people into refugees with some of them eventually having settled down in Europe.

It may be interesting to note in this regard that refugees were generated both in the developed and developing countries. For instance, 'major refugee flows' in the 1990s were generated from:

> 'Bosnia, Kosovo, the former Soviet Union, the Horn of Africa, Rwanda, Iran, Afghanistan and East Timor ... In 2014, UNHCR (Office of the United Nations High Commissioner for Refugees) reported almost 20 million refugees, and this number has certainly increased in 2015 in particular as a result of the crisis in Syria. The most important countries of origin for refugees in 2014 were Syria, Afghanistan, and Somalia. The most important host countries were Turkey, Pakistan, and Lebanon. Overall, developing countries hosted 86 per cent of the world's refugees in 2014'.[23]

In 2015, 1.9 million Syrian refugees were concentrated in Turkey, 1.1 million in Lebanon, 60,000 in Jordon and 2,50,000 in Iraq. The wealthy Arab States (Saudi Arabia, Qatar, Kuwait, and the United Arab Emirates) have not signed the Geneva Convention on refugees and have closed minds to the reception of refugees.[24]

In this connection, however, an overall review of the factors directly or even indirectly responsible for the generation of refugees should not only go further back than recent years but are also varied in their character. As a matter of fact, one has to go as far back as 1917 when the Russian Revolution took place and was followed by a Civil War (1917-1921) which gave rise to a large-scale flow of people as refugees, estimated between 8,00,000 to 2 million, seeking refuge across Europe 'without protection and status'. This was followed by the Second World War, mentioned before, creating more refugees, making some 60 million Europeans displaced by conflict. Along with this, a number of internal wars between Middle East countries, such as the Iranian Revolution of 1979 followed by Iran-Iraq war between 1980 and 1988 leading to Iranian refugees seeking asylum in Europe. Likewise, the Gulf War of 1990-91 following Iraq's invasion of Kuwait gave rise to a large number of Iraqi refugees fleeing to Europe. Similarly, the wars in former Yugoslavia in the 1990s displaced over 4 million people, and though the number was slowly declining, the Kosovo conflict in 1998-99 reversed the downward trend.

Over and above these, the military intervention made by the USA in Afghanistan in 2001, coupled with armed attack on Iraq based on a flimsy plea of non-existent chemical weapons in 2003 turned millions of people homeless seeking refuge, many of those from Afghanistan going to Europe. In 2002, 2.37 million refugees were concentrated in the countries of European Economic Area (EEA). Another instance of internal conflict giving rise to refugees is provided by the Ugandan Government in 1972 expelling people of South Asian descent from the country including 27,000 British citizens who finally settled down in Britain. Similarly, following the overthrow of the socialist government in Chile in 1973, many people were turned into refugees, many of them seeking asylum in the UK and Germany. The cessation of the long-term Vietnam War (1955-1975) gave rise to over 2,30,000 Indochinese refugees from Vietnam, Laos and Cambodia who settled down in Europe, half of them going to France, their colonial power.

In 2011, civil unrest in Syria developed into an armed uprising against the government, turning into a full-scale civil war which with renewed conflict in Iraq produced millions of refugees. According to UNHCR, in 2016 there were 5.7 million Syrian refugees and asylum-seekers in the world. Though the majority of them are currently settled in neighbouring countries like Turkey, Lebanon, and Jordan, another 80,000 are in the European Union, including about 4,75,000 in Germany alone. Those fleeing Syria and Iraq since 2014 have been joined by increasing number of refugees escaping conflict and persecution in Afghanistan, Eritrea, Nigeria, Pakistan, Somalia, and Sudan moving across the Mediterranean from Turkey and North Africa mostly on flimsy boats, many of them drowning to an untimely death.

Why EU came to be the main target of refugees instead of North African countries may be explained by the fact that,

> 'the comparatively high standard of living, the level of public assistance service and the largely well-ordered asylum procedures'[25]

proved supportive for the new-comers. The drowning of 3500 refugees in 2015 in the Mediterranean and more than 5000 in 2016, clinched the issue in favour of the refugees seeking asylum. The major European countries taking share of asylum-seekers originating from the Sub-Saharan region, Pakistan and Afghanistan were Germany where the number of applicants increased six times between 2008 and 2015 going up further in 2016, while it increased four times between 2015 and 2016 in Italy. The Syrian war, as mentioned above, turned almost half of its total population of 23 million into refugees by 2013.[26]

Incidentally, Greece, from its location closer to North African countries was used as a footboard for refugees constituting primarily Syrians, representing almost 60 per cent of the total plus Afghans, Somalis, and Eritreans comprising in all about 43,500 in 2015 who arrived across the Mediterranean in most overcrowded boats likely to capsize any moment. As a matter of fact, both Greece and Italy acted as the transit point for these refugees before many of them moved further into the other European countries seeking asylum.

An estimate of refugees given asylum at first instance in 2016 compared with that of 2015 by EU gives a clear idea about how it varied for different countries of origin (Table 2.1).

Table 2.1: EU + Asylum Decisions on First Instance by Applicant's Countries

Country of Origin	2015	2016
Syria	1,67,101	4,12,308
Afghanistan	18,504	1,06,636
Iraq	26,277	1,03,611
Eritrea	37,966	43,703
Albania	42,737	43,378
Pakistan	18,599	32,523
Nigeria	17,448	25,553
Kosovo	36,757	23,310
Serbia	22,390	23,098
Iran	8,474	21,046

Source: Pries L. *Refugees, Civil Society, and the State: European Experience and Global Challenges*. Edward Elgar Publishing. 2018:40.

It is interesting to note that altogether EU accorded outright asylum to 11,30,100 applicants at first instance in 2016 amounting to 98 per cent of the Syrian refugees and 92 per cent from Eritrea as the highest rate of not negative decision which is, indeed, the most remarkable humanistic treatment of people living at life-risk.

The reasons behind such large-scale exodus of people seeking asylum away from their own homeland cannot hide the truth that violent political situation endangering lives of innocent citizens in each of the affected country mentioned in Table 2.1 is at the root of the emerging situation. For instance, in Syria, as mentioned above, the internal war between the government in power and the so called *Jihadis*, claimed to be violent terrorist outfits, made life unbearable for common people threatened with severe consequences which led almost half of the whole nation on to seeking relocation elsewhere. Entangled in conflicts for decades with the rise of terrorist power forced many Afghans from their home country for an undefined future for his own and his family, seeking asylum mostly in Europe. On the other hand, the political misadventure of America destroying the economy of Iraq and handing over its rule into the unwelcoming hands of the Islamic terrorists exposed the common people to imminent danger of losing their lives and thus compelled them to seek safety as refugees in other places.

In the same way both in Eritrea and Somalia, the military or armed groups subjecting people to join the army irrespective of age left no alternative for common people to leave their own country as refugees forced to seek asylum elsewhere. Organized violence by certain local terrorist groups like Boko Haram in Nigeria has been at the root of migration from Nigeria as well as some other Sub-Saharan countries, such as Somalia forcing out common, innocent people for rootless existence elsewhere while civil war, as mentioned earlier, in the Balkans forced people out of their own countries as refugees from Albania, Kosovo, Macedonia, Serbia and Bosnia-Herzegovina seeking shelter mostly in developed countries.

Looking at the potentials of the refugees one is not much encouraged at the prospect of any contribution by them to their places of asylum. According to Ludger Pries (2018), 28 per cent of the refugees from Afghanistan, 41 per cent from Iraq and 36 per cent from Syria:

> 'claimed having gone to school for nine years at the most; 38 per cent of those entitled to asylum from the following six countries – Afghanistan, Eritrea, Iraq, Iran, Sri Lanka and Syria – indicating that they had completed, started or terminated some kind of professional or university education … Among the refugees from countries long plagued by war and civil war such as Afghanistan, areas bordering Pakistan, Somalia and Sudan, the percentage of respondents who dropped out of school or never started school is especially high'.[27]

In other words, lack of technical skill makes these refugees rather poor assets for contributing to economic advancement of the society they have joined as asylum seekers though they are not going to be a burden as whatever education they have, they are likely to improve it and pursue it to have a greater grip on their individual career in future.

III. International Migration as Global Force of Development – Skills and Remittances

International migration irrespective of its form (not including slavery) contributes to development in global perspective. For instance, currently brain-drain or movement of skilled labour plays a very important positive role in filling the shortage of skilled labour in the country inviting and absorbing them, such as the USA, or Europe and Australia. India, for instance, unfortunately could not offer similar opportunities and suffers from losing their services (resources). However, it is not a total loss since in most of the cases the migrant earning a good salary sends money home, to his/her country of origin, and according to an estimate of the World Bank, such world-wide remittances amounted to US$586 billion in 2015.[28] Among the recipient countries, India had the leading role in 2014 with US$70 billion followed by China with US$64 billion and the Philippines with US$23 billion. However, as proportion of respective country's GDP, the remittances were the highest in small countries, such as in Jordan it was 23 per cent, in Lesotho 27 per cent, and 37 per cent in Tonga. Such remittances play a significant role in lifting people out of poverty in poor countries, as in Somaliland it doubles the average household income, while in Lesotho such remittances 'represent up to 80 per cent of the rural household'[29], though according to the same author, Sub-Saharan Africa on the whole was the recipient of the lowest level of remittances, amounting to about US$33 billion for the entire region, which might indicate its poor participation in providing skilled labour'.

Apart from remittance-incentives, the diasporas themselves frequently came to the aid of their home countries in different ways. Coming from the same region or country, diasporas living in considerable numbers in their destination-countries, such as London, New York etc., often are represented by informal organisations of different types, bringing people together, diasporic people of various professions, and form organisations based on a variety of activities, such as 'sport, religion, gender, charitable work and development, keeping in view an idea of helping people of their country of origin in profitable manner.[30]

IV. Migrants and Ethnicity

According to UN definition, there were 232 million migrants worldwide in 2013, making one in every thirty-five people an international migrant. In other words, '3 per cent of world's population is an international migrant'.

The emerging trend of increasing number of international migrants makes an interesting study. The number rose by 77 million between 1990 and 2013, or 50 per cent when 135 million of them lived in the developed countries and 95 million in the developing world. Incidentally, Europe had the largest number, amounting to 72 million, while Asia altogether had 70 million, North America 53 million, 18 million in Africa, while Latin America and Australia together had about 8 million each. In other words, almost 20 per cent of the international migrants in 2000, amounting to 46 million, were concentrated in the USA, the second place in this regard going to the Russia Federation with about 11 million followed by Germany, Saudi Arabia, the UAE (United Arab Emirates), and the UK with between 8-10 million each.[31]

In this connection, it may be noted that in 2013, most migrations took place 'within and not between' major areas. Almost 82 per cent of the international migrants living in Africa and 76 per cent in Asia were born there. Further:

> 'there are far more refugees in the developing world than the developed world. Equally, more Europeans come back to the UK each year, for example, than do people from outside Europe; and many of the Europeans and British citizens returning from stints overseas'.[32]

However, there has been a significant change in the proportion of migrants in recent years who are women. Almost half of the international migrants 'were women in 2013', and an increasing number of them are dependent migrants without being part of the family as used to be earlier, and thus becoming major 'bread winner' of the family they leave behind. The reasons behind that is the growing demand for skilled female labour in developed countries required in the specialised fields of 'services, healthcare and entertainment', including providing domestic service termed as 'maid trade', migration for marriage besides supporting sex-trade, the last one representing the most deplorable side of the migration of females.[33]

International migration undoubtedly makes a great impact where immigrants settling down take a part in the economic development of the country of their residence, making an inescapable effect on changing the overall character of the society. The immigrants representing the ethnic minorities play a distinctive role in characterising the whole community. The entire situation may give rise to two contrasting cases. For instance, when immigrants are allowed citizenship and there is 'gradual acceptance of cultural diversity', allowing the formation of ethnic communities contributes to a harmonious existence. On the contrary, denial of citizenship rights and rejection of cultural diversity leads to the emergence of ethnic minorities treated as 'undesirable and divisive', making them an unwelcome entity, remaining disgruntled all the time, barring a healthy growth of the society. Racism emerges from such as intolerant situation.

Racism is, perhaps the worst manifestation of immigration, keeping the situation far from conducive with a question of non-acceptance of a component of the society, denied on the basis of skin-colour, cultural or religious differences.

Women, though taking a growing share of the immigrants, in fact, receive worse treatment than non-immigrants in these societies and could be paid:

> 'lower wages and controlled more easily than men .... They tend to be overrepresented in the least desirable occupations, such as repetitive factory work and low-skilled positions in the personal and community service sectors ... Professional employment is often linked to traditional caring roles. Minority women have experienced casualisation of employment and increasing unemployment'.[34]

V. Recent Growing International Migration

It has been argued that focusing on the South, comprising developing countries within the Arab, African, and Latin American regions on the one hand and the Asia-Pacific regions on the other is

> 'an essential precondition for formulating the future policies of the developed world'.[35]

The term 'Arab Region' includes Arab countries of North Africa and Western Asia, as well as non-Arab States of Turkey, Iran, and Israel. It contains four major migrant labour sub-systems such as 'emigration from the Mediterranean littoral to western Europe, Arab labour migration to oil-producing states, migration to non-oil producing Arab states, and East and South Asian labour migration to oil-producing states.' Besides immigrants, there are also large flows of refugees, and the entire situation is characterised by 'deprivation of basic rights' in the absence of a sound political system. Lack of adequate employment opportunities for a fast-growing population in rich river valleys have given rise to massive recruitment potential for emigration.

> 'By 2002, Morocco and Turkey had the largest populations of expatriates in the EU, with 2 and 3 million of their citizens respectively residing as third country nationals. Large Moroccan communities lived in Italy, Spain, and the Netherlands in addition to France, where just over 5,00,000 Moroccans resided in 1999. The vast majority of Algerians and Tunisians, 5,00,000 and 1,50,000 respectively, lived in France. The colonial legacy shaped all North African flows, but less completely in the Moroccan case'.[36]

Masses of foreign-workers were recruited by the oil-rich states of the Persian Gulf following the price-rise of oil in 1973, who came from Arab and Asian countries employed for construction and industrialisation along with employing female domestic servants coming particularly from the Philippines and Sri Lanka. There were 1.1 million foreign workers in Iraq at the beginning of the Gulf War (1990-91) between Iraq and Kuwait while Kuwait had 1.5 million. The migrants largely came from Egypt, Sudan, Jordan, Palestine, India, Sri Lanka, Pakistan, and Bangladesh. But there had been mass migration on the occupation of Kuwait by Iraq, and a million Yeminis were displaced after Saudi Arabia 'sided' with Iraq. Altogether 5 million migrants were displaced which had a severe backlash on remittances made to the countries of the migrants' origin. The Gulf War brought a big change in the composition of the labour-force in oil-rich countries, with greater dependence on migrant labour from South and East Asian countries replacing politically suspect Arab States including Egypt. As a result, non-national migrant-population came to represent in 1995 almost one-third of the total population of the states belonging to Gulf Cooperation Council (GCC), comprising Saudi Arabia, Kuwait, Oman, Qatar, Bahrain, and the United Arab Emirates.[37]

Immigration of foreign workers in non-oil producing areas of Arabian region is much less spectacular. Nevertheless, the employment of almost 40 per cent of domestic, skilled workers abroad mainly in the Gulf Region, needed replacement and thus immigration took place from adjoining states like Iraq, Egypt and Syria which included a big flow of unskilled labour from the last two countries. There had been a decline in Palestinian workers after 1991, but immigration of foreign workers from Romania and the Philippines and Thailand was encouraged which naturally hit very hard on the economy of the Palestinians having long been dependent on employment in the Gulf States. In contrast, there were Jewish immigrants from former Soviet Union accommodated by Israel in 1990s, with net migration accounting for 40 per cent of the total population which was 6 million in 1998.[38]

According to social scientists, Africa has a very mobile population, its 'crushing poverty' or death 'due to malnutrition' pushed people out for sustenance and as such Sub-Saharan Africa generates 'significant outflows of intercontinental migrants' directed mainly to Western Europe and North America as well as the Arab Region. But what is highly interesting in this respect is that the flow of migrants largely follow the route to former colonial powers, such as the 'Congolese migrating to Belgium, Senegalese to France or Nigerians to Britain'. Though some of these Sub-Saharan migrants are educated, the majority constitute labour migrants going in significant number to Spain, Portugal, Canada and USA, but the majority portion of the Sub-Saharan migrants 'stays within the continent'.

In comparison to Africa, Latin America, and the Caribbean present altogether a different picture of migration. The entire region presents four disparate cases of migration. For instance, the region comprising Brazil, Argentina, Chile, Uruguay, and Paraguay had witnessed massive flows of immigrants from Europe settling down permanently and making up majority of the population of European origin plus Brazil receiving African slaves up to the nineteenth century as well as Japanese workers until the 1950s. It is interesting to note that according to an estimate almost 21 million Italians forming the largest group of immigrants settled in Argentina alone while another 3,32,000 mostly of Italian origin settled down in Venezuela. However, immigrants from Spain as well as Portugal also formed a part of the entire lot of immigrants mentioned here.

In contrast, immigration from Europe during the nineteenth and twentieth century was of less significance in the Andean area where Indians and people of mixed European-Indian (Mestizos) origin dominated the population. On the other hand, Central America is largely populated by people of Indian origin or Mestizos. The region has been subjected to continuous conflicts, particularly involving El Salvador, Nicaragua and Guatemala, and migrants from these countries mostly sought asylum in the USA employed in labour-intensive activities. At the same time, the Caribbean, forming the fourth segment of Latin America, is mainly populated by people of African origin along with people of Asian and European descent. Since the 'colonial period', Caribbean migrants have been concentrating in the eastern and southern shores of the USA, employed mostly in the agricultural sector. However, one of the most notable migrations was represented by seasonal migrations of the Haitians to the Dominican Republic during sugarcane harvest taking place every year in November, many of whom have settled down permanently in spite of living in abominable conditions, termed as 'slavery', and in spite of political changes, the condition of the Haitians working in Guatemala did not improve much in later years.[39]

International migration has been taking different roles in different situations. For instance, migration from Asia has taken a great momentum since the mid-twentieth century taking place both inside Asia between countries as well as outward, involving almost 6.2 million employed within Asia outside their own countries and another 5 million employed in the Middle East by 2000. Among the major labour-exporting countries are China, the Philippines, India, Bangladesh, Pakistan, Sri Lanka, and Indonesia. The migrants have taken different destinations no doubt and those going to the Middle East are a very prominent group, starting since the rise of oil price in 1973, making for a great supply particularly from India and Pakistan, and then from the Philippines, Indonesia, Thailand, and Korea. There were 3.2 million migrant workers from Asia by 1985 working in the Gulf States of which over 2 million were employed in Saudi Arabia alone. In 1997, a total of 4,16,000 labourers came from India of which 93 per cent went to the Middle East, 1,54,000 from Pakistan 96 per cent of that for the Middle East and 1,50,000 from Sri Lanka of which 85 per cent came to the Middle East while 75 per cent of migrants from Bangladesh out of a total of 2,31,000 were employed in the Middle East. This shows an overwhelming dependence of the Middle East on migrants representing almost 28 per cent of the population of Saudi Arabia, and this came to be higher for smaller countries, such as for Kuwait it was 65 per cent, for Bahrain 37 per cent, as much as 77 per cent for Qatar and 73 per cent for United Arab Emirates, though dropping to 27 per cent for Oman. The women workers came mostly from the Philippines, Indonesia, Thailand, Korea, or Sri Lanka, but Pakistan and Bangladesh sent none. They often worked under exploited conditions subjected sometimes to sexual abuse. However, an attraction of higher wages for unskilled workers is the major factor for the migrants which was eight times more for the Sri Lankan workers than they could earn at home and thirteen times higher for the Bangladeshis though one of the major handicaps was the extortion made by the agents or brokers providing them the opportunities costing sometimes as high as 25 per cent of what each of them earned as a salary.[40]

The migration process in the Middle East, nevertheless, gradually became complex including more undocumented migrants leading to the expulsion of many migrants consisting of unauthorised workers, subjecting 1,60,000 from the United Arab Emirates in 1996, while Saudi Arabia expelled 3,50,000 to 4,50,000 per year. Interestingly, as mentioned above, it is the attraction of higher wages that worked for these migrants to join the force in spite of highly volatile working conditions.

Apart from the flow of migrants, mostly unskilled, to the Middle East there was another flow of Asian migrants to Western Europe, North America and Australia becoming effective since the withdrawal of the discriminatory rules against Asian migrants to the USA in 1965, Canada in 1962 and 1976, and Australia in 1966 and 1973. Three European countries experienced this migration as a result of decolonisation, the Netherlands from its former colony Indonesia; France from Vietnam; and Britain from the Indian subcontinent and Hongkong. In addition, small colonisers like Portugal experienced this from Goa (in India), Macau and East Timor which ultimately declined in course of time replaced by migration of both skilled and unskilled labour from Asia to Europe since the 1990s including the migration of female domestic workers from countries like the Philippines and China.

Since the change in the Immigration Act in 1965 in the USA, there had been movement of Asian migrants to the USA, increasing from 17,000 in 1965 to 'an average of more than 2,50,000 annually in the 1980s and over 3,50,000 per year in the early 1990s'. Asia had been the source of about 'one-third of all migrants' rising to over 7 million by 2000. China was the second largest source following Mexico, followed by India, the Philippines, Vietnam and Korea.[41]

The repeal of the White Australian Policy in the late 1960s in the early 1970s, the door was opened for immigrants to Australia and by the beginning of the 1990s, almost half of new migrants came from Asia, comprising those from China, India, the Philippines, Taiwan and Vietnam, which, altogether amounted to over 1 million in 1999.

Canada came to be another country where following the withdrawal of 1976 Immigration Act, opened up for migrants of Asian origin, recording 6,74,000 of them in 1981 and since 1993 over half of all migrants arrived from Asian countries. The most important source of migrants between 1995 and 1998 were China, Taiwan, Hongkong, India, Pakistan, and the Philippines.

New Zealand, on the other hand, has been 'a traditional immigrant country' represented by people from only the UK, and has encouraged immigration of people with professional skill and capital, originating mostly from Hong Kong, Taiwan, Korea, and Japan. With permanent entrants amounting to 22,000 from Asia out of the total 55,000 in 1995, migrants from Asia, however, declined to 11,000 by 1999. In spite of that Asia has ultimately turned out to be the main source of highly skilled personnel for the global labour market.[42]

VI. Source of Immigration

In the perspective of growing emigration of skilled as well as non-skilled labour to the industrialising countries of the West and the Asia Pacific region along with the Middle Eastern oil-rich countries, it becomes imperative to assess the future potential, or, in other words, to find out the dependable sources of meeting the supply of skilled to highly skilled labour for the global market as a whole.

Industrialising Asia had its own reserve of labour mostly based in countries like China, the South Asian countries, the Philippines, Indonesia, and India providing labour for Asian countries as well as the entire world when many of these countries had established special departments dealing with the supply of labour. Though most of the labour was low skilled workers, there is also a growing number of skilled to high skilled labour including 'professionals, executives, technicians etc.' forming this group, giving rise to 'brain-drain', mentioned earlier, in the country of origin. They are mostly destined for highly developed countries like Europe, North America and Australia receiving:

> 'thousands of doctors and engineers from India, Malaysia, Hong Kong and similar countries. Britain recruits nurse from the Philippines for the National Health Service, Germany competes with other highly developed countries to attract Indian Information Technology (IT) Specialists. The USA obtains highly trained workers from Asia. According to US State Department, 69 per cent of employer-sponsored H-IB Visas from 1990 to 1997 were issued to persons from India, the Philippines, Japan and China'.[43]

One should warn that brain-drain at this scale has a crippling effect on the countries of origin in the developing world, so much so that, as mentioned before, the Philippines provides one of the glaring examples to this effect where, it is reported, hospitals are closing down operating theatres 'in the absence of trained doctors who have left for Britain attracted by higher salaries'. In addition, many companies send their highly qualified executives, professionals, and experts to developed countries to gather experience. At the same time, movement of skilled workers from developed countries represents an opposite flow of migrants to developing countries, such as there were 2,00,000 foreign specialists in China in 2000, while Malaysia had 32,000 and Vietnam 30,000 coming from other Asian countries as well as USA, Europe, and Australia. In addition, another group of emigrants consisted of short-time travellers for business amounting to 2.6 million from Japan in 2000, 1.6 million of whom went to Asian countries.

Skilled emigration also includes students, 3,66,000 of whom were visiting the USA by late 1980s, nearly half of them coming from Asia, while Australia issued 86,277 student Visas in 2000-01, the majority of them coming from Asia. Many of them on completion of their studies stayed on, for example 23,599 science and engineering faculty members of Asian origin stayed on in the USA in 1997.[44]

Another very important component of migration is represented by refugees, mentioned earlier including asylum seekers, internally displaced persons etc., who, according to the estimate of the UNHCR amounted to 7 million in Asia and Pacific alone, out of the global total of 12.1 million. Majority of them, amounting to about 4.5 million came from Afghanistan, followed by Pakistan, Iran, Burma (Myanmar), Iraq, Vietnam, China, East Timor, the Philippines, and North Korea.

More than 3 million people left Vietnam following the Vietnam War between 1955 and 1975, triggering exodus on a massive scale with 2.5 million finding new homes. Over a million Vietnam refugees settled in the USA, and a small number of them found asylum in Australia, Canada, and Western Europe. On the other hand, as mentioned earlier, Russian military intervention in Afghanistan in 1979 turned almost one-third of its 18 million population into refugees of which 3.3 million settled in Pakistan and another 3.1 million in Iran. Further intervention of fundamentalist Taliban in Afghanistan discouraged the return of Afghan refugees who formed the world's largest refugee population.

This was followed by a flow of refugees from different other sources adding to the numbers of refugees worldwide, which touched 20 million in 2014 according to the UNHCR, increasing further in 2015 following the Syrian crisis. Most important countries by then for origin of refugees were Syria, Afghanistan, and Somalia while Turkey, Pakistan and Lebanon were the most important host countries, and developing countries together absorbed 86 per cent of them. According to the UNHCR, the number of Syrian refugees increased further to 5.7 million in 2016, giving rise to an unprecedented movement of people across the Mediterranean.

The religious and ethnic persecution of the Rohingyas from Myanmar presents the most recent case involving the movement of nearly 7,40,000 people seeking asylum in the adjoining state of Bangladesh.[45] India was planning to move 40,000 of Rohingya refugees to Myanmar. Incidentally, India faced a problem earlier in rehabilitating the Chakma and Hajong refugees resulting from religious persecution in Bangladesh and rehabilitating them 'mostly in Arunachal Pradesh between 1964 and

1969, granting citizenship to more than one lakh Buddhists and Hindu Chakma' which later on gave rise to a local political dilemma.[46]

VII. Ethnic Minority and Social Problems

Immigration involving migration of labour, both unskilled and skilled, has resulted in the growth of ethnic minorities accepted as a normal process of change in some countries while in some others it has given rise to marginalisation and exclusion. A current example in this respect perhaps, is at the root of the 'Brexit' movement in Britain.

The USA provides one of the greatest mixes of population resulting from immigrants arriving from different races and cultural background over the period of almost five centuries.

The native American societies, wrongly called Red Indians, were destroyed in most cases under the unrelenting pressure of whites from European countries pushing westward in the vast expanse of North America where millions of African slaves were brought to work in the growing plantations of the South. Even after the abolition of slavery in 1865, the African American descendants suffered from 'segregation and powerlessness'. However, changes in the Immigration Law in 1865 allowed new immigrants mainly from Latin America and Asia, comprising main Asian countries like the Philippines, China, South Korea, Vietnam, and India. As a result, in 2000, 10 per cent of the total population were foreign-born and six states – California, New York, Florida, Texas, New Jersey and Illinois – 'received over two-thirds of all immigrants' in 1999. As such ethnic minorities represent 'a quarter of USA's population' making the greatest divide between blacks and whites. Indeed, the number of Hispanics of Mexican and Central American origin exceeds the number of blacks. The proportion of US population according to 2000 US Census brings out the demographic characteristics highlighting the importance of ethnic minorities with black population along with other ethnic groups representing almost 25 per cent of the total white population at 75.1 per cent. The position of the ethnic minorities did not, however, improve. As observed by Castles and Miller (2003):

> 'In the long term, many white ethnics achieved upward mobility while Afro-Americans became increasingly ghettoized. Distinction between blacks and whites in income, unemployment rates, social conditions and education are still extreme'[47] (Table 2.2).

Table 2.2: US Population by Race and Hispanic Origin, 2000 Census

	Millions	**Per cent**
White	211.5	75.1
Black	34.7	12.3
American Indian, Eskimo or Eleut	2.5	0.9
Asian or Pacific Islanders	10.6	3.7
Other Race	15.4	5.5
Two or more Races	6.8	2.4
Total Population	281.4	100.0
Hispanic or Latin Origin	35.3	12.5

Source: Castles & Miller. *The Age of Migration*. Palgrave, MacMillan. 2003:233. (Primary source: US Census Bureau, 2000).

In general, residential segregation becomes the most identifiable feature of ethnicity where immigrants coming from different cultural background, mostly of a lower standard, get isolated in the community which they join for finding work. It generally means poor housing and social amenities, though in other cases it allows the opportunity for 'community formation and the development of ethnic infrastructure and institutions'.[48]

However explained, it does not conceal the fact that in the USA whites and blacks including the Hispanics are completely separated in their residential areas, making racism and social exclusion very palpable. In Britain, as well, London has 49 per cent of Britain's ethnic minorities in 2001, and 28 per cent of London's population were ethnic minorities with some of the groups such as those from Bangladesh largely concentrated in disadvantaged areas. From another point of view ethnic neighbourhoods give rise to small business activities primarily catering to the needs and requirements of the ethnic population making life more enjoyable and act to promote community formation.

In France, however, ethnic segregation has taken a serious turn even though more than a million immigrants have been naturalised, giving equal social rights to them except the right to vote. In spite of that there are immigrants, such as Algerians, Tunisians and Moroccans, black Africans and Turks who may have formal rights as French Citizens, but still they suffer from 'socio-economic exclusion and racism' marked by 'low status insecure jobs, and high unemployment rates especially for youths'. Such racial discrimination sometimes leads to violence particularly involving North Africans. However, the socialist government (1997-2002) took steps for creating a 'secure situation' for legal migrants.[49]

As recent data show, it is quite evident that a declining trend in immigration has already set in the industrialised countries. By the end of 2010 there were:

> 'about 214 million migrants in the world. Of those, 60 per cent were living in 'so-called' developed countries. It's a majority – but not an overwhelming majority'.[50]

Lately, migration is mostly non-economic representing large number of refugees leaving conflict-torn countries like Iraq, Afghanistan, Somalia and Syria, and environmental migration, such as rising sea level which is growing in alarming proportion in Bangladesh where saltwater entering freshwater aquifers and estuaries 'contaminating drinking water and farmland' threatening to shrink the **country** by '18 per cent' with one metre rise in sea level. This is taking a more frustrating form with further rise in ocean water temperature making typhoons, cyclones, and storms more frequent as well as devastating particularly for island countries (such as Japan devastated by a recent typhoon) in the Pacific region giving rise to a greater number of environmental refugees, the latter ending up in adjoining countries seeking shelter and livelihood. These environmental refugees are going to be a great headache for the countries threatened by rising sea level with the growing rate of global warming.

Presumably, environmental refugees are going to be a more common feature in near future with fast deteriorating climate changes. For instance, warmed up ocean water is at the back of a phenomenon like 'Hagibis', an extremely powerful typhoon which hit Japan very recently, worst in six decades, making landfall Southeast of Tokyo on 12 October, 2019, with gusts of wind up to 216 kilometres (134 miles) per hour unleashing unprecedented rain triggering landslides in its wake, causing '76 rivers, mainly in eastern and northern Japan to burst their banks. Landslides burying homes and vehicles killed at least 72 people and left on the third day some 75,900 homes without power and water cut off to 1,35,000 homes affecting 36 out of 47 prefectures of the country.[51]

Another case of climate change giving rise to environmental refugees in very recent time is presented by a deadly forest fire which broke out 'as hot, windy conditions spread south towards Los Angeles' making more than a million Californians without power after electricity had to be switched off 'in a bid to prevent a repeat of last year's catastrophic inferno which killed 86 people', and devastated the homes of 26,000 people at a place called 'Paradise'. Some 50,000 people had been ordered to leave their homes on the third day of the fire which by then spread over 5,000 acres,

40 miles north of Los Angeles turning into a '16,000 acres inferno' in no time fed by wind gusts 'topping 113 kilometres per hour'. Wildfire raged across California on Friday (the fourth day), destroying homes, and forcing evacuations ... tens of thousands of residents near Santa Clarita, north of Los Angeles'.[52] The blaze continuing – called Kincade Fire – spread over 30,000 acres put about 1,80,000 people under mandatory evacuation orders was being fought by over 3000 fire fighters backed by air tankers and helicopters, compelling to turn off power to nearly one million customers across northern and central California.

NOTES

*Harari, Y.N. *Sapiens, A Brief History of Humankind.* Vintage. 2011, p. 20.

'Whether Sapiens (*Homo sapiens*) are to blame or not no sooner had they arrived at a new location than the native population became extinct. The last remains of *Homo Seloensis* are dated to about 50,000 years ago. *Homo Denisova* disappeared shortly thereafter. *Neanderthals* made their exit roughly 30,000 years ago. The last dwarf-like humans vanished from Flores Island about 12,000 years ago. They left behind some bones, some tools a few genes in our DNA and a lot of unanswered questions. They also left behind us, *Homo Sapiens*, the last human species.'

**Harari, Y.N. *Sapiens, A Brief History of Humankind.* Vintage. 2011, p. 54.

'In most habitats, Sapien bands fed themselves in an elastic and opportunistic fashion. They scrounged for termites, picked berries, dug for roots, stalked rabbits, and hunted bison and mammoth. Notwithstanding the popular image of 'man the hunter', gathering was Sapiens' main activity, and it provided most of the calories as well as raw material, such as flint, wood and bamboo.'

1. Childe, G. *What Happened in History*. U.K.: Penguin Books, 1886, p. 40.
2. Childe, G. *Man Makes Himself.* 4th ed. U.K.: Spokesman Books, 2003, p. 23.
3. *Ibid.*, pp. 24-25.
4. Harari, Y. N. *Sapiens: A Brief History of Humankind.* London: Vintage, 2011, p. 9.
5. *Ibid.*, p. 23.
6. *Ibid.*, p. 14.
7. *Ibid.*, p. 77.
8. *Ibid.*, p. 79.
9. *Ibid.*, p. 87.
10. *Ibid.*, pp. 87-88.
11. *Ibid.*, p. 104.
12. Childe, G. *Man Makes Himself.* 4th ed. U.K.: Spokesman Books, 2003, p. 35.

13. *Ibid.*
14. *Ibid.*, p. 36.
15. Koser, K. *International Migration: A Very Short Introduction*. 2nd ed., U.K.: Oxford University Press, 2016, pp. 2-3.
16. *Ibid.*, p. 4.
17. Castles, S., Miller, M.J. and Ammendola, G. *The Age of Migration: International Population Movements in the Modern World.* 3rd ed., New York: The Guilford Press, 2003, p. 51.
18. *Ibid.*, pp. 52-53.
19. *Ibid.*, pp. 53-55.
20. *Ibid.*, p. 55.
21. Koser, K. *International Migration: A Very Short Introduction*. 2nd ed., U.K.: Oxford University Press, 2016, p. 4.
22. *Ibid.*, p. 64.
23. *Ibid.*, pp. 67-68.
24. Pries, L. *Refugees, Civil Society, and the State: European Experiences and Global Challenges*. U.K.: Edward Elgar, 2018, p. 49.
25. *Ibid.*, p. 13.
26. *Ibid.*, pp.13-14.
27. *Ibid.*, pp. 34-35.
28. Koser, K. *International Migration: A Very Short Introduction*. 2nd ed., U.K.: Oxford University Press, 2016, p. 38.
29. *Ibid.*, p. 40.
30. *Ibid.*, p. 42.
31. *Ibid.*, p. 5.
32. *Ibid.*, p. 7.
33. *Ibid.*, pp. 7-8.
34. Castles, S., Miller, M.J. and Ammendola, G. *The Age of Migration: International Population Movements in the Modern World.* 3rd ed., New York: The Guilford Press, 2003, p. 37.
35. *Ibid.*, p. 122.
36. *Ibid.*, p. 123.
37. *Ibid.*, pp. 130-131.
38. *Ibid.*, pp. 133-135.
39. *Ibid.*, pp. 144-151.
40. *Ibid.*, pp. 159-160.
41. *Ibid.*, p. 158.
42. *Ibid.*, pp. 158-159.
43. *Ibid.*, p. 170.
44. *Ibid.*, p. 171.
45. Mukherjee, S. Perspective. *The Statesman*. Kolkata. 28 August, 2019.
46. Lahiri, H. *Diaspora: Theory and Transnationalism*. Hyderabad: Orient Blackswan, 2019, p. 65.

47. Castles, S., Miller, M.J. and Ammendola, G. *The Age of Migration: International Population Movements in the Modern World.* 3rd ed., New York: The Guilford Press, 2003, pp. 222-223.
48. *Ibid.*, pp. 228-229.
49. *Ibid.*, pp. 232-233.
50. Baird, V. *The No-Nonsense Guide to World Population.* U.K.: New Internationalist, 2011, p. 80.
51. *The Statesman.* Perspective. Kolkata. 13-16 October, 2019.
52. *Ibid.,* 12 October, 2019, 24 and 26 October, 2019, 27 and 28 October, 2019.

3
An Analysis of Recent Migration

I. International Migration and the Current Trends

Man has never been static in his place of birth; one or other reason has always pushed him out in quest for new locations. Adventurism could have been one of the many compelling reasons. In short, numerous factors like 'economic prosperity, inequality, demography, violence and conflict and environmental change' are there at the back of migration, or, in other words, continuous flow of people over space and time settling down either permanently or temporarily at newer locations mostly alien to his/her culture, belief as well as personal habits risking adjustment/adaptation often in uninviting situations. This worldwide movement of people taking place all the time, more so in recent years called international migration has involved 244 million people globally in 2015 representing 3.3 per cent of total global population, increasing from 155 million in 2000 with further involvement of another 740 million people having migrated within their own place of origin (inter-country or inter-continental).[1]

The most striking feature of international migration is its fast, steady increase, rising from about 84 million in 1970 to over 243 million in 2015 (nearly three times in four and half decades) of whom around 72 per cent people are of working age (20-64 years), giving an idea about the growth in number of the international migrants (Table 3.1) over the recent years.

Altogether, 62 per cent of the international migrants, or about 75 million of them are concentrated in Europe and Asia combined, while the second highest concentration – 54 million – moved to North America, or 22 per cent of the global migrants, Africa hosting 9 per cent of the total with another 4 per cent concentrated in the Caribbean and 3 per cent in the Oceania. In other words, migrants represented 21 per cent of the total population of Oceania, the global highest, 15 per cent and 10 per cent of

North America and Europe, respectively. It is very important to remember that since 1970 USA has been the major destination of the international migrants, increasing four-fold from 12 million in 1970 to 46.6 million in 2015 while the second place as a host country went to the Russian Federation prior to 2005.

Table 3.1: International Migrants, 1970-2015

Year	Number of Migrants	Migrants as a % of World Population
1970	8,44,60,125	2.3
1975	9,03,68,101	2.2
1980	10,13,83,149	2.3
1985	11,32,06,691	2.3
1990	15,25,63,212	2.9
1995	16,08,01,752	2.8
2000	17,27,03,309	2.8
2005	19,12,69,100	2.9
2010	22,17,14,243	3.2
2015	24,37,00,236	3.3

Source: UN: *World Migration Report*, 2018, p. 15 (UNDESA 2008 and 2015a).

Looking from another angle, it is more important to note that nearly 'half of all international migrants in 2015 were born in Asia, the largest contingent coming from India, over 17 million, followed by China with nearly 15 million' and all others in the list of top ten were from Asian countries except Mexico happening to be the third largest contributor. Among the recipient countries, on the other hand, USA topped the list among the ten countries hosting over 46 million immigrants in 2015 followed by Germany and all others were also part of the developed world. It may further be interesting to know about the preference of the migrants regarding choice of their residence which shows that almost 'two-thirds' of the international migrants, amounting to about 157 million of the total took residence in 2015 in **high-income** countries, while 77 million, or a third of the total number of migrants chose to settle down in **middle-income** countries in 2015 but only about 9 million settled in **low-income** countries.

II. Migration Flows and Migration Paths

In the absence of dependable data available for international migration flows we have to satisfy ourselves with the latest data made available by

UNDESA (United Nations Department for Economic and Social Affairs) for 45 countries in 2015. The data collected in this connection shows an increase in 'permanent migration flows' to OECD (Organisation for Economic Co-operation and Development) countries which 'increased from 3.85 million in 2000 to 7.13 million in 2015', and Germany hosting over 2 million new international migrants topped the list as a destination followed by USA with over 1 million while UK hosted about 4,80,000 new migrants in 2015.[2]

It becomes necessary now to find out the migration paths usually followed by migrants in the expectation of 'greater opportunities and a better life' avoiding persecution or faced with conflict or natural disasters. These movements obviously take place from low/middle income countries to more affluent countries, as such the most dominant of that is (a) South-North Migration. However, there are three more pathways used by the migrants which are – (b) 'from one high-income country to another high-income country, such as the UK to Canada (**North-North**) in the expectation of better opportunities; (c) from high-income to a low-middle-income country, such as from Portugal to Brazil (**North-South**) movement; (d) from one low-middle-income country to another such as from Indonesia to Malaysia (**South-South**).[3] In other words,

> 'North refers to high-income countries and **South** to low-middle-income countries, as classified by the World Bank'[4] in 2010.

According to the World Bank, the largest migratory flow takes place along a South-North path, representing 45 per cent of the total followed by South-South with 35 per cent, North-North 17 per cent and only 3 per cent of the total number of migrants taking North-South pathway. The number of international migrants taking different pathways, however, slightly varied according to the classifications made by two different authorities at global level, UNDESA (United Nations Department of Economic and Social Affairs) and UNDP (United Nations Development Programme). For example, the number of migrants travelling **N-S** was 13 million in 2010 according to UNDSA, as against 7 million claimed by two other sources (WB and UNDP). Further, movement of migrants along **S-S** pathway is the second largest volume of the total as claimed by each of the sources, but it varied rather widely from 73 million (UNDESA) to 75 million (WB) and 87 million (UNDP) as estimates made by respective sources. Put against this, movement from **N-N** is comparatively less, but much larger than from **N-S**, falling to 54 million (UNDESA), 37 million (WB) and 33 million

(UNDP). In comparison, movement of migrants from **S-N** represents the largest one by each source (Table 3.2).

Table 3.2: Movement of Migrants along different Pathways According to Different Sources (in millions)

Source	Pathways			
	N-S	S-S	N-N	S-N
UNDESA	13	73	54	74
WB	7	75	37	95
UNDP	7	87	33	87

Source: IOM (International Organisation for Migration), World Migration Report 2013.

It may be interesting to observe that origin of migrants is overwhelmingly more in the South than in the North, the former ranging between 147 million to 170 million according to different sources though the migrant share of the total population is less than 2 per cent in the South but ranges between 10 and 12 per cent in the North. And it is important to note that more than half of the top 20 migration pathways for migration along South-South corridor involve the largest volume of migrants moving from Russian Federation to Ukraine and Kazakhstan and *vice versa*. Other important corridors represented by this **S-S** group is provided by movement from Bangladesh to India, both ways from Afghanistan to Pakistan and Iran, and from Indonesia to Malaysia, while the only corridor maintaining movement as one of the top 20 from S to S is in Africa, represented by migration from Burkino Faso to Cote d'Ivoire.

Henceforth, the top 'migrant-sending' countries, that is, wherefrom the migrants originate, and 'migrant-receiving', or where the migrants go, are the USA, the Russian Federation, Ukraine, and India. Further, Germany, Italy, Poland and the UK are the 'major countries' of origin, or sending out migrants in the 'North-North' context. In the same context, USA receives migrants from many 'nationalities' such as – Canada, China, Mexico, Puerto Rico, the Philippines and the Republic of Korea, thus representing destination for both 'South-North' and 'North-North' migration, receiving to the tune of '35 per cent and 27 per cent' respectively of migrants representing two of the flows (**S-N** and **N-N**). Contrarily, USA also happens to be the major migrant sending country for North-South migration (to Mexico and to South Africa).[5]

III. An Analysis of Migrants

Sub-headings: A. Gender of migrants, B. Work by migrants, C. Home Remittances of migrants, D. Refugees and asylum seekers, E. Climate refugees, F. Migrants in Regional Perspective – (a) Africa, (b) Asia, G. Migration, Violent Extremism and Social Exclusion

A. Gender of Migrants

The proportion of females in the migrant population taking an important role in many respects shows that female participants considered as a 'share of total migrant population' were in the majority only in the North-North context as computed individually for each of the three sources (UN DESA, WB, and UNDP) in 2010. But the situation changes in all other migratory flows, female migrants falling in share compared with men with one exception for **N-N** where according to one source (UN DESA), females were in majority.

> 'About 60 per cent of all female migrants live, like their male counterparts, in the North and about 10 per cent of them are international migrants'.[6]

Another interesting aspect of proportion of females in each of the migration flows shows their share of the total female migrants involved in each flow. It shows that in terms of the share of the total female migrants, both **S-N** and **S-S** flows had the larger share of the total number of female migrants than along the two other flows (**N-N** and **N-S**) (Table 3.3).

Table 3.3: Proportion of Female Migrants as per cent of the Total Female Migrants in Corridors of Flow

Source	Pathways			
	N-S	S-S	N-N	S-N
UNDSA	7	31	27	35
WB	3	36	18	42
UNDP	3	40	16	41

Source: IOM (International Organisation for Migration), World Migration Report 2013.

B. Work of Migrants

According to data made available by UN sources for 2013, a total of 150.3 million out of a total of 232 million migrants of working age – 15 years or older comprising a total of 207 million or 70 per cent – were engaged in activities for earning a living though, as mentioned, it may be an underestimate. As per UN Report, male migrant workers outnumbered female migrant workers by 'almost 17 million in 2013 with 83.7 million males (55.7%) and 66.6 million females (44.3%).'

There are, however, wide differences in the volume of migrant workers – males and females – between economic status of their destinations. For example, the highest number of migrant workers of both sexes are found in the High-Income countries (112.3 million) with a systematic decrease for lower-income countries, from 112.3 million in the High-Income countries to 17.5 million in Upper-Middle income countries to 16.9 million in Lower-Middle income countries to the lowest of 3.9 million in Low Income countries. The proportionate share of men and women is shown in Table 3.4. [7]

It is interesting to observe that according to the same Report, majority of migrant workers, 106.8 million, or 71.1 per cent, were engaged in services, almost 8 per cent of whom were in domestic services. On the other hand, 26.7 million, or 17.8 per cent were employed in manufacturing and construction while agriculture absorbed 16.7 million, or 11.1 per cent of migrant settlers. On the whole, however, domestic workers, an estimated total of 11.5 million in 2013 constituted by migrant labour, comprising more than 17 per cent of all domestic workers (67.1 million) in 2013, representing over 7 per cent of all migrant workers comprising 8.45 million females and 3.07 million males were 'overwhelmingly' engaged in High-Income Countries.[9]

C. Home Remittances by Migrants

Migrants usually give financial help to their families at places of origin – one of the main causes for migrating abroad, often at family-cost, for better earning as well as working opportunities at their better economic situation. Though information available on this count is debatable, it is estimated that global flows of annual remittances were 'USD 598 billion in 2014', though contracted to 'USD 582 billion in 2015'.

Since annual remittances received by the country, particularly in the developing world play a significant role in lifting many families out of poverty, as mentioned in Chapter I, it is imperative to take a closer look at the existing position. The USA, by far, has turned out to be the top remittance-providing country, 'with a total out-flow of USD 61.38 billion in 2015' with Saudi Arabia in second place with remittances amounting to USD 38.79 billion and Switzerland providing remittances to the tune of USD 24.38 billion a year. In this regard, however, China makes a

Table 3.4: Migrant Workers, by Sex and Income-Level of Destination Countries, 2013

	Low Income			**Lower Middle Income**			**Upper Middle Income**			**High Income**			**Global Total**		
	M	F	T	M	F	T	M	F	T	M	F	T	M	F	T
Migrant Workers (millions)	1.8	1.8	3.6	9.4	7.5	16.9	10.4	7.2	17.6	62.1	50.1	112.2	83.7	66.6	150.3

Source: UN: World Migration Report 2018: Table 3 (Based on ILO, 2015).

M= Male **F** = Female **T**=Total

highly interesting case when herself being the recipient of the second largest amount in both 2010 and 2015 (first in 2005) she provided USD 20.42 billion annually in 2015. Table 3.5 gives a comprehensive idea how migrants give their families in their country-of-origin beneficiaries money earned by them in a foreign country.

Table 3.5: Ten Top Countries as Beneficiaries from Migrants' Remittances (2000-2015) (Current USD Billions)

	2000		2005		2010		2015	
1.	India	12.84	China	23.63	India	53.48	India	68.91
2.	France	8.61	Mexico	22.74	China	52.46	China	68.94
3.	Mexico	7.52	India	22.13	Mexico	22.08	The Philippines	28.48
4.	The Philippines	6.96	Nigeria	14.64	The Philippines	20.56	Mexico	26.23
5.	Republic of Korea	4.86	France	14.21	France	19.90	France	23.35
6.	Spain	4.86	The Philippines	13.73	Nigeria	19.75	Nigeria	18.96
7.	Turkey	4.56	Belgium	6.89	Germany	12.79	Pakistan	19.85
8.	United States of America	4.40	Germany	6.87	Egypt	12.45	Egypt	16.58
9.	Germany	3.64	Spain	6.66	Bangladesh	10.85	Bangladesh	15.38
10.	United Kingdom	3.61	Poland	6.47	Belgium	10.35	Germany	15.36

Source: UN World Migration Report 2018: Migration and Migrants: A Global Review: Table 4.

The same source, mentioned above, also provides information about sending remittances and according to that USA takes the leading position remitting annually USD 61.38 billion followed by Saudi Arabia with USD 38.79 billion and as mentioned above, the third position in ranking order goes to Switzerland and with USD 24.38 billion while China as one of the leading (second in rank) recipient countries takes fourth position remitting USD 20.42 billion in 2015. Altogether, USD 234.65 billion were remitted in 2015 by top ten countries which include six Western Countries (USA, Switzerland, Russian Federation, Germany, France, and Luxemburg) while three oil-producing countries of the Middle East (Saudi Arabia, Kuwait and Qatar) also take a part in this employing a large number of migrants who are actually the source of these remittances. The most important route for the flow of remittances is the North-South corridor and the top recipient countries are in Asia.

D. Refugees and Asylum Seekers

According to the UNHCR (United Nations Higher Commissioner for Refugees) record, there were 22.5 million refugees in 2016 to which was added another 5.3 million by the United Nations Relief and Works Agency counting Palestine refugees in the Near East (UN RWA). To this was added another 2.8 million as asylum seekers, bringing the total number of the refugees to almost 30.6 million in 2016 of which Germany provided asylum to 7,20,000 followed by the USA to 2,62,000 and Italy to 1,23,000.

Age-wise, refugees below 18 years constituted about 51 per cent of the total global refugee population by the end of 2016 (UNHCR) making the entire child population very high, indeed, including an estimated 75,000 orphans seeking asylum. At the same time, the proportion of females remained more or less stable between 47 and 49 per cent of the total refugee population and majority of the refugees, almost 60 per cent of the total number, were settled in urban areas. Among the top 10 countries turning their citizens into refugees under the threat of 'conflict dynamics' at this time (by the end of 2016) according to UNHCR were – Syrian Arabic Republic, Afghanistan, South Sudan, Somalia, Sudan, the Democratic Republic of the Congo, Central African Republic, Myanmar and Burundi – together accounting for about 13.5 million or 79 per cent of asylum seekers, with many of the countries being among the 'top sources of refugees for at least five years'.

In country-wise assessment, the number of refugees has reached about 5.5 million from Syria while continued 'instability and violence' have turned Afghanistan with 2.5 million (2.7 million in 2015) refugees into the second top country of origin of refugees in the world. South Sudan with over 1.4 million in 2016 has become the third largest source of refugees in 2016 under large scale violence. Altogether, three countries – Afghanistan, South Sudan, and Syria – represent almost 55 per cent of the total number of refugees in 2016 according to UNHCR's mandate. However, the most ironical fact is that while the number of refugees never crossed 30,000 a year in 2010, the number came to 10,05,500 refugees in 2015 primarily coming for safety in life.[10]

It may be of great importance to mention that apart from the USA, Germany and others, there had been some extremely benevolent countries, providing shelter unasked for to the hapless people uprooted by severe violence in their home countries and one of them had been Turkey which, for the third consecutive year in 2016, was the largest host country in the world taking in 2.9 million refugees, 'mainly Syrians (2.8 million)', plus two other middle-east countries, Jordan and Lebanon featured among the top 10 countries playing host to displaced persons followed by Uganda, Ethiopia, Germany, the Democratic Republic of the Congo and Kenya. It should be appreciated that least developed countries like 'Cameroon, Chad, the Democratic Republic of the Congo, Ethiopia, Kenya, Sudan and Uganda together hosted 28 per cent of the global refugees (4.9 million in 2016, UNHCR)' between them while high-income countries like Sweden and Malta took fifth and ninth place among the 10 host countries.

Interestingly, refugees given asylum in safer locations by different countries may, on some occasions, prefer returning to their countries of origin, that is home country. For example, in 2016, over '5,50,000 refugees' returned to their home country, more than double the number in 2015, and majority of them belonged to Afghanistan, earlier settled in Pakistan.[11]

E. Climate Refugees

Apart from political disturbances and internal conflicts displacing people from their roots, there is another reason not less virulent 'triggered by climate and weather-related hazards, such as floods and storms' accounting for displacing almost 25.3 million people every year since 2008.

> This is far greater than the average for conflict and violence and reflects the indiscriminate, unpredictable and uncontrollable nature of certain hazards. These dimensions are strikingly apparent when considering the number of countries hosting the newly displaced: '118 for disasters, compared with 37 countries for conflict and violence'.[12]

In short, climate induced disasters make a much more challenging issue than man-made violence or conflict since the former is beyond our control (though reluctantly man is the cause for such disasters) while the latter may be controlled. Between 2008 and 2017 'an average of 25.3 million people have been displaced by natural disasters, far greater than the number of displaced by conflict and violence. In 2016, 23.5 million or 97 per cent of the total displaced persons were the victims of nature's fury as recorded by UNHCR, and such geophysical hazards have displaced on average 2 million people every year since 2009 with China experiencing it for 74,34,000, the Philippines for 59,30,000 and India for 24,00,000 in 2016 – the highest numbers.[13]

F. Migrants in Regional Perspective

A continent-wise study brings out the prevailing character of migration on the one hand and on the other the existing scope of development aimed at migrants on the other.

(a) Africa

Taking Africa as a case for observation in this respect the most striking factor that appears first is that almost equal number of migrants move 'either within or out of the region'. In other words,

> 'in 2015, over 16 million Africans were living in another African country, while an additional 16 million were living in a different region'.[14]

The number going outside the continent has more than doubled since 1990, more to Europe, 9 million in 2015, followed by 4 million to Asia and 2 million to North America while in the same year 2.3 million came to Africa originating from Asia and Europe.

In the continent, the most emigration takes place from the northern regions with the largest number of people from Egypt living abroad in 2015 followed by Morocco, Somalia, Sudan, and Algeria. In relation to immigration to Africa, South Africa received the largest number of immigrants, about 3.1 million, making 6 per cent of its total population followed by Gabon with 16 per cent of its total population, Djibouti (13%), Libya (12%), Cote d'Ivoire and Gambia 10 per cent each.

Factors like geographic proximity, previous labour recruitment agreements, and post-colonial ties, along with growing unemployment in North African countries have acted as 'drivers of migration' for 10.6 million Africans in 2015, about half of them seeking fortune in Europe with another 3 million in the Gulf States. On the other hand, much interregional migration involving labour mobility was caused by communal and ethnic tensions,

> 'while UNHCR notes that the socio-economic context (one of the world's poorest countries when measured by gross national income per capita), combined with insecurity and access constraints present significant challenges for protection and assistence'.[15]

Extreme weather variability with increasing occurrences of droughts and floods have further worsened the situation in West and Central Africa.

At the time 'intractable politics, political and communal violence' and setbacks in peace building efforts have displaced millions in East Africa, have pushed people to seeking refuge.

> 'Recently, drought influenced by El Nino climate cycle in 2015 and 2016 has caused a humanitarian crisis related to widespread food shortages and famines, contributing (in addition to other non-environmental factors) to human displacement in a number of countries. Rapid-onset disasters such as flooding in 2016 also displaced around 3,00,000 people in Ethiopia, 40,000 in Kenya, 70,000 in Somalia, and thousands more in the Republic of Tanzania and Madagascar.'[16]

(b) *Asia*

Over 40 per cent of global international migration originated in Asia in 2015 of which over half – 59 million – was interregional, making a significant increase over the years from 35 million in 1990. At the same time, there has been considerable increase in migration outside the continent, 15.5 million going to the USA in 2015 and 20 million to Europe in the same year. Migrants from India and China make the largest absolute numbers living abroad though representing a very small share of their total population. More than 2 million Chinese emigrants resided in the USA and other large groups of Asian migrants included India, the Philippines and Vietnam, besides migrants from Bangladesh and Pakistan have gone to Gulf countries.

As mentioned earlier, migrants to Gulf countries in many instances 'make up high proportions' of the total population of their destination – countries, such as in 2015 it was '88 per cent in the United Arab Emirates, about 74 per cent in Kuwait; 76 per cent in Qatar; and 51 per cent in Bahrain.'

Interestingly, India takes the premier position among 20 top Asian countries in sending out migrants (emigrants) followed by China in 2015 while as regards receiving immigrants United Arab Emirates followed by Kuwait, Jordan, and Saudi Arabia – all oil-producing countries – maintained leading positions. Similarly, considering 20 migration-corridors, India was at the top, sending about as many as 3.5 million migrants to the United Arab Emirates in 2015 closely followed by Bangladesh in sending migrants to India. Among the top 20 of the other migration-routes, Indian emigrants took further important position in those between India and Pakistan, India, and the USA, and between India and Saudi Arabia.

Apart from migrants, Asia is also facing great pressure from politically displaced persons, called refugees, or asylum seekers when Syrian and Afghan refugees together constituted 'more than a third of world's refugees' at the end of 2016. The vast majority of Asian refugees, as mentioned earlier, were hosted by neighbouring countries like Turkey, Lebanon, Jordan, Pakistan, Iran, and Iraq.

Another side of the problem is 'unprecedented demographic change' happening particularly in Eastern Asia where low fertility has already created 'negative population growth in Japan' while the Republic of Korea is facing 'lowest birth-rate and as much proliferation of aged population ultimately creating labour shortage and increasing dependence on imported labour (migrants)'. Besides, another development taking place in recent years is 'outward and inward' student-mobility urged by the need of better-quality education prompting movement of a 'high number of international students from Eastern Asia' to countries like the USA, Canada and the United Kingdom.

> 'In the academic year 2015/16, China, the Republic of Korea and Japan were among the top countries of origin of international students in the United States, with more than 3,00,000 students from China alone. In 2014, of the world's total population of students studying abroad, one out of six were from China. However, Eastern Asia is not only a major origin of international students, but it is also gradually becoming an important destination for foreign students, many of them coming from within the sub-region. More students from the Republic of Korea, for example are choosing to study in China, with those from the Republic of Korea accounting for the largest number of international students in China in 2015. Japan plans to attract around 3,00,000 international students by 2020'.[17]

It has been mentioned earlier that China is one of the largest recipients of remittances in the world sent by its emigrants, the latter in 2015 constituting the fourth largest group of migrants, nearly 10 million living abroad following India, Mexico, and Russia, receiving annually USD 61 billion out of global total of USD 575 billion in 2016 from its own people settled (temporarily) abroad. On the other hand, since economic as well as social reforms in the 1980s, the hapless poor in China started moving into urban areas in China in 'hundreds of millions' seeking better sources of livelihood.

Migration in Asia from one subregion to another, particularly in the oil-producing Gulf States since the rise in oil price in 1973 has attained mindboggling dimensions, as mentioned earlier, in many instances forming the largest section of the total population of the receiving countries. Southern Asians now constitute the largest migrant labour force in these countries making 'Southern-Asians among the largest recipients of remittances in the world', which amounted to USD 62.7 billion in 2016, and such remittances sent by their respective migrants to home countries like Pakistan, Sri Lanka, and Bangladesh 'exceeded 5 per cent' of respective GDP in the same year.

As in China, interregional migration in Asia's subregions takes a very important economic role with 'over 85 per cent of the 14.1 million international migrants in Southern Asia originated from other countries in the subregion. As mentioned above, the major corridors of interregional migration happen to be 'Bangladesh-India, Afghanistan-Pakistan, India-Pakistan, and Nepal-India'. Millions of migrant labourers from Bangladesh and Nepal are working mainly in the informal sector, constituting the most important sector of economy primarily based in the growing urban sector employed in construction as well as domestic services. In addition, rural-urban migration, as in China, makes a very lucrative channel for the rural population often facing extreme hardship from failure of crops dependent mostly on climatic vagaries aggravated further by scarcity of storage, marketing as well as transport facilities on top of which they are often subjected to playing in the hands of extremely dishonest intermediaries and moneylenders in the absence of credit or insurance facilities.

Apart from migrants going abroad or moving inside the continent, Asia is also faced with a large number of displaced persons requiring help, numbering about 3.6 million resulting from inadequate infrastructure to tackle 'slow-onset or rapid-onset of disasters related to natural hazards and climate change'. India, Bangladesh and Sri Lanka are among the 10 top-ranking countries for disaster-related displacements, such as cyclone Mona in May 2017 displaced 'hundreds and thousands' of people in Bangladesh while in Nepal severe earthquakes in 2015 caused displacement of people on a large-scale, and almost half-a-million people in Sri Lanka in May 2017 were displaced.

While people in Southern Asia are perpetually plagued with different types of problems magnified by both natural and man-made causes, people in the South generally, especially from lower-income countries, were subject to a massive flow of their citizens which absorbed nearly 10 million international migrants within this subregion, 6.9 million of whom migrated to other countries within this subregion. Two major destinations of migrants from this subregion (South-East Asia) are economically advanced Malaysia and Singapore.

G. Migration, Violent Extremism and Social Exclusion

This sub-title has been borrowed from the report entitled, 'UN World Migration Report 2018' to underline another type of development related to migrants, though correct information in this regard is far from adequate. However, looking at the world as a whole, it is becoming gradually less peaceful than, say, even a few decades back, with violence often of unspeakable scale affecting people in many parts of the world.

Hence, we need to find out how far the responsibility for the deteriorating situation lies with migrants since many of them coming from different economic and cultural backgrounds are the offshoots of such violence.

> 'It is necessary to analyse the linkages between migration and violent extremism for a number of reasons: First, there have been isolated incidents of violent extremism perpetuated by migrants and we need to try to understand why these occurred. Second, it is important to bring data and evidence to bear on an often-misinformed public debate, acknowledging from the onset important research and data gaps. Third, there are linkages between migration and violent extremism, but not those that normally attract attention. Finally, looking to the future, the risk of radicalisation among migrants may grow unless evidence-based policies and interventions to prevent violent extremism are developed now'.[18]

In analysing the available data in this regard about the involvement of migrants with terrorism, the Global Terrorism Index (GTI) 2016 gives the information that 72 per cent of all deaths due to terrorism in 2015 took place in 'just five countries', Iraq, Afghanistan, Nigeria, Pakistan and Syria. But according to this World Migration Report 2018, there is lack of data from non-OECD (Organisation for Economic Cooperation and Development) countries which host 'at least half of the world's migrants' where the 'majority of violent extremist attacks occur'.

It can, however, be confidently stressed that there is no direct link between migrants and occurrences of violent extremism simply because of the fact that millions of migrants living together in many countries are not linked to cases of violent extremism, and if there is any, they are not the product of migrants. There may be quite a number of extreme cases of violence, such as those in the USA on occasions, in each of which killing people indiscriminately had no political agenda but mental derangement. Contrarily, what happened in Paris or elsewhere involved individuals, no doubt, migrants by definition, but they could not be identified as acting with hatred as a group.

In spite of that one cannot deny the instances of migration leading to suffering from 'violent extremism' or actions of violent extremist groups. One can cite the instance of Christian minorities in Levant where 'over half a million of 1.8 million Syrian Christians' have been displaced in 2014 having been targeted by violent extremism. Nigeria provides another example of displacement as targets of Boko Haram, a case of religious violence, with another similar case in northern Uganda. Besides, as expressed by the United Nations Resident Coordinator in 2015, there was every possibility of using the refugee camp in Minawao in northern Cameroon by the Boko Haram. More cases involving population of different religious minorities fleeing occur in South-East Asia which includes Rohingya minorities from Rakhine State in Myanmar, and Chakmas from Bangladesh, as mentioned earlier.

In speaking about violent extremism perhaps a line needs to be drawn between migrants and refugees, the former going on own accord/decision or choice while the latter fleeing oppression. In the case of migrants, they take their own decision without being forced by anybody apart from their own desire of improvement of self-career. Whereas refugees are under mortal-stress saving life from the hands of extremists (mostly religious). Hence, while migrants do not face a situation of any kind of extremism in the country they go on a career-improving mission, and they are never the victims of extremist violence apart from very rarely facing a situation like that individually, and that too one in a million.

> 'Despite recent high-profile terrorism incidents carried out by Central-Asian militants – the April 2017 St. Petersburg metro bombing, the January 2017 Istanbul Night Club attack, and the June 2016 Ataturk Airport bombing – there is no clear evidence that religious, economic or political root causes in Central Asia are responsible for *exporting* terrorism'.[19]

However, migrants going for better financial opportunities are not likely to be treated as equal in consideration of social status, particularly in the USA or European countries or even in Australia but left undisturbed to socialise within their own or similar communities. As such they do not bear any revengeful grudge and keep to their primary as well as ultimate aim of realising the best from the offer obtained.

On the contrary, however, the refugees are quite often at the mercy of the host country and suffer from an uncertain situation though given enough opportunity for improving individual status in a secure situation. The question of inferiority complex is always there and may vitiate the mind in certain circumstances by fortune-seekers exploiting the weaker section to join the violent groups, the process known as 'radicalisation', examples of which are provided by at least four situations: (1) the 'use of Namibian Refugee Settlement in Angola by the South-West Africa National Army'; (2) use of Afghan Refugee camp by Taliban; (3) use of border camps by Nicaraguan Contras, and (4) the case of Cambodian Red Khmer. In addition, the Daesh fighters using the refugees in Yarmouk Camp outside Damascus as **human shields** provide one of the latest most outrageous cases of this type. Concerns have further been expressed that the 'Daesh may be recruiting within refugee settlements in Turkey and Lebanon'. There are definitely more instances of refugees getting 'radicalised to violent extremism' as instances found in Pakistan at 'the Jalozal camp' for Afghan refugees, in Yemen at the 'Somali refugee camp in Kharas', and in Jordan at 'the Zaatari camp for Syrian refugees'. A Syrian refugee boy aged 16 was arrested in Cologne, Germany living in a Syrian refugee camp since 2015 possessing bomb-making devices maintaining connection through internet with Daesh members. Obviously, these are very stray cases to draw any firm conclusion on the influence exerted by Islamist-Jihadists on the refugees in general.

That Jihadists have taken opportunities to enter Europe in the guise of refugees is proved by the case in April 2016 when a man arrested in 2018 at a refugee camp in Salzburg was part of the original group of terrorists that carried out the November 2015 attacks in Paris. As admitted by himself, he an Algerian man along with a Palestinian man were involved in the case. Besides, Daesh at one time in 2015 threatened to flood Europe with half-a-million refugees through Libya, obviously with *Jihadists*. According to a study made in the USA in 2015 (Cato Institute) a total of 154 foreign-born terrorists have so far been identified who 'killed 3,024 people between 1975 and 2015 (including 3,000 victims of the 11 September, 2001 attacks) and of the 7,45,000 refugees 'settled in the USA since 9/11 to 2015, only three have been charged with terrorism'. Perhaps this evidence alone shows how limited are the links between refugees and radicalisation.[20]

What is needed to avoid even such sporadic incidents is a more humane approach to the general condition of the refugees.

> 'Reducing the risk of radicalisation among refugees goes beyond providing humanitarian assistance and requires a

> multipronged approach that gives refugees viable choices for their future. There is, however, no system as yet to evaluate each situation in sufficient depth to create such an approach. The study demonstrates that any effective programme will require the collaboration, sharing of information and alignment of objectives among donors, non-governmental organisations (NGOs), the local population and the host government, as much as with refugees'.[21]

Every host country essentially should give top most priority to the feelings of the people constituting the refugees who have suddenly got uprooted from their country, home and dear near-ones (maybe even from children/parents/siblings/all possessions acquired through long period living in own home, the surroundings and friends/relatives, even shops and sites they had grown up with) on a stroke leaving frantically on a moment's notice to avoid facing death at the hands of people that they had never known or come into any clash with. Leaving home on a moment's notice when the lucky ones came to places alien in every respeet without any promise or idea how life was going to shape up for him or her and the family having survived the death-trap.

Refugees make up, so to say, a race by themselves after they get settled in a host country. Even outstanding citizens distinguish them from the society around as an alienated group. This is very much palpable for any unbiased observer there where they are temporarily (even after permanently) settled, an unseen curtain of alienation keeps them separate from the society around enjoying independent existence. This alienation arises primarily from their status of full-dependence, the very low economic status, the language they speak, dress they wear, (sometimes), religion they follow, food they eat, general habits they pursue, cultural habits they exhibit, and, at times the skin-colour keep them very much alienated from the society (mainstream) that had adopted or hosted them. In most cases, they arrive in large numbers joined later by others arriving from same or other sources and are usually huddled together for a long time in makeshift, or most temporary accommodations often bereft of proper lighting, running water, toilets, sanitation of the meanest order and such other facilities like roads, or any private space, and live with often roofs leaking, flimsy walls incapable of stopping cold/hot winds creeping through walls during summer/winter and children go often without schools. With utter deprivation all around and no hope of future one cannot expect full sanity with these people having nothing to look forward to as 'future', dream of a happy independent life but left with memories of a happy life left behind felt as a big joke for which they never bargained. What happened to these rudderless people at the hands of some of the cruellest people on earth sometimes reminds this author about the doer's similarity with *Homo sapiens*.

However, one looks at the problem of acute isolation felt/suffered by the refugees in a foreign country it cannot be slighted away as a normal or unavoidable happening. The host country has full responsibility for making them feel at home through a process of deep sympathy, compassion and understanding approach them with all humanitarian concern. It is very important to build absolute trust in them so that they get completely rid of a feeling of isolation, so they can feel one with the society around.

In this respect, it is necessary to remember that the refugees belong to an entirely different stock of new arrivals than the migrants in general. The migrants do not move in mass in modern times as they did in the sixteenth to the eighteenth centuries with the primary intention of colonisation. Both slave and indentured labour migration taking place in large numbers travelling together are not considered mass-migration made wilfully. Migrants moving today even in large numbers are fortune-seekers having obtained prior permission to enter and settle down in a country of their choice maintaining an amicable relationship with the employer which is not the case with the refugees. Inclusion through trust-building along with proper living facilities as well as educational opportunities along with the scope for better livelihood may go a long way in the rehabilitation of the refugees so that they can feel as a part of the society, which is not merely the host, but one they are growing up with. In the same spirit, attempts may be made to deradicalize the Jihadists with an open mind which might prove highly beneficial for both sides not only rehabilitating them but bringing them back to the mainstream would lessen the burden of precaution. India provides a large number of such instances of rehabilitation of people who grew up under a different name (Maoists).

NOTES

1. "Migration and Migrants: A Global Review" in *United Nations World Migration Report*, 2018, p. 13.
2. *Ibid.*, p. 23.
3. "World Migration Report: Migrant Well-being and Development" in *International Organisation of Migration*, 2013, p. 25.
4. *Ibid.*, p. 36.
5. *Ibid.*, p. 63.
6. *Ibid.*, p. 65.

7. "Migration and Migrants: A Global Review" in *United Nations World Migration Report*, 2018, p. 28.
8. *Ibid.*, p. 29.
9. *Ibid.*
10. *Ibid.*, p. 33.
11. *Ibid.*, p. 34.
12. *Ibid.*, p. 38.
13. *Ibid.*
14. *Ibid.*, p. 44.
15. *Ibid.*, p. 51.
16. *Ibid.*, p. 54.
17. *Ibid.*, p. 59.
18. *Ibid.*, p. 209.
19. *Ibid.*, p. 219.
20. *Ibid.*, pp. 215-216, 217.
21. *Ibid.*, p. 214.

4
Migration Leading to Slavery
Its Changing Phases

I. The Earliest Phase

Man, the descendants of *Homo sapiens*, has been the cruellest of living animals on earth, even unprovoked, having succeeded in complete annihilation of all other-human-species (Neanderthals etc., numbering altogether six) as well as large animals to make his own life unimpeded through the passage of time. It may not be surprising, therefore, that at one stage he turned some of his own species not fortunate enough to enjoy similar status into slaves used for deriving bodily pleasure (physical) by the more powerful in society that had grown up by that time. Who knows if from the earliest phases of man there existed markets for buying/selling slaves made out of men/women belonging to the lower rungs of the society. As a matter of fact, the slave trade, as evidenced by archaeologists happens to be one of the oldest practices of humankind.

Undoubtedly, slavery is a social construct born of deriving services of the weakest section of the society by higher-ups, including physical enjoyment of all sorts (obviously including free, forcible sex) free of any cost in return of food and shelter of the meanest order, barring freedom of any kind, slaves living always under the threat of facing instant death without trial.

However conjectural the entire picture may look like, the prevalence of slavery cannot be wished away as we find undisputed instances of its presence dating back to the Greek and Roman days, long before the birth of Christ.

According to archaeological evidence, slavery existed before 2000 B.C. among the Sumerians of Mesopotamia and in citing the instance of the Code of Hammurabi which ruled Babylon in the 18th century

B.C., it may be learnt that slaves were allowed to be liberated on certain conditions defined by Hammurabi. It came to be in vogue during the period of Greek-City States. Slavery did exist during the Classical Greek Period (800-500 B.C.) when having slaves added special status to the citizen in the society. During this period most of the labour in agriculture, mining and milling was provided by slaves, they could also hold posts of 'civil servants, clerks and prison attendants' along with some police functions but were barred from holding 'public office'. Besides, a small number of them were used as Gladiators, providing the instance of one of the cruellest games in human history.

> 'By the 4th century B.C. Athens had a slave population of nearly 100,000 amounting to perhaps half the city's population. Piraeus and Attica had roughly the same ratios. One author estimated that between 317 and 308 B.C., the slave population in Athens, Corinth and Aegina out numbered the free population by about four to one.'[1]

It is quite interesting to observe in this respect that the 'institution of slavery' was inherited from the Greeks by the Phoenicians and the Romans to utilise slaves in wars of conquest to expand the territorial domination and for this purpose they brought slaves 'from North Africa, Iberia, Gaul, Britain and Germanic lands' (including, indeed, blacks and whites). The wars they pursued obviously provided prisoners who were converted into slaves. Apart from the natural increase in the slave population, more slaves were available:

> 'by taking and enslaving prisoners; by convicting and sentencing to slavery those free citizens, who committed common crimes; through the sale of infants or orphans into slavery by their parents or guardians; by the sale of waifs by their finders; and by enslaving victims of piracy and plunder who could not pay ransoms'[2].

Corroborating evidence shows that Caesar's Western campaigns provided 'about 5,00,000 slaves from Gaul (modern France) between 58 and 50 B.C. besides Rome having acquired more slaves from Syria, Greece and Egypt. As noted by Frankopan, the Roman empire 'required 2,50,000 -3,00,000 new slaves each year' to maintain its business in slave trade, the market for which was provided by the Arabic speaking lands:

> 'stretching from Spain through to Afghanistan, which would suggest that the number of slaves sold may have been far

> greater even than those for Rome … a Caliph and his wife owning a thousand slaves each, while another was said to own no fewer than four thousand. Slaves in the Muslim world were as ubiquitous – and silent – as they were in Rome'.[3]

Rome further shows how slaves were brought and sold and in this perspective 'personal preferences' of buyers (usually the noblemen or aristocrats) insisting varyingly, such as at some instances on 'matching slaves', meaning 'all equally attractive and of the same age', while in the eleventh century women of a 'particular tribe' (Beja) coming from Egypt, Sudan and Eritrea' were in high demand because of having 'golden complexion, beautiful faces, delicate bodies and smooth skins', making,

> 'pleasant bed-fellows if they are taken out of their country while they are still young. A thousand years ago, money could not buy love, but it could help you get what you wanted'.[4]

Though slavery existed and provided the major labour force even two centuries before the birth of Christ, the very wish for freedom gave rise to slave revolts at times, two of which, occurring in Sicily in Second Century B.C., were serious enough that they lasted for two years before being supressed.

The Greek and the Roman empires are not the only instances of encouraging slavery. It developed later even in Central Europe, concentrated mostly in Germany turning war-prisoners into slaves besides getting slaves from 'long distance slave-traders' operating around the Black Sea area. They were distinct from the Serfs, and

> 'could be whipped, chained, sold, tortured or killed at his master's pleasure. Also, like other property, slaves could be inherited'.[5]

Precolonial Africa had developed a slave industry generally confined within the continent till the entire system underwent a sea-change during the later colonial period. In the precolonial period slaves used to be considered as part of the extended family 'sharing the duties of other members of the society', their children 'accepted as free and equal' with others. With European intervention later the entire system gradually obtained very much a commercial character, to be discussed later.

Slaves constituted a very important element of the 'pre-American populations', particularly thriving in the old empires of South America – the Mayans, Incas and Aztecs. For example, slaves formed a very important expendable commodity in the Mayan society utilised in warfare where slavery was 'perpetual and hereditarian', occupying the lowest rung in the society, and as with the cruellest instances of sometimes being sacrificed in 'religious ceremonies'. Among the Aztecs as well where slavery was very much prevalent for use as labour in agriculture, domestic chores, and porterage they fell into: (a) those acquired as prisoners of war consisting primarily of women and children since men had invariably been sacrificed; (b) contractual slaves sold by parents quite often in debt; and (c) criminals with 'wide range of offences'. Interestingly, Aztec slaves could own property and even slaves of their own children were treated as 'free and equal Aztec citizens'. In contrast, however, the Inca slaves were labourers while the female slaves designated as 'chosen women' consisted of young girls taking part in religious ceremonies and acting as 'royal concubines'.[6]

II. Slavery in the Medieval Period

The merchants from Scandinavia, popularly known as Viking Rus (or Rhos, perhaps due to their red hair. They gave their name to the country of Russia[7]) headed east and south for trade from the beginning of the ninth century lured by the 'trade and riches in the Islamic world'. It involved a journey of almost 3000 miles from Scandinavia to the area around the Caspian Sea and among the various commodities shipped south were 'wax, amber, honey, fine swords' and silks but the 'most important were slaves'. The Rus are considered to be the most ruthless in 'enslaving local population and transporting them south'.*

The river systems were used for transporting the slaves further south 'though not before their captors had sexual intercourse with them one last time! The Slave-trade turned out as an 'important part of Viking economy'. Many slaves were earmarked for Scandinavia where the society consisted of three categories: the aristocrats, freemen, and slaves. The usual routes for transporting slaves by the Viking Rus followed northern and southern Europe terminating at Novgorod where the slaves were traded through Baghdad and 'elsewhere in the Muslim world' and some other Asian cities beside cities in North Africa and Spain 'with greater spending power' had a high demand for slaves. According to archaeological findings, the vibrant economy of northern Europe in the later part of the ninth century boosted trade-relations while 'cash-rich locations' like Samarkand, Tashkent, Balkh etc., made a high demand for slaves imported from Sub-Saharan Africa in 'huge numbers', taken even from Turkic tribes of Central Asia, considered as 'the most precious' ones, with nothing equal to them.

> 'Slave markets thrived across central Europe, stocked with men, women and children waiting to be trafficked to the east

> – and also to the court at Cordoba, where there were more than 13,000 slaves in 961. By the mid-tenth century, Prague had become a major commercial centre attracting Viking Rus and Muslim merchants to buy and sell tin, furs, and people ... slaves were often sent as gifts to Muslim rulers. At the start of the tenth century, an embassy from Tuscany to Baghdad ... offered as a token of friendship ... twenty Slavic eunuchs and twenty particularly beautiful Slavic girls'.[8]

Interestingly, it was not only the Viking Rus 'who profited from the almost insatiable demands for slaves', but Jewish merchants as well traded slaves brought from Europe consisting of boys and girls, while castrating of young men to turn them into eunuchs enjoyed a high demand.

According to Frankopan (2016), Muslim traders were highly active in the slave-trade in the Mediterranean where the slaves consisting of men, women and children brought from all parts of the northern Europe were assembled in Marseilles, taking the role of principal markets wherefrom slaves passed through 'subsidiary' markets of Rouen etc., while Rome itself was another major slave-trading centre. However, in 776, Pope Hadrian I openly derided this system of slave-trade though to no effect.[9]

Ultimately, the slave-trade started dwindling – 'at least from eastern and northern Europe as Viking Rus started losing interest in it, facing too many obstacles including growing resistance from common people when they found trading in other goods more profitable involving less risk but greater profit and hence focused on building up better relationship with the Byzantine empire and its great city of Constantinople instead of the Muslim world centred on Baghdad. Besides:

> 'the adoption of Christianity by the Rus ruler Vladimir in 988 was important too, both because it led to the creation of an ecclesiastical network ministered at the outset by clergy sent from Constantinople, and because of the inevitable cultural borrowings that flowed northwards from the imperial capital ... As the Rus' economy became more mercantile, the warrior-like society became increasingly urban and cosmopolitan. Luxury items like wine, oil and silks were imported from Byzantium and sold on, with trades recording invoices and receipts on birch bark.[10]

III. Slave Trade During the Modern Period

However dormant, the slave-trade does not seem to have stopped at all, making a vigorous presence in early sixteenth century as will be detailed here. Modern slavery owes its origin to that of the Middle Ages, though instead of having a wider sweep covering large parts of Europe and the Middle East countries across white nationalities as well as North Africa, it came to be more oriented to the two emerging European Colonies of North and South America. But instead of different types of status enjoyed by slaves in different situations – even like owning property or buying freedom, in some instances slavery during the colonial period could be described as making the sharpest dividing line between the master and the slave, not even little more were children born of forcible sex able to enjoy any better chance than being considered as slaves providing cheap, additional labour. In both Americas, the growing European colonies, familiar with plantation-slavery introduced by the Christians in the 'Levantine Mediterranean and South-West Iberia'[11] and with the African slave-trade existing even a century ago through the discoveries of Christopher Columbus.

> 'In 1488, Ferdinand the Catholic, King of Spain presented Pope Innocent VIII with some 100 Moorish slaves, which the Pope distributed to his Counsellors'.[12]

The trans-Atlantic slave-trade got special impetus from the growing importance as well as demand for such specialities as sugar, coffee, indigo, cotton, and tobacco. According to the *Encyclopaedia Americana*, nearly 9.6 million Africans were engaged as slaves between 1510 and 1870 in two Americas.[13]

According to Hirsch (2018), the first cargo of five hundred slaves of African origin to the Americas made by Sir John Hopkins in 1562 marked the beginning of the slave-trade, a venture highly appreciated by Queen Elizabeth I of England, as mentioned earlier, and had far-reaching consequences involving every monarch in Britain since then down to George III giving 'direct support to the trans-Atlantic slave-trade'. In 1672, the establishment of Britain's first 'slave trading' corporation, the Royal African Company with the support of King Charles II clinched the issue, turning it into the most lucrative source amassing huge wealth for royalty in particular.

> 'It was not just the British royal family but also the aristocracy and banking and industrial classes who grew rich from slavery but also fuelled the Industrial Revolution, the railways and other key parts of the physical and financial infrastructure that continue to serve us today. Preparing a vessel for a slave voyage, as Olusaga has shown, was complex and expensive,

> the average cost of fitting one out to carry hundreds of humans, in the currency of 1790, was about £10,000. That's more than half a million pounds today'.[14]

As mentioned earlier, European consumption of sugar having leaped twentyfold between 1663 and 1775 sustained the supply of slaves in greater number through this period to be used as free labour obviously collected from Africa in the most clandestine manner. Interestingly, production of cotton overtook sugar as a slave-produced commodity and in the 1840s, the import duties on 'free-grown and slave-grown cotton and sugar were equalised' providing rich profits for Britain from the 'unpaid labour of kidnapped Africans' (Hirsch, 2018).

It is highly astonishing to believe the impact of slavery on Africa continued for almost four centuries at a stretch where millions of 'often the strongest and most able' people of working-age were kidnapped on an industrial scale and murdered thus making the most debilitating effect on the supply of manpower required for the continent's own need. At the same time, the most blood-chilling accounts of sexual abuse of slave-women cannot be ignored as a natural event which makes an essential part of the slave-trade pursued by colonial powers. For example, the Slave Forts of Cape Coast at Elmina Castle, the oldest European building south of the Sahara Desert still standing after about 55 hundred years now was utilised for keeping African slaves holed-up in cells before they were loaded on to ships for transport to their final destinations – obviously one of the two Americas – undergoing the 'most grotesque and prolonged' suffering in human history.

> 'In the dungeon where female slaves were held in filth and anguish for up to three months, a trapdoor leads directly to the master's luxurious bedrooms above, where they would be washed before he raped her. It is estimated that at the peak of the slave trade, 10,000 people a year was transported onto the boats from its haunted cells'.[15]

As mentioned in Chapter 2, even a conservative estimate puts the number of slaves smuggled out of Africa forcibly consisting of able-bodied men and women at 12 million, 40 per cent of them carried by British ships, while 15 per cent of the total died on the way with a million landing in Spanish and Portuguese colonies, with four million going to Brazil alone while more than a million ended up in British colonies to work till death intervened. Finally, according to this author, Hirsch (2018), the share of Britain's profit out of slave-trade was the highest among all colonial countries.[16]

Further, it is quite strange to observe that the slaves were not spared to give free labour even after Britain legally abolished the trans-Atlantic slave-trade which happened in 1807. It is argued that the value of 8,00,000 or so slaves still then owned by the British in the Caribbean was £47 million. Of this amount £20 million was paid to slave-owners for losing the right to have slaves,whereas the slaves themselves 'losing family, income, dignity, heritage, identity or life', had to provide free labour for another four years even after the abolition of slavery to compensate for the remaining sum of £27 million. It, thus, makes obvious that abolition meant little to British consciences, who treated the Africans as their own property free of any obligation to avoid utterly inhuman treatment.

Unfortunately, the slave-trade did not end with its abolition in 1807, but continued unabated in best of disguises, such as:

> 'By 1840, there were more slaves crossing the Atlantic than there had been before and British investors and businesses were among those profiting. Conditions for slaves were becoming even more hideous ... British traders set up partnerships with traders in Cuba where slaves continued to arrive until 1870 – and Brazil, where the trans-Atlantic trade was only abolished in 1888. There was nothing to stop Brits investing in the actual ownership of slaves in these nations, and in slave-worked mines and plantations, and they did in significant numbers'.[18]

A. *Life of Slaves*

The lives of slaves used to be patterned on the principle of chattel according to which it was treated as a movable property by the master, treated as commodities when,

> 'a tall well-proportioned slave man or woman in case of a sale, would always command the highest price paid'.[19]

In such a society, slaves felt themselves treated as property of the owner. Whenever the master was not pleased with them or when he needed more cash, he was likely to sell them which the slaves wanted to avoid because of facing a worse situation, separated from their family and friends, in unknown territories. In a situation like this, a slave would run away since he had nothing more to lose:

> 'isolation, hunger, exposure, tracking dogs, and threats of violent capture and sadistic punishment that their owners generally used to keep them from slipping out they could no longer provoke enough fear to keep these men from running away'.[20]

The author, Walter Johnson (1999) mentions an incident in this connection, which happened in January 1833 when 153 slaves bought from their master by another master to work in his sugar plantations, involving movement from Florida to Louisiana – 'about forty' ran away and later 120 out of the total of 153 'disappeared'. As a matter of fact, the most identifying feature dominating the treatment of slaves as 'commodities' made the relationship between masters and slaves most unfavourable.

The slave-trade, as it appears, from the accounts, was very much dominated by seasonal pressure of work which pulsated in agricultural work with different phases of cropping, for example, more 'hands were needed in the summer and to tend crops'. Demand for more labour at those times giving rise to 'seasonality' in the movement of slaves made the situation highly disagreeable for them as they could be highly reluctant to leave their adopted places living with family and acquaintances (friends) already having made a niche for themselves.

In contrast, movement of slaves purchased by a buyer (new master) portrayed a heart-rending scene enough to explain why the slaves did not want to move. One particular case giving a real idea about such an incident where the slaves were kept in chains overnight when taking about three hundred slaves:

> 'they (the master and his team) had a caravan of nine waggons and single-horse carriages, for the purpose of conducting the white people, and any of the blacks that should fall lame, to which they were now putting the horses to pursue their march. The female slaves were, some of them, sitting on logs of wood, whilst others were standing, and a great many black children were warming themselves at the fires of the bivouac. In front of them all, and prepared for the march stood, in double files about two hundred male slaves, manacled and chained to each other'.[21] They had to go on foot, covering about twenty miles a day for seven or eight weeks to reach their destinations.

This interstate trade in slaves came to be a very common feature to stop slaves running away when sold to new masters, having purchased them through a dealer, used to keep man-slaves in chains while the women, less likely to run away, were kept 'bound with ropes'. In order to stop slaves plotting revolt, or run away, they were not allowed to speak to each other. However, the distance from original place where they were engaged first and made their home came to be so far that gradually it became more difficult for them to run away. Perhaps, nothing makes it more clear how the slaves felt about their life having been sold time and again to new customers as stated here by Walter Johnson (1999):

> 'sale into trade was more than they could bear. Separated from the world that had given their lives meaning, some slaves were overwhelmed by the traders' brutality, the numbing privation of the slow southward march, and the terrifying contingency of lives put up for sale. To the social death experienced by those torn from their histories and identities and the physical death they faced in the killing fields of the lower south must be added the psychic deaths – the 'soul murder' – that left many of the trader's victims with little will to resist'.[22]

There is obviously no doubt that slave owners, in general, irrespective of their locations treated slaves with 'extreme callousness and cruelty'. This was possible because of the fact that products like 'gold and sugar' commanding international markets were in the hands of the slave-holders and even though the number of slaves increased sharply in America by importation from Africa, sometimes forming the majority of the population pushing other forms of labour, such as 'small farmers and wage workers to the margin' sometimes giving rise to revolts made by the slave communities – such as those called the rice revolution in Carolina in the early eighteenth century, and the cotton revolution in the Mid-West in the early nineteenth century.[23]

However, in the absence of competitors, the slaveholders 'solidified their rule' and utilising their control of the state framed more rigorous laws in no time sharply reducing the latitudes slaves enjoyed earlier and subjecting them to absolute rule of the master vigorously curtailing the advantages the slaves enjoyed previously, such as 'ability to travel, to meet among themselves, to hold property, and to trade at market'.

In the process of growth of slave communities slave societies came into being. However, the evolution of the slave societies went through three distinctive phases, (a) *the charter of generations* which consisted of the first arrivals including their children and, in some cases, their grandchildren; (b) *the plantation generation* who were forced to grow the great staples; and (c) *the revolutionary generation,* who understood the 'promise of freedom and faced a resurgent slave regime'. In other words, it shows the development of a gradual process of change in the status of slaves. All these express how generations of African slaves realised the realities of life they had been forced into and realised they had to make a life of their own in the new circumstances. In this context it is essential, as (Ira Berlin, 2003) says, to understand the basic changes in the status of African slaves through the period of two centuries. Such as:

> 'In mainland North America, slaves (like their owners) were simply not the same people in 1819 that they had been in 1719 or 1619, although the origin and colour (perhaps the most defining factor) of the slave population often had not changed'.[24]

The growing importance of the slave-trade, originating with slaves from Africa may be recognised from the fact that Elmina, in West Africa. as one of the most important bases of slave-trade, as mentioned in Chapter 2, grew in size so that it had a population between 12,000 and 16,000 most of eighteenth century larger in size than Charles Town in South Carolina, which later became the largest slave-port on mainland North America. The importance of places like Elmina can be ascertained from the fact that:

> 'they served as both field headquarters for great European mercantile companies and collection points for trade between the African inferior and the Atlantic rim. Depending on the location, the exchange involved European textiles, metal-ware, guns, liquor and bids for African gold, ivory, hides, pepper, beeswax, and dyewoods ... Everywhere slaves were bought and sold, and overtime the importance of commerce-in-persons grew'.[25]

As a matter of practice, the African slaves purchased for life worked alongside indentured servants, many of them from Ireland, 'convicts' or political refugees. This happened in the tobacco plantations in Chesapeake during the seventeenth and the eighteenth centuries and the relation between the master, servant and slaves was more amicable than it was elsewhere. The situation in New Amsterdam, renamed New York by the English, was amicable between the master and the slave. However, the entire situation changed fast with white farmers migrating west during the last decades of the seventeenth century and slaves started replacing indentured servants. By 1700, the slaves constituted one-third of the labourers growing tobacco in Maryland and Virginia and by 1740 'black people' made up 40 of the population in parts of Chesapeake. The nature of treatment took sharp change in the early years of the eighteenth century than it had been in the previous century. For example:

> 'In the previous century maimings, brandings and beatings had occurred commonly, but the level of violence increased dramatically as planters transformed the society with slaves into a slave society. Chesapeake slaves faced the pillory, whipping post, and gallows far more frequently and in far larger numbers than ever before. Even as planters employed the rule, the lash, the branding iron, and the fist with increased regularity, they invented new punishments that would humiliate and demoralise as well as correct.'[26]

Sadly, all these most inhuman as well as heinous practices got support from the state 'affirming master's right to take a slave's life without fear or retribution'. The nature of torture is further revealed in the fact that, the slaveholders reduced the number of holidays in a year to three by the early eighteenth century: such as Christmas, Easter, and White sun tide while Saturday came to be a full working day and many slaves had to work on Sundays as well and even at night during winter by firelight to compensate for the shorter length of days. 'Violence, isolation, exhaustion, and alienation often led slaves to profound depression culminating in 'self-destruction' in many cases. In some cases, the slaves used to run away but when caught, had to face brutal treatment, and if they survived that, they were sold to more distant places.

However, there was a welcome change in slave-life during the concluding period of the eighteenth century representing a local-born new generation of African Americans consisting of native-born black people increasing in number through procreation, healthier, living longer than African new-comers. With English as their native tongue (may be in a 'Scottish-Irish dialect' or 'Virginia accent') enjoying a better grip on the situation with better knowledge of plantation agriculture acquired through a generation of experience and as such taking up greater challenges of management moving from the position of mere labourers on the field to more important responsibilities. For example:

> Travelling through the countryside as messengers, watermen, and jobbing tradesmen, native-born slaves exuded confidence as they mastered the terrain, perfected their English, and incorporated the icons and institutions of the owners' culture

> into their African inheritance. The culture that emerged enabled African American to challenge their owners from a position of knowledge'.[27]

In spite of this, the slave-owners were determined not to allow slaves a 'modicum of domestic stability, continuously intervening in family' affairs forcing them to seek prior permission even for family-contacts, even declining permission to visit Kinfolk 'in their own time'. Nevertheless, in course of time the slave-owners had to relent, at least on some of the prerogatives, such as entitlement to free Sundays, taken as a right during the middle of the eighteenth century along with part of Saturdays free of labour.

All these originated from the fact that by this time the slaves with their knowledge in their work had given them an upper hand when without applying this the complex process of raising tobacco as a crop could completely fail, ruining the entire economy that the master enjoyed. This was fully realised by the master who needed to be in a compromising position to save fortune.

However, quite naturally the situation demanded some change in the crop schedule in order to stop a monopoly of tobacco as the major crop in the seventeenth century while other crops such as wheat, changing tobacco areas into cereal producing areas particularly in the eastern shores of Maryland and Virginia from where tobacco was gradually eliminated by cereals like rye, oats and especially wheat, thus making cereal production more profitable in value far exceeding that from tobacco in the third and fourth decades of the eighteenth century, on the eve of American revolution.

This further brought a kind of revolution in the working process unlike that of tobacco requiring slave labour working round the year in the fields since cereal production needed most labour at the time of sowing and planting while releasing it for a profitable use in other associated activities like transporting the grain 'to market it, store it, mill it, reship it as bulk grain, flour or bread'. On the other hand, draft animals used for transporting provided raw material like hides on their death could be 'tanned, and used for bridles, saddles, and shoes, the manufacture of which gave rise to new professions like 'tanners, blacksmiths, saddlers and harness makers', besides providing jobs for the slaves in the growing industries such as 'flour mills, iron foundries, weaving houses and other non-agricultural ventures'. In other words, greater stress on cereal cultivation revolutionised the work of the respective landowners with greater diversification swelling the earnings and reducing uncertainties of producing a single crop like tobacco requiring greater care.

This brought in further changes in the work-schedule of slaves. They were allowed to work on 'little spots allotted to them' besides rearing flocks of chickens, geese and ducks to provide them extra income by selling products, improve their own diet and 'expand their wardrobes'.

Meanwhile, low country South Carolina went through another revolutionary change in crop production with the introduction of rice and indigo in the last decade of the seventeenth century for which the inland swamps and coastal marshes were reclaimed which demanded more African slaves imported and in '1720 more than half the value' of all exports from South Carolina was derived from the export of rice, its production by 1760 spreading from North Carolina to East Florida, but the most promising of the new crops, indigo, was 'a rapidly growing weed that could be transformed into a much-valued blue dye' involving a very complicated process of production which became a great burden on overworked slaves. Nevertheless, it accounted for 'one-quarter' of South Carolina's export by the time of American Independence. But the increase in the level of violence which accompanied the entire process of production was decried by Christian missionaries as:

> '*Profane and inhuman practices*, as planters turned to the lash, the faggot and the nooses to discipline slaves unfamiliar with the requirements of rice and indigo. Even punishment for small faults took on monstrous quality, as with the planter who placed slave miscreants in a *coffin where they are almost crushed to death*, keeping them *in that hellish machine for twenty-four hours* ... The State – which was nothing more or less than the planters themselves – naturally affirmed this judgement'.[28]

As a result, slave-unrest, from the first decades of the eighteenth century, gave rise to an uncertain condition and created a sort of heart-change among some slaveholders which made some, though very little, changes in their dealing with slaves, henceforth 'demanding deference and loyalty in return for benevolent oversight'. Gradually, the attitude of slave-owners changed further and by mid-eighteenth century they recognised 'slaves' right to produce independently and accumulation of property in this way strengthened their familial attachment, reducing their intention of running away.

B. *Freedom from Slavery: A Slow Process*

The Declaration of American Independence on July 4, 1776, made by thirteen states severing their role with Great Britain as the ruler opened a new vista not only for them but also had a longstanding effect on other related activities. One of them was very closely related to the freedom of slaves.

> 'Thoughtful men in both the south and north (of the thirteen liberated states) agreed that Negro bondage was not morally justifiable, and that slavery and the slave-trade should be ended. Abolition of slavery was much easier where slaves were few. Within 30 years after the Declaration of Independence, slavery had largely disappeared in New England States, New York, New Jersey, and Pennsylvania; and the North-West Ordinance 1787 forbade the institution in the North-West Territory, from which the States of Ohio, Indiana, Michigan and Wisconsin were eventually formed'.[29]

However, freedom of slaves did not come immediately with the Declaration of Independence and the Declaration of the Rights of man as many white Americans 'rarely welcomed the new order' as it would mean the greatest loss of working hands which once purchased will give free labour round the clock over the years as long as slavery survived. As such there had been strong opposition to liberating the slaves and giving them freedom from life-long bondage. As such the 'demise of slavery was a slow, fortuitous process'. It took most of the northern independent states more than one or even two generations until they passed anti-slavery laws in the mid-nineteenth century.

> 'Still, whatever the limits northern lawmakers placed on their freedom, black people moved quickly to give meaning to their freshly won liberty and to give form to a rapidly emerging African-American culture. They chose their own names, took their own residences, and found their own jobs. Having created individual identity as free men and women, they built institutions to protect and expand their liberty as free people. Along with churches, schools and fraternal societies, a leadership class emerged and laboured to maintain the unity of African American Society'.[30]

However, this was a turbulent period with strongly opposing views, some states in northern New England like Vermont, Massachusetts, New Hampshire conceding to the slaves while such a move was very strongly resisted in southern New England and Middle Atlantic states where ultimately this involved movements of troops to bring a solution to the emerging problem, making the entire situation more complex than it had been before with many slave owners transferring their slaves to their friends for 'safekeeping', or sending them to distant places. The expected emancipation was very slow to come, so much so that even in 1780, the process of 'legal liquidation of slavery' had not even started in some states like Connecticut, Rhode Island, New Jersey and New York.

In response to such characteristic reticence the slave hitherto 'took seriously the liberation promise of American Independence and would accept nothing less. According to a report between half and three-quarters of the young slave men' did not report for duty in Philadelphia in the 1780s. But the slave-owners still refused to yield to the growing pressure of emancipation which became slow and spasmodic. Still then it was not being taken seriously, such as in 1784 Connecticut and Rhode Island lawmakers legislated emancipation while it took two more decades for New York and New Jersey to take the same step. As a matter of fact, the New York abolition law of 1799 and the New Jersey Act of 1804 were nothing but a great mockery since they,

> 'mandated the eventual liquidation of slavery but actually freed no slaves. In New York, the children of slaves born after the law went into effect on July 4, 1799 would remain in the service of their mothers' owner until age twenty-eight for males and twenty-five for females. It would take nearly another twenty years for New Yoɪk to free the slaves who had been born before 1799. A similar formula delayed even longer the arrival of freedom in New Jersey'.[31]

In short, slavery remained in practice in one form or another serving the masters' interests who could easily connive as they were the lawmakers protecting their own interests to the hilt for which no step was wrong. However, unlike the Civil War of Emancipation, Abraham Lincoln's Proclamation freed the black people in a 'single stroke' in the Southern States while it took sometimes more, a generation, in some of the northern states, as mentioned before, but eventually it came in starts and fits, making white domination perpetually dead. Altogether, though it gave rise to two nationalities in the long run, strongly divided by a line of separation never to meet and give rise to one undivided society, and this line of demarcation keeping both sides very much different from each other was the line dividing black and white. In fact, it is white domination which speaks for America with full authority keeping Black America at the whim and dictation of the White America. However, one can agree, the Whites determine, and Blacks follow. Arguably, the one-nation theory stumbles when one considers barring entitlement of the Blacks to many things sustaining the Society. However, this Black and White distinction is also in many actions which, if not all, European countries manifest sometimes in quite subtle manner. For example, since the money and the power of selection for some great achievement in a field of arts/science etc. remain in White hands, the final selection in many cases is very strongly influenced by the colour of the skin of the awarded person. This has happened time and again in the case of awarding the most prestigious award of the Nobel Prize. The domination in the selection of the right person in arts, science or other field is very much prevailed upon by the colour of the skin which is preferred to be White than non-White. However, it is not that skin colour other than White is the only criterion, but it is the dominating un-hesitant one. It is, as mentioned earlier, not difficult to find that the origin of the idea of Brexit in Britain has a deep connection with the division between White and non-White and immigration.

IV. Indentured Labour: Another Instance of International Mass-Migration

Both Slavery and Indentured Labour mean mass migration, the primary distinction between the two being that the former is forcible and the latter voluntary. Besides, the former, slavery – as the word defines – meant forcible capture of unwary people who never offered their labour to the captor, who were taken out of Africa (mostly) against their will or any consent, leaving no address behind and thus becoming rootless once taken out to work for their whole life receiving no renumeration, and thus becoming out and out the personal property of the owner (master) to be treated as he liked who purchased them from the Agent/Supplier. In sharp contrast to this, indentured labour were taken out on contract for a stipulated period on a fixed salary for a fixed period but based on entirely false hopes of a better future with a freedom of returning home if they wished on completion of the tenure.

The word 'indentured' was introduced by the British in the 1800s when they ruled India, and 1.3 million labourers of Indian origin called indentured labour or coolies were taken out between early nineteenth and early twentieth centuries, sent to the Caribbean and other British Colonies to work mainly in the sugar plantations (Table 4.1).*

The Act of Emancipation in 1833 passed by the British Government leading to the abolition of slavery brought in a great change in the history of the West Indies or the Caribbean world, wherefrom 6,55,000 African

Table 4.1: Indentured Indian Migration to the Caribbean

Colony	Period	Immigrants
British Guiana	1838-1917	2,38,909
Trinidad	1845-1917	1,43,939
Guadeloupe	1854-1889	42,326
Jamaica	1854-1885	36,420
Dutch Guiana	1873-1916	34,304
Martinique	1854-1889	25,509
French Guiana	1856-1877	6,551
St. Lucia	1858-1895	4,354
Grenada	1857-1885	3,200
St. Vincent	1860-1880	2,472
St. Kitts	1860-1865	337
St. Croix	1862	–
Total		**5,38,642**

Source: Vertovec, S., *Indian Indentured Migration to the Caribbean from the Cambridge Survey of World Migration.* Cambridge University Press (Ed. R.Cohen). 1995: p. 59.

slaves earned their freedom with similar action taken by the French and the Danish in 1848 and the Dutch in 1863. It came to be an extremely hard decision for the European planters since their entire economy hinged on cheap labour which ultimately found a way-out in bringing indentured labour on easy terms mostly from their colonies, particularly from India to replace the slavery system. As a matter of fact,

> 'From the 1820s (even before the abolition of the slavery system) sugar planters in Reunion and Mauritius had experienced some success in importing labourers from India'.[32]

British Guiana was the first Caribbean Country to bring indentured Indian labour in 1838 and according to Steven Vertovec (1995) 'more than half a million Indians were brought to the Caribbean' through the system though it was temporarily halted under local pressure from 'nationalist Indians'.[33]

It was a common practice for British rulers in India to employ an Indian, called 'Arkati', an unlicensed agent, or middleman, to recruit coolies (unskilled labour) for indenture. Loitering in temples, in markets or train stations, they used to catch people looking for jobs, or those who appeared vulnerable telling them about the prospect of the job going to be offered as indentured labour, sometimes even giving a little money in advance which undoubtedly exerted a great deal of influence in believing the Arkati's story about the entirely false prospect of working abroad. They were told that if they worked in the plantation, they were likely to be taken to, there was a prospect of earning rupees 'five a month' as compared with what they could earn in India which even with hard labour was 'three rupees a month'. Hence such an offer acted as a very strong attraction for going abroad when anywhere in India at the time unskilled people's earning was very low (Table 4.2).

Table 4.2: Daily Wages in North, Middle and South India (in Rupees)

Region	Nature of Labour	1810	1830	1850	1871	1896
North India	Coolies/ Labourers	0.10	0.08	0.09	0.14	0.14
	Bricklayers	0.16	–	0.19	0.25	0.28
	Carpenters	0.13	–	0.16	0.25	0.31
	Blacksmiths	–	–	0.13	0.19	0.31
Middle India	Coolies/ Labourers	0.11	0.11	0.15	0.22	0.16
	Bricklayers	0.31	0.31	0.43	0.66	0.66
	Carpenters	0.31	0.31	0.43	0.66	0.66
	Blacksmiths	0.31	0.31	0.43	0.66	0.66
South India	Coolies/ Labourers	–	–	0.05	0.10	0.13
	Bricklayers	–	–	0.17	0.25	0.38
	Carpenters	–	–	0.17	0.25	0.38
	Blacksmiths	–	–	0.17	0.25	0.38

Source: Gubili, K., *Craftsmen and Labourers Wages and Rice Indices in India in 1913 Constant Rupee, 1800-2000*. Viriah, Notion Press, Chennai (India) 2018, p. 59.

The persons willing to go as indentured labour needed to sign a contract for going abroad but, interestingly, the assurances made for available facilities at the time of signing the contract, were never fulfilled, i.e. 'of a free house to live in, of garden ground for cultivating fruits and vegetables, of doctors that would be available, and of families that would never be split'.[34]

All these had a dream-like effect on the poor, uneducated rural people who hardly could make an existence during the British rule when complete closure of rural industries left no alternative for earning though it is maintained that economically India was very much well-off before colonial rule set its grip on the country's economy when,

> 'India's share of world economy was about 25 per cent, which was equal to that of Europe at that time. In three (?) hundred years of British occupation, India's share fell to a miniscule 4 per cent'.[35]

In those days, all the ships carrying indentured labour from India left from only two ports – Calcutta (Kolkata) and Madras (Chennai). Though most of the migrants as indentured labour mainly came from 'north-east and south-India', the planters' prejudices against South-Indian labour 'ceased between 1861 and 1906'. Thus, henceforward the migrants came from 'western Bihar and eastern Uttar Pradesh', aged within their twenties 'with an average sex ratio of three males to one female', the voyage between Calcutta and the Caribbean taking three to four months, though reduced to six weeks by the beginning of the twentieth century.[36]

The indentured labourers, referred by Krishna Gubili (2018), included his own great grandfather, Viriah (named after the goddess, Viramma) taken to South Africa in 1904 where he was working in the sugar plantations in Natal as a conscripted labourer under very severe working conditions without proper sustaining food and any medical care. It is, however, interesting to record that:

> 'The South Africa-bound ships, 384 trips were made to transport 1,52,184 coolies at an average of 400 coolies per ship, 534 trips were made for Guyana to transport 2,39,000 coolies there at an average of 450 coolies per ship. The ship carrying great grandfather had more than 600 coolies on it'.[37]

By 1911, there were about 1,52,184 indentured Indian labourers in Natal including Viriah where even the pavements in Durban were forbidden to be stepped on as the signs bore the words for 'Whites only'.

The episode is only a lone instance of 1.3 million indentured labourers taken to British colonies – considered much cheaper than buying a black slave – alone between the early-nineteenth to the first quarter of the twentieth centuries and the countries benefited with the service of almost free labour in consideration of their very low wage. The experience of some of those British colonies in this respect is worth noting. Among the four major British Caribbean colonies Jamaica 'stands apart' with its geographical setting containing vast tracks of unsettled mountainous areas whose sugar export had been declining since the abolition of slavery. This, naturally initiated labour immigration and India offered unlimited scope for this where from already 25,468 Indian coolies had migrated to Mauritius between 1834 and 1839 and within another about twenty-five years from 1842 onwards, 3,40,718 fresh Indian recruits arrived from India in Mauritius comprising 2,61,074 males and 79,644 females channelled through three Indian ports of Calcutta, Madras and Bombay. Although 87,617 of the indentured labourers went back home on completion of their period of contract, the 'balance remained' back on the island making it their permanent home.[38] In contrast demand for such labour was quite low in Jamaica for political reasons having only 2000 labourers in 1847 to work in the sugar plantations where they were found 'more efficient and thorough' than African slaves. In 1858, it was advocated by the Government of Jamaica that Indian immigration to Jamaica's sugar plantations was the only way to revive Jamaica's prosperity. Accordingly, between 1867 and 1914, the colony introduced 27,215 Indian workers on lengthy indentures which helped in restoring the sugar plantation industry from further downfall.[39] There is no doubt that the somewhat half-hearted approach of the local government was responsible for the production of sugar gradually sliding down which, otherwise, could be the most important export for Jamaica (Table 4.3).

Table 4.3: Average Annual Production of Sugar in British Colonies

(in tons)

Years	Jamaica	Barbados	Trinidad	British Guiana
1824-1833	68,465	14,838	12,322	55,936
1887-1896	20,891	54,667	50,000	109,718
1910-1914	14,996	27,682	46,344	87,615

Source: Saunders, K., *Indentured Labour in the British Empire 1834-1920*, 2018. Taken from Noel Deerr, *A History of Sugar*, Chapman and Hall, London. 1949-1950; 2: pp.193-203.

There cannot be any doubt that the abolition of slavery hit very hard on the economy of the British Caribbean and, the sugar industry in particular. To fill in the gap of labour vacated by slaves from Africa, indentured labour was brought to British Guiana from 'India, Madeira, the West Indies and Africa'. There were 46,514 of them arriving between 1834 and 1848 but unfortunately by 1851 only 7,670 of East Indians remained due to the death of the 'unseasoned immigrants', besides many of them running away whenever they got the opportunity.[40]

Ordinarily, the contract made for indentured labour, particularly with those from India, was for five years but renewable including 'provisions for return passage, free housing, medical attention and standard rations' for which the labour was required to work nine hours a day and six days per week. But the most depressing aspect was that of very poor accommodation in wooden barracks left by slave-workers with 'leaky roofs, bad ventilation and poor drainage' without latrine, worse in every respect than houses back in their villages in India where they came from.[41]**

It is, indeed, very revealing to note that the indenture system primarily sourced from India, surviving almost eighty years between 1830 and 1916 was, in fact, preceded by the Dutch bringing 6,000 South Indian slaves in 1800 to the French planters in Mauritius and thousands to Reunion to work in the plantations. On the other hand, the beginning of the indentured labour system was the result of the Indian colonial rules:

> 'discriminatory taxation on Indian goods, persistent famines and pestilence were among the many reasons for migration which offered the only avenue of hope to many. While all sectors of Indian Society were affected by these profound changes, the lower agricultural classes, who predominated among the recruits were the worst affected'.[42]

Mauritius was the first British colony to receive indentured labour from India in 1834, receiving altogether half-a-million between 1834 and 1911 while 60,965 Indian labour were recruited by Fiji between 1879 and 1916, majority of them coming from the United Provinces (Uttar Pradesh), Bihar and Central Provinces (Madhya Pradesh), 75 per cent of them boarding at Calcutta (Kolkata), which became the Principal 'Coolie Catchment' port and the remaining 25 per cent from Madras (Chennai).[43]

Talking about British Guiana, mentioned above, between 1854 and 1917, such contrasts as death of Indian indentured labour as well as many of them running away made it essential the Guianese economy to stop the renewal of contract for those who had gone back to their country without permission from 1904. In spite of that the number of labourers from India resident on estates rose from '15,392 to 18,552 to 72,793 in 1904'. But the rise in the number of those Indians who stayed back was followed by a very unethical practice imposed by the planters in reducing their wages which, starting from 1860s down to mid-1870s, however, was lifted for a short while when the European sugar beet crop failed. As a matter of fact:

> 'indentured immigration can be seen as an essential part of that complex process through which the sugar economy in British Guiana survived the double blow of slave emancipation and free trade ... sugar has kept British Guiana the one civilised spot in the continent of America'.[44]

However, because of the fall in sugar prices in 1883 and the fall again at the 'second sugar crisis of 1894-97', the practice of indenture was discontinued entirely from 1917 which finally closed the legacy of 200 years of sugar in British Guiana.

Trinidad, coming into British possession in 1834 from the hands of Spain, took measures to combat the shortage of labour following the emancipation of slaves by bringing indentured labour from India from 1838 to 1865, resulting in 29,254 recruits on a three-year contract, raised later to a five-year contract in 1862 (as well as black labour being brought from other areas of the Caribbean). Highly improved methods and technology were used in agriculture in Trinidad and the gradually falling price of sugar in the international market between 1860s to early 1880s, though it 'remained relatively high', enabled a great expansion in the sugar industry in Trinidad as recorded in Tables 4.4 and 4.5.

Table 4.4: Estimated Average in Principal Crops for Selected Years in Trinidad

Year	Sugarcane	Cocoa	Rice	Ground Provisions
1879	19,556	24,158	NA	16,720
1899	50,256	1,50,683	7,449	34,349
1907-08	58,300	2,26,880	11,800	41,850

Source: Saunders, K., *Indentured Labour in the British Empire 1834-1920*. Routledge. 2018 : p. 58.

The system of increasing production of sugar depended largely on reliable workforce provided by the indentured labour force, an increasing number of them finding occupation not only in sugar plantations but also in the production of cocoa and rice along with vegetables.

The sugar industry, however, retained its favoured position even during the twentieth century when cocoa surpassed it in extent and value[45] though sugar and cocoa growers together decided by the end of the nineteenth century about using more immigrants than indentured labour as the latter appeared costlier. Nevertheless, the role of indentured labour has been very important in sustaining particularly the sugar estates in providing a 'reliable and disciplined work-force between 1895 and 1917' to replace the previously employed slave-labour.

Table 4.5: Sugar Exports and Values, Trinidad 1831 to 1907

Year	Sugar Exported	
	Quantity (tons)	Value (£a)
1831	14,997	2,04,029
1841	13,103	4,09,416
1851	19,899	2,94,248
1861	30,147	3,76,865
1871	58,592	9,38,000
1881	43,608	6,68,153
1891	45,357	6,62,789
1901-02	45,254	4,53,304
1906-07	45,004	4,30,182

Note: £a sterling = Trinidad $4.80.
Source: Saunders, K., *Indentured Labour in the British Empire 1834-1920*. Routledge. 2018 : pp. 58-59.

In talking about the role and results of the involvement of indentured labour, especially from India, Mauritius presents the most successful case among the British colonies, making a remarkable expansion of industry even after emancipation of slaves, presenting a case of highly successful transition from 'slavery to indentured'. In this respect, colonial slavery abolished on 28 August, 1833 meant great hardship for many colonies to readjust for the new situation. In fact:

> 'slave emancipation jolted the British colonial sugar industry leading to universal decline in sugar production during the period of Apprenticeship and after ... The slaves were legally freed but in practice remained bonded to their former owners as apprentices for further terms of four to six years'.[46]

For instance, as mentioned earlier, Jamaica provides a good example where 'sugar industry experienced permanent decline' though before 1834, Jamaica produced 'twice as much as British Guiana, seventy per cent more than Mauritius', which twenty years later turned into the position of 'Britain's premier sugar colony' increasing to more than double British Guiana's production and almost five times greater than that of Jamaica's. Table 4.6 shows sugar production fluctuations in four of the most important sugar-producing British colonies between 1824-28 and 1854-58, though Barbados alone shows signs of increase in its production during the period.

Table 4.6: Average Annual Sugar Production in Britain's Four Most Important Sugar Colonies (in metric tons)

Period	Mauritius	British Guiana	Jamaica	Barbados
1824-28	17,119	46,914	68,514	12,889
1829-33	33,158	58,115	70,618	16,029
1834-38	32,713	52,099	55,035	20,636
1839-43	33,713	33,160	33,939	15,457
1844-48	50,777	36,544	32,977	18,851
1849-53	69,886	38,114	28,335	29,675
1854-58	1,13,014	49,829	23,218	32,812

Source: Saunders, K., *Indentured Labour in the British Empire 1834-1920*. Routledge. 2018, p. 80.

Indentured labour was at the root of Mauritius's flourishing sugar industry.The end of apprenticeship in 1839 was instrumental in the importation of 34,401 indentured labourers from India and by 1840, Mauritius had become Britain's first-ranking sugar colony. As Table 4.6 shows, there was a spurt in sugar production from 1844-48 maintained without any disruption, far surpassing all other colonies and this helped in building up the 'local fortunes ... which tied up colonial and metropolitan elites'.[47] The boom in sugar production is clearly reflected in the unobstructed flow of Indian labour, such as in the 'quarter-century after 1842' altogether 3,40,718 Indians came to Mauritius and only 87,617 of them returned to India on completion of the indentured period. However, there is also a very interesting side of the whole process which involves the development of a practice of accumulating sufficient funds to pay for licences enabling the indentured labour to carry on a:

> 'wide range of petty trading and manufacturing ventures, or to purchase or lease land and acquire cows, draught animals, carts, and carriages, which could be used to earn an independent livelihood on the expiry of their contracts. These activities included market gardening, dairying and freight and passenger transport services'.[48]

This clearly indicates a very important fact that many Indian labourers intended staying back on expiry of the contract-period since the situation back in home country of their origin, India, as a matter of fact, was not at all inviting for them as they represented the 'lowest and most ignorant classes of their countrymen' having no prospect of a better future. But here, where they came on indenture, they had an opportunity to eke out a better life where they had worked for some years. This led to a rise in a peasantry class as well as petty traders and artisans and as such they preferred to stay on permanently in the colony turning in the long run a part of the existing society.

Fiji shows another case of immigration of Indian labour which started with the abolition of slavery in 1834 involving over one million Indian labourers transported across the oceans to different British colonies including '60,965' of them – the Indian coolies on indenture – brought to Fiji 'between 1879 until 1916' when it finally ceased.

As mentioned above, Calcutta (Kolkata) came to be the major centre of transportation handling almost seventy-five per cent of them while Madras (Chennai) transported the rest. Most of the migrants came from the United Provinces (eastern part of Uttar Pradesh), Bihar (Bihar and Jharkhand) and Central Provinces (Madhya Pradesh) as well as North-Western Provinces (including Punjab) etc., to work in the plantations on a contract for 'five or more years' but required to obtain 'prior approval' to see his 'indentured wife'. Such inhuman behaviour was due to the attitude of the CSR (Colonial Sugar Refining Company, an extensive Australian Enterprise) given authority by the Fiji government to organise plantation agriculture, supporting such treatment. On the whole, the working conditions for the labourers were very badly managed, being put in overall charge of overseers who had full authority for exploitation.

> 'Indeed ... the labourers complained that tasks were altered at the overseer's whim ... Another yardstick overzealous overseer's ... used was the amount a task set on other plantations ... when conditions on different plantations varied enormously. There could be variations in soil, terrain, and the number of times the ground had been worked over. Thus to set the standard of one plantation on the basis of another without careful thought was, once again, to put extra pressure on the labourers. Overtasking was a major problem'.[49]

This was one of many problems faced by the indentured labour beside pay-cuts on flimsy reasons so that the majority of the labourers did not receive the 'minimum statutory wage', thereby failing to have adequate food and rest, which resulted in very poor health becoming naturally a reason for absence from work. The real intentions of the planters was 'to squeeze the last ounce of work from the indentured labour and thus increase production without incurring any extra expenditure'. There was also another practice when in many plantations the Sirdars (or the overseer employed by the planters) opened up stores from which the Labourers were compelled to buy provisions and thus incur unending debts. Some of these Sirdars thus 'acquired fortunes from unscrupulousness and extortion'.

It is, therefore, not surprising that the labourers would revolt in the long run, which culminated in a strike taking place in May 1886 joined by 130 men and a demonstration when men carrying their working implements marched into the office of the Agent General of Immigration to explain their grievances and though 'subsequent investigations revealed' that they were 'indeed overtasked', they did not receive justice.

The inhuman treatment, the most horrible living conditions where a room 10 feet by 7 feet, improved later to 10 feet by 12 feet after 1908 without any window provided to the family next to an unmarried man giving no privacy, made life unbearable for those most hardworking people cheated by everybody which led ultimately to suicide as shown in Table 4.7, varying between indentured and free men/women.

Table 4.7: Suicide Among Fiji Indians in the Indentured Period

Years	**Indentured**		**Free**	
	Male	**Female**	**Male**	**Female**
1887-1895	16	3	–	–
1896-1905	50	5	16	3
1906-1915	104	12	31	4
1916-1921	20	2	18	3

Source: Saunders, K., *Indentured Labour in the British Empire 1834-1920*. Routledge. 2018, p. 149. (Taken from Annual Reports on Indian Immigration 1881-1921).

> 'The everyday reality for workers was marked by grinding overwork, low wages, malnutrition, persistent illness and poor housing, social and medical facilities, as well as a range of punitive measures, including beatings, fines and imprisonment. Little attention was paid to their mental and emotional needs since workers were viewed as little more than vehicles of labour ... Indian managers (Sirdars), speaking the workers' language, were appointed to ensure effective running

> of the estates and many gained notoriety among the workers. Assault on both men and women by overseers and Sirdars were commonplace; women particularly were forced to provide sexual services. Workers in turn found it difficult to prove assault and, when found guilty, overseers and Sirdars escaped with light sentences. As a result, few workers registered complaints for fear of reprisal from employer'.[50]

Incidentally, many of the indentured labour after completion of the period of mandatory indenture for five years preferred to stay back as free citizens, settling down on their own land initially taken from planters, or CSR contractors trying 'market gardening, banana cultivation, poultry farming', majority of them turned to 'sugarcane farming', made living as free citizens. It is interesting to note that these freelancers produced '1700 tons' of sugarcane in 1889 which increased to '1,32,000 tons' in 1901. Meanwhile, the size of free population among the Indians increased from 11,392 in 1901 to 29,758 in 1911 out of 44,220 Indians including those who were still then on indenture, the former, undoubtedly, started playing an important role in the society.

Unlike that in Fiji, migration of indentured labour to another British colony, Malaya, was different in many respects. Spatial proximity between the two countries – Malaya and India – played a defining role, with recruitment concentrated particularly from South India. Over the hundred years, between 1830 and 1930, Tanjore provided the indentured labour for most of the British colonies. Between mid-1840s and 1910 indentured Indian labour was recruited for Malayan sugar plantations from South India where from it is claimed, even Indian slave-labour comprised 'as many as one-seventh of them' were sent to Mauritius as late as 'February 1835'.

According to an estimate, Malaya received about 2,50,000 indentured labour from India between 1844 and 1910 on periods of contract stretching from one to three years but unlike that for other British colonies, the labourers had to pay their passage, thus beginning their life in debt in Malaya. The migrants, with the exception of a few hundred from Bengal were entirely composed of South Indians, taken mainly from 'Tanjore, Trichinopoly, Madras and occasionally from Salem and Coimbatore', 80 per cent of them were employed in sugar plantations while the remaining 20 per cent were absorbed by 'coffee plantations'. The highest number of indentured labour that came in one year to Malaya was recorded as 9,174 in 1900 along with another 30,752 'non-regulated migrants' organised by 'labour-agents' when some of them went on their own to meet the heavy demand for labour. They were mostly adults 15 to 45 years old, accompanied by a small proportion of females (20%) and children (10%). But the wages were 'barely sufficient' to feed themselves 'alive' and as a result they ran into debt. Besides, the high rate of mortality led to the flight of the labourers, ultimately failing to 'ensure a regular and reliable labour supply for Malaya plantations'.

On the other hand, colonial Queensland of Australia earned an exceptionally barbaric reputation for its treatment of bonded labour in their sugar plantations, which covered a large area encompassing most of western and northern Queensland, the Northern Territory and the coastal areas of Western Australia where it is alleged, the enslavement of Australian Aborigines was customary', and a ghastly picture shows:

> 'an aboriginal woman being flogged by a native trooper ... The buying and selling of Aboriginal children in frontier Queensland was instanced 'as the custom of the place (along with) ... murdering, abducting children for immoral purposes and stock-whipping defenceless girls ... the atrocities mentioned have even been exceeded'.[51]

An English journalist, Arthur J. Vogan, gives an account of this time quoting from *The Black Policies: A Story of Modern Australia* (1890), and states further in his later pamphlet, *The Case for the Aborigines* saying that:

> they (the aborigines) were shown as the *defenceless victims*, victims of *land-greedy* pioneers, *a rough consciousless crowd*, who save for some notable individual exceptions behaved *enmass* as ruthless *scoundrels*.[52]

It is stated that the intervention of law into these 'unequal, imperious interventions did have no effects where the master had the 'power of life or death' on the aborigines, in completely disrupting family life, as clearly stated by Mestor, the Southern Aboriginal Protector as late as 1901 in the following statement:

> 'scattered among the stations of Western Queensland are small parties of aborigines among whom the family ties have long been severed ... This isolation of solitary men and women, and couples, and small groups old people and children separated widely from friends, family and class relations is a source of much fretting and grief among those Western Aboriginals. I met the fathers and mothers of boys and girls whom they had not seen for years. That is a common complaint over a large area of Queensland'.[53]

However, it is maintained by many authors that Queensland was a 'society of paradox' by the late nineteenth century. It employed a large number of convicts and sheep farmers who were whites, and this labour was 'cheap and servile'. It is interesting to note that instead of depending on indentured labour from India, Queensland preferred a policy of diversion in this matter perhaps not leaving scope of concerted action on the part of the indentures who enjoyed numerical superiority. The labour was drawn from different nationalities such as Chinese, Indian, Japanese, and other Asian sources. For example, Pacific Islanders headed the number of indentured labour in Queensland, over 70 per cent of them originating from the Solomon Islands after 1890. In their policy Queensland wanted to avoid the mistake committed by the USA where African slaves brought in the sixteenth and seventeenth centuries became permanent residents after abolition of slavery. Of the 18,231 Pacific Islanders who came between 1863 and 1904, those after completion of first three years of indenture chose other forms of labour but Melanesians were specifically restricted from such work as 'mill operatives, carriers, domestic servants and tradesmen', thus keeping them separated from white working class primarily aimed at maintaining the 'white Australian policy' not threatened and contaminated by non-Whites. In order to achieve this goal, an Act was passed in 1885 prohibiting further introduction of Pacific Islanders after 1890. By the late 1890s, political pressure increased further to keep the continent 'White' with the expulsion of the Pacific Islanders from the Queensland sugar industry. Interestingly, in spite of all pressure from the lawmakers for White-Australia, 'Melanesians continued as the main source of cane cutters and sugar farm labourers', mainly in the north and there were 9,324 Melanesians in Queensland, but 4,269 of them were deported in 1906 and 1907, and these two years witnessed a 'substantial transition from black to white labour in cane fields' and (with some change in an Act in 1916) by the 1920s, Queensland sugar industry finally adopted the 'principle of White labour only'.

In contrast, South Africa, another British colony, presents an altogether different picture later in the early twentieth century which used to bring slave labour from the Malayan archipelago since the seventeenth century to work in sugar plantations. But later, in the mid-nineteenth century the source of labour with change of venue for plantation agriculture to Natal shifted to India wherefrom labour came till it was stopped in 1911 by the Government of India. But the discovery of diamonds followed by the discovery of extensive gold deposits in Witwatersrand in Transvaal after 1886 and the extensive use of coal as fuel to drive the machinery further increased the demand for Indian labour after 1886. By 1910, South Africa came to be the largest gold producer in the world, providing almost 35 per cent of it. The total value of gold was put at £3,09,87,665 in 1909 employing 1,55,000 miners. But with the growing pressure of work and non-availability of Indian labour, South Africa ultimately turned to bringing Chinese labour on 'three-year indenture', and between 1907 and 1910 altogether 53,828 Chinese indentured labour were imported to Transvaal. Two important provisions were laid down in the contracts for the Chinese indentured labourers, such as, they were employed only to 'metalliferous mining and the employment had to be confined to Witwatersrand district, remaining exclusively at the disposal of the gold mining industry'. It is claimed that Chinese labour made a 'major contribution' to the 'structural transformation of the gold mining industry'. But ultimately the contract expired, and the shipment of time-limited indenture took place in February 1910.[54]

V. Cultural Impact of Indentured Labour

It is very important to note that the indentured labour as a case of mass-migration has a great role in changing the very composition of the present population, making an indivisible part of the existing society each of which had participation of their forefathers as immigrants contributing to building up the economy of the country they came to. Thus, according to Krishna Gubili (2018), mentioned earlier, at present altogether '4.5 million grandchildren and great grandchildren of the 1.3 million indentured coolies are thriving across the globe' taking a key-role in all activities of the related countries. To highlight the role of these descendants Krishna Gubili (2018), mentions famous names of the descendants of the coolies:

> 'Vijay Singh, 2004-2005 World No.1 Professional Golfer; Sir V.S. Naipaul, Nobel Literature prize-winning author; Shivnarine Chanderpaul former captain of the West Indies Cricket Team; Anerood Jugnauth, former Prime Minister of Mauritius. All of the above are offspring of indentured coolies'.[55]

The brief outline given by Krishna Gubili (2018) is worth noting such as among all the British colonies receiving Indian emigrants taken as indentured labour, the largest number, about 5,50,000 came to the Caribbean.

> 'The number of their descendants has grown to about 1.8 million Indians now and comprise the largest ethnic group in Guyana, Surinam and Trinidad and Tobago. They are the

second largest group in Jamaica, Grenada, Saint Vincent and Grenadines, Saint Lucia, Martinique and Guadeloupe'.[56]

In Guyana, the first batch of indentured labour from India arrived in May 1838. The 'Indo-Guyanese' represent today 40 per cent of the total population of this country, representing the largest ethnic group and 60 per cent of the indentured coolies hailed from present Uttar Pradesh and Bihar. Many of their descendants have shot into prominence, most noted among them being Bharrat Jagdeo as former President of Guyana while Cheddi Jagan was also the President of the country from 1992 to 1997 besides others holding very important positions.

Trinidad also has a diverse population with 'diverse ethnicity, religion and culture' comprising 20 per cent Hindus and 5 per cent Muslims as descendants of indentured labour who came mostly from Uttar Pradesh, speaking Bhojpuri, a Hindi dialect having become a shared language of the East Indians in Trinidad today. The most famous person representing these people is V.S. Naipaul, the Nobel Laureate.

The first indentured labour landed in Jamaica in 1845 and all the labourers coming afterwards were collected from present-day Uttar Pradesh and Uttarakhand, Bihar, Jharkhand, Rajasthan, Chhattisgarh and Madhya Pradesh. The contribution of their descendants towards the economic and cultural development of the country is gratefully recognised by the country observing 'Indian Heritage Day' since May 1995. The most illustrious characters representing the cultural milieu of the country include a large group of renowned artists in various fields.

According to Krishna Gubili (2018), South Africa with its 1.3 million Indians today makes a vibrant part of South Africa's social, economic, and political fabric[57], with Durban as the largest Indian city outside India. It was in South Africa that Mahatma Gandhi started the freedom struggle in 1913, and one of the Indians, Ahmed Kathrada, spent 27 years of his life with Nelson Mandela in Robin Island in his struggle against apartheid. The Indian society has produced a large number of people renowned in many fields.

Another small country, Reunion, an island near Mauritius as a French colony used to get indentured Indian labour from Pondicherry, another French colony in India at that time, and those who did not go back on expiry of their indenture contract settled down retaining their Indian heritage till date celebrating Indian festivals. As in other colonies, enjoying Independence from colonial rule, Reunion has a significant number of celebrated citizens of Indian heritage.

Fiji, consisting of about 800 tropical islands lying close to Australia and New Zealand, was another British colony depending on indentured labour from India, in those days to run sugar plantations. As in other colonies, many of the indentured labour coming mostly from present Uttar Pradesh and Bihar did not go back on completion of indentured period as life back home at that time had no better prospect than what they could make staying back. Thus, slowly they became a part of the existing society contributing to its growth both economically as well as culturally, making up a third of the islands' population with 3,30,000 people of direct Indian origin. However, the military coup of 1987 followed by racial violence led nearly 1,00,000 Indo-Fijians to migrate to Canada, Australia, and other countries. Among the most illustrious men of Indian origin had been Mahendra Pal Chaudhury who became Prime Minister of Fiji, another one was Imrana Jalal, the human rights adviser to the United Nations, Rajen Prasad, an M.P., Rajesh Chandra, the first Vice Chancellor of the University of Fiji.

Another country, Mauritius, a French colony until it became a British colony in 1810, becoming an independent country in 1968, depended very much on Indian coolies, brought on indenture for its plantation agriculture, the first lot of them coming from Bihar landed in 1834 followed by the arrival of a total of 45,063 migrants altogether, arriving mostly from Bihar, Uttar Pradesh, and Andhra Pradesh. Interestingly in Mauritius, Indians always had a prominent place in society unlike in other British colonies, so much so that almost 70 per cent of the Island's 1.5 million population are of Indian origin. The importance of Indians is very much reflected in the fact that it was Sir Seewoosagur Ramgoolam the first Prime Minister of the Country who led the island's independence movement while Anerood Jugnauth had been the recent President and Prime Minister of the Country. Among other illustrious sons as descendants of the Indian coolies are Ariranga Govindasamy Pillay, the Chief Justice of Mauritius, Navin Ramgoolam, another Prime Minister, Rama Sithanen, Finance Minister and Vice Prime Minister.[58]

Portrayal of the background of the independent colonies by Krishna Gubili (2018) shows a very striking change in the life of each of the previous colonies, thriving today in their economic as well as cultural affluence owing very much to the efforts of the descendants of the indentured coolies who did not go back to their country of origin after finishing their contract-period, as mentioned above showing their choice of staying back as a mark of great resilience on the accessibility of the host country. But this could not happen in a hostile environment.

It is very important to note the presence of a sharp dividing line between the indentured labour wishing to settle down permanently in the country of their immigration and the slaves smuggled out of Africa in the most secretive way leaving no address behind to trace their roots afterwards, if and when necessary, and had to settle down on emancipation in the country of immigration, such as the USA, as one of them – were never accepted by that or other such white countries as part of the existing population. The slaves and their descendants through generations remained separate in the country of immigration never accepted as a part of the society represented entirely by the whites alone, maintaining a sharp division between the Whites and the Blacks, based on skin-colour. In contrast, there was no distinctive line of difference in the colour of the skin between the local population and the indentured coolies to make such a dividing line between the two in British colonies so that both sides got easily mixed-up in course of time in contrast to the Whites and Blacks in the USA or other White-dominated countries (the riots in Fiji are an exception).

The so-called 'Whiteness' has maintained its dominating superiority even in European countries, becoming a defining factor in the choice of merit or any achievement for acceptance sharply affecting the lives of non-Whites in many fields.

One should not forget that skin-colour is a direct manifestation of the ultra-violet radiation.

> 'Skin pigmentation plays the role of the UV-B rays. In tropical Africa whereas per current knowledge the origin of *Homo sapiens* are said to be, the high intensity of UV-B rays led to more production of a compound called melanin to serve as a natural sunscreen and consequently, darker skin. Closer to the poles, or at higher latitudes, the annual average UV radiation on the earth's surface is far less than in the tropics. Also, the UV-B rays are more scattered by the atmosphere due to earth's tilted rotational axis. As human beings moved outside the tropics, they were moving to areas that received less intense UV-B rays. The evolutionary response was a change in pigmentation or less production of melanin to absorb UV rays more efficiently. Consequently, this led to higher skin colours'.[59]

In other words, skin-colour is nothing but a natural phenomenon giving no special quality of its link to superiority. It was, rather, historical events that put white races in the lead-role of cultural progress which they could achieve partly because of some natural advantages like the presence of coal and its use for power generation replacing manual labour leading to scientific achievements putting them, particularly Britain, ahead of other countries but at the same time the emergence of colonial powers from Europe putting colonial rule on many of the countries including the Indian Subcontinent in the process, completely destroying the existing economic affluence of the subjugated countries in the process and thus establishing the rule of whites on non-whites lasting in the case of India-Pakistan-Bangladesh for a long stretch of almost two hundred years. The noted historian and writer William Dalrymple (2019) brings this out very clearly saying:

> 'We still talk about the British conquering India, but that phrase disguises a more sinister reality. It was not the British government that began seizing great chunks of India in the mid-eighteenth century, but a dangerously unregulated company head-quartered in one small office, five windows-wide in London, and managed in India by a violent, utterly ruthless and intermittently mentally unstable corporate predator Clive. India's transition to colonialism took place under a for-profit Corporation, which existed entirely for the purpose of enriching its investors'.[60]

He states further that in the minds of the Victorian period of the mid-nineteenth century there was a strong sense of embarrassment about the 'shady, brutal and mercantile way the British founded the Raj', that is, British rule in India, followed by Clive buying up both 'MPs and Parliamentary seats' using his wealth he carried on in India in unscrupulous ways.

The 'White' ego remained unashamedly present at all levels of public life even in the late nineteenth to early twentieth centuries in India. The most striking case in this respect is provided by Sir J.C. Bose when obtaining a Doctorate degree from Cambridge University he joined Presidency College in Calcutta (Kolkata):

> 'reckoned as the premier educational institution in India ... (where) an Indian Professor's income, even if the Imperial Service, was two-thirds that of a European's (Bose succeeded later in getting this distinction abolished) ... As his protest was disregarded, he resolved never to touch the cheque received by him as pay; and continued this for three years ... After

> three years' work in this temporary post both the Principal (Mr C.H. Tawney) and the Director of Public Instruction (Sir Alfred Croft) came fully to realise the value of Bose's professional work, and to understand his character, and they became henceforth his staunchest friends. The Director had found that Bose could be inflexible when questions of principle were concerned. Bose on his part also realised more fully than ever that the best way to get on with an Englishman is to stand up to him .... In consequence of this change of view of the Director, Bose's appointment, by help of a special order from the Government, was not only made permanent, but this with retrospective effect. He therefore received his full pay for the last three years in a lumpsum'.[61]

But 'white-distinctiveness' happened more painfully later when the Nobel Prize for the success in Wireless Transmission accomplished first by Bose was not acknowledged by the Nobel Prize Award Committee who gave it to Marconi from Italy instead which long after the incident was clearly acknowledged by Marconi's grandson, Francesco Paresco Marconi, who admitted in writing when he visited the Bose Institute in Kolkata on November 30, 2006, in the following words:

> 'This is a wonderful experience for me, since Sir J.C. Bose actually performed the first wireless experiment before that of my grandfather Guglielmo Marconi. Many thanks for your hospitality. I appreciate the honour'.[62]

Incidentally, this was not the first time that Bose was deprived of the honour. It happened again later when his next earth-shaking discovery followed by several types of demonstrations proving the existence of life in plants went unacknowledged by the Nobel Committee, simply ignoring him for the second time. It is true that this discrimination for not being a 'white' person (though not explicitly recorded) palpably indicates the hidden truth when another Noble Laureate (in Chemistry), Professor Richard R. Ernst visiting Bose institute in Kolkata on 25 September, 1999 recorded in writing his views as follows:

> 'I was very much impressed by the ingenuity of Professor Bose, especially his way of informative experimental set-ups for biological and physical measurements. He was really very much ahead of his time. I also like very much his interdisciplinary approach so essential for mastering our future'.[63]

Here, referring to Sir Patrick Geddes (1930), we may mention a list of publications of Sir J.C. Bose:

1. *Response in the Living and Non-living*, with 117 illustrations, 8 vol., 1902.
2. *Plant Response: As a Means of Physiological Investigation*, with 278 illustrations, 8 vol., 1906.
3. *Comparative Electro-Physiology*. Physico-Physiological Study, with 406 illustrations, 8 vol., 1907.
4. *Research on Irritability of Plants*, with 190 illustrations, 8 vol., 1913.
5. *Life Movements in Plants*, Volume I, with 92 illustrations, 8 vol., 1918.
6. *Life Movements in Plants*, Volume II, with 128 illustrations, 8 vol., 1919.[64]

However, this is not the lone case of deprivation. There are a few more instances of similar denial of achievement, citing cases from West Bengal alone. For example, Dr. Meghnad Saha, the noted astrophysicist, renowned for discovering the thermal ionisation equation, it is rumoured his name had been proposed to the Nobel Committee seven times but was ignored while Professor Satyen Bose who formulated the Bose statistics and whose paper was translated for publication by no less a person than Einstein was similarly ignored though proposed for the same three times. Further, it is equally very sad and disheartening when a prolific filmmaker like Satyajit Ray, owner of life-time Oscar when the Committee has gone out of the way to acclaim the work of many other fields far beyond perhaps what was intended by Alfred Nobel.

Nevertheless, admittedly two very powerful forces – the constant operation of (two very powerful forces) emigration and immigration taking place across the world have already blurred the difference between white dominance with infiltration of growing 'coloured' prominence. For example, it is very much visible in the present population of the United Kingdom in 2019 when people from only two non-white countries, India and Pakistan together have about 1.3 million people and so comprise a significant part of her total of 67 million population in 2019, when large presence of other non-white people particularly from Bangladesh, China, Sri Lanka and many more non-white countries are yet to be included to outshine 'Whiteness' (Table 4.8).

Table 4.8: Overseas Population in the UK, 2019

1.	Poland	8,31,000
2.	India	7,95,000
3.	Pakistan	5,03,000
4.	Ireland	3,82,000
5.	Germany	2,86,000
Total	**UK's Population**	**6,76,22,643**

Source: *World Population Review*, United Nations.

Further, the growing trend of immigration has a very strong role in changing the character of population in major countries as revealed in the following Table 4.9.

Table 4.9: Total Number of International Migrants (i.e. Foreign-born Residents) in Selected Countries as per cent of Total Population

Country	Year	No. of Foreigners (million)	% of the Total Population	Year	No. of Foreigners (million)	% of the Total Population
Canada	1990	4.3	15.7	2019	7.96	21.3
Brazil	1990	0.8	0.5	2019	0.8	0.4
France	1990	5.9	10.4	2019	8.3	12.8
Germany	1990	5.9	7.5	2019	13.1	15.7
Portugal	1990	0.4	4.4	2019	0.8	8.7
Peru	1990	0.05	0.3	2019	0.7	2.4
Spain	1990	0.8	2.1	2019	6.1	13.1
UK	1990	3.6	6.4	2019	9.5	14.1
USA	1990	23.2	9.9	2019	50.6	15.1

Source: UN Population Division 2019.

An indication of the growing trend of immigration sustained through the time-space for nearly three decades, 1990-2019, for the countries mentioned above leaves no doubt about greater possibility of increase in the presence of non-whites in utilising the opportunity of using their skill replacing local residents in the competitive work-places and thus change composition of the resident population turning it more coloured in the long run.

NOTES

*Frankopan, P. *The Silk Roads: A New History of the World*. Bloomsbury (First Published 2015). 2016 : p.117.

'Renowned for 'their size, their physique and their bravery' the Viking Rus had 'no cultivated fields and lived by pillaging', according to one Arabic writer. It was the local population that bore the brunt. So many were captured that the very name of those taken captive-slaves-became used for all those who had their freedom taken away: slaves'.

**Vertovec, S. *Indian Indentured Migration to the Caribbean*, in 'The Cambridge Survey of World Migration Edition'. Cohen R. Cambridge University Press. 1995 : p. 60.

'The work performed by Indians on sugar plantations varied according to sex, age, ability and experience. The primary tasks of forking and cutting cane dominated the labour of men, who were organised into gangs under a driver or overseer (often an Indian himself). Women concentrated on weeding while young boys were expected to tend livestock. The most skilled estate workers were in the sugar mills.... Indian indentured or unindentured, also served as estates' carpenters, stock keepers, grooms, and watchmen. Indian labour stimulated a major upswing in British Indies sugar trade'.

1. *The Encyclopaedia Americana*. New York: Americana Corporation, 1973, Vol. 25, p. 48.
2. *Ibid.*
3. Frankopan, P. *The Silk Roads: A New History of the World*. Great Britain Bloomsbury, 2015, p. 119.
4. *Ibid.*
5. *The Encyclopaedia Americana*. New York: Americana Corporation, 1973, Vol. 25, p. 20.
6. *Ibid.*
7. Frankopan, P. *The Silk Roads: A New History of the World*. Great Britain: Bloomsbury, 2015, p. 119.
8. *Ibid.*, p. 120.
9. *Ibid.*, p. 122.
10. *Ibid.*, p. 126.
11. *The Encyclopaedia Americana*. New York: Americana Corporation, 1973, Vol. 25, p. 20.
12. *Ibid.*
13. *Ibid.*, p. 21.
14. Hirsch, A. *Brit(ish): On Race, Identity and Belonging*. London: Vintage, 2018, p. 65.
15. *Ibid.*, p. 202.
16. *Ibid.*, p. 54.
17. *Ibid.*, p. 61.
18. *Ibid.*, p. 62.

19. Johnson, W. *Soul by Soul, Life Inside The Antebellum Slave Market*. Cambridge, Masschursetts, London, England: Harvard University Press, 1999, p. 21.
20. *Ibid.*, p. 31.
21. *Ibid.*, p. 49.
22. *Ibid.*, p. 64.
23. Berlin, I. *Many Thousands Gone: The First Two Centuries of Slavery in North America*. 4th ed. Cambridge: The Belknap Press of Harvard University Press, 2003, p. 9.
24. *Ibid.*, p. 13.
25. *Ibid.*, p. 22.
26. *Ibid.*, p. 115.
27. *Ibid.*, p. 126.
28. *Ibid.*, p. 150.
29. *The Encyclopaedia Americana*. New York: Americana Corporation, 1973, Vol. 1, p. 732.
30. Berlin, I. *Many Thousands Gone: The First Two Centuries of Slavery in North America*. 4th ed., Cambridge: The Belknap Press of Harvard University Press, 2003, pp. 228-229.
31. Vertovec, S. "Indian Indentured Migration to the Caribbean", in *The Cambridge Survey of World Migration*, ed. R. Cohen. Cambridge: Cambridge University Press, 1995, p. 57.
32. *Ibid.*, pp. 57-59.
33. Berlin, I. *Many Thousands Gone: The First Two Centuries of Slavery in North America*. 4th ed. Cambridge: The Belknap Press of Harvard University Press, 2003, p. 234.
34. Gubili, K. *Viriah*. India: Notion Press, 2018, p. 69.
35. *Ibid.*, p. 168.
36. Vertovec, S. "Indian Indentured Migration to the Caribbean", in *The Cambridge Survey of World Migration*, ed. R. Cohen. Cambridge: Cambridge University Press, 1995, p. 59.
37. Gubili, K. Viriah. India: Notion Press, 2018, p. 65.
38. Saunders, K. *Indentured Labour in the British Empire 1834-1920*. Oxon and New York: Routledge. 2018, pp. 87, 92.
39. *Ibid.*, p. 29.
40. *Ibid.*, p. 43.
41. Vertovec, S. "Indian Indentured Migration to the Caribbean", in *The Cambridge Survey of World Migration*, ed. R. Cohen. Cambridge: Cambridge University Press, 1995, p. 60.
42. Thiara, R.K. "Indian Indentured Workers in Mauritius, Natal and Fiji", in *The Cambridge Survey of World Migration*, ed. R. Cohen. Cambridge: Cambridge University Press, 1995, p. 63.
43. *Ibid.*, pp. 63-64.
44. Saunders, K. *Indentured Labour in the British Empire 1834-1920*. Oxon and New York: Routledge, 2018, p. 50.

45. *Ibid.*, p. 71.
46. *Ibid.*, p. 79.
47. *Ibid.*, p. 91.
48. *Ibid.*, p. 111.
49. *Ibid.*, p. 133.
50. Thiara, R.K. "Indian Indentured Workers in Mauritius, Natal and Fiji", in *The Cambridge Survey of World Migration*, ed. R. Cohen. Cambridge: Cambridge University Press, 1995, pp. 66-67.
51. Saunders, K. *Indentured Labour in the British Empire 1834-1920*. Oxon and New York: Routledge, 2018, p. 184.
52. *Ibid.*, p. 185.
53. *Ibid.*, p. 197.
54. *Ibid.*, pp. 260-281.
55. Gubili, K. *Viriah*. India: Notion Press, 2018, p. 193.
56. *Ibid.*, p. 195.
57. *Ibid.*, p. 199.
58. *Ibid.*, pp. 201-204.
59. Tumbe, C. *India Moving: A History of Migration*. India: Vikings Penguin Random House, 2018, p. 3.
60. Dalrymple, W. *The Anarchy: The East India Company, Corporate Violence and the Pillage of an Empire*. London, New Delhi: Bloomsbury Publication, 2019, p. xxv.
61. Geddes, P. (Sir). *The Life and Work of Sir Jagadish C. Bose*. London: Longmans, Green & Co., 1920, pp. 35-39.
62. Remarks of Francesco Paresce Marconi. Rome, Italy, Institute of Astrophysics, Marconi Society, New York, USA, Former Chairman & Director, The Italian Astrophysicist, and grandchild of renowned scientist Guglielino Marconi.
63. Remarks of Professor Richard R. Ernest. Zurich, Switzerland, Nobel Prize in Chemistry in 1991.
64. Geddes, P. (Sir). *The Life and Work of Sir Jagadish C. Bose*. London: Longmans, Green & Co., 1920, Flyleaf.

5
Theories of Migration and Development, with Special Reference to India

I. Theories of International Migration and Development

In studying the evolution of international migration one of the most important observations made by Massimo Livi-Bacci, the noted 'historical demographer' made in 2010 is that the USA, the leading global economy today,

> 'owed its birth and expansion to immigration'[1]

which in other words means that the emergence of the USA as the most economically as well as politically powerful country in the world today was entirely the product of those people who came from outside as immigrants and settled down permanently shaping it to the USA today, to its present eminence.

As such Livi-Bacci (2010), calls migration the 'key element of social and biological evolution.[2] Migration as a general process of human history consists of two opposing elements – emigration and immigration – and both may involve any country at the same time when people go for other destinations called 'emigrants', and the same people become 'immigrants' to the new destinations they go to settle down in either permanently or temporarily. Thus, it turns out to be quite intriguing when we look at the movement of people, its connotation in terms of going out as 'emigration', and going in as 'immigration'.

As pointed out by Livi-Bacci (2010), ancient men going out of their birthplace, or place of origin in East Africa and slowly spreading out into 'Western Asia, then into Europe and then into Eastern Asia, finally reaching the Americas and Australia is considered as expansion, providing instances of global-scale movements of emigration while at the same time such movements are considered as immigrants for regions or countries they went to. Naturally, such movements took a very long time giving rise to widely changing effects on the land and people the immigrants came into contact with, for example, as mentioned in Chapter 3, men representing *Homo sapiens*, our forefathers, completely annihilating other races of men, like Neanderthals in Europe, and early other human species belonging to separate races elsewhere, besides large animals in Asia and America during their movements into those areas where the former had survived undisturbed for millions of years. Large animals wiped out of existence were namely mammoths in Siberian Asia, giant ground sloths reaching up to six metres in height weighing up to eight tons, giant armadillos measuring over three metres in length and weighing up to two tons in North America, elephant birds, a flightless creature three metres tall and weighing nearly half a ton, are only a few instances of life which survived till, perhaps, the ancient people, the *Homo sapiens*, managed to cross the land-bridge, the Bering Strait, providing access from Asia to North America, some '20,000 or more years ago'.

The pre-historic migrants, as much as we can presume today travelling across Europe, Asia and into the two continents of Americas, were in search of more food, no doubt, faced little resistance as we realise and such emigrations were not entirely wanderlust, but necessary in a way to find out greater resources for these foragers slowly increased in number requiring more space without coming into direct conflict. Their choice of areas like north Asia, the Americas and later Australia, were, in all likelihood devoid of any living human races but offering unending resources for survival.

In contrast, however, many of the migratory movements in the first millennium of the modern era were 'movements of invasion and settlement' made by Germanic peoples 'driven by ambitions of conquest directed eastward 'continuing from the ninth to almost the mid-nineteenth century displacing Slavs, happens to be the largest of all migratory movements, made in three directions, south-eastward following the Danube in Hungary, northward following the Baltic Coast, and the 'great eastward migration ultimately resulting in the colonisation of 'almost 30 million people' living east of the Elbe-Saale line at the end of the nineteenth century.[3]

> 'This wave of migration seems to have owed more to the high level of technology and organisation of the emigratory population and the correspondingly less developed state of the native Slavic population .... in the zone of immigration. Moreover, the settled lands presented extremely favourable

conditions to farmers and the distances were fairly short. The German immigrants had ploughs, axes and tools that allowed them to deforest and cultivate difficult land'.[4]

At this time there was also happening eastward migration movements of people, led by the farming population in Russia settling down in the Asiatic Russia beyond the Urals involving 4.5 million emigrants of which over a million were convicts. Similarly, China also witnessed cases of huge movement of emigrants into Manchuria, intensified during the nineteenth century, consisting mostly of peasants, increasing population sixfold between 1850 and 1904.[5]

Apart from Europe-Centric and Chinese counterparts, another interesting scene involving the 'New World' was opening up by this time presenting highly interesting cases of turning almost vast uninhabited territories, especially in North America, into freshly fast-populated countries. For example, America, which was '100 per cent Native American in the year 1500', became mostly populated by Europeans three centuries later, providing a very strong case of immigrant-migration.

North America, in this respect, offers the most striking case of getting populated by the Europeans as settlers, who, later brought African slaves in huge numbers to work for them free of charge on the plantations. It is interesting to observe that there were 4.5 million settlers of European descent (immigrants) in North America in 1800 while South and Central America had 3.5 million besides 2.5 million African slaves by 1770 in two Americas.

> 'An estimated 12 million slaves were taken to the Americas before 1850. For the women, hard labour in the mines, plantations and households was frequently accompanied by sexual exploitation. The children of slaves remained in the chalets (personal property) of the owners. In 1807 ... slave trafficking was abolished within the British Empire ... while other European states followed suit by 1815. Yet slavery itself was not abolished until 1834 in British colonies, 1863 in Dutch colonies and 1865 in the southern states of the USA'.[6]

The colonial exploitation made by Western Europe provided huge wealth much of which led to the beginning of the Industrial Revolution during the eighteenth and nineteenth centuries, happening first in Britain which, besides encouraging new forms of manufacture attracting people from agricultural work into industries and turned arable land into pastures and made people jobless to look for opportunities elsewhere. The unskilled labour naturally looking for other opportunities started emigrating to the Americas along with other opportunity seekers from other European countries who joined the stream of emigrants to the Americas.Thus 66 per cent of the emigrants to the USA between 1800 and 1860 were from Britain along with 22 per cent from Germany while people from countries like Ireland, Italy, Spain, and East European countries where the benefits of industrial revolution came late also joined the flow of emigrants pouring into the USA between 1850 to 1914. The dream of a better achievement, however, was not fulfilled in many cases.

> 'Often this dream led to disappointment: the immigrants became wage-labourers building roads and railways across the vast expanse of the New World; 'cowboys', gauchos, or stockmen on large ranches; or factory workers in the emerging industries for the North-Eastern USA. However, many settlers did eventually realise their dream, becoming farmers, white-collar workers, or business people, while others were at least able to see their children achieve education and upward social mobility'.[7]

As a matter of fact, the USA by this time had emerged as the 'most important of all' destinations for immigrants mostly of European or Latin American origin (racist laws kept Chinese and Asians out from the 1880s). It is estimated, emigrants amounting to 54 million people from Europe entered North America between 1820 and 1887, followed by another 30 million between 1861 and 1920. Among the immigrants, the Irish, Italians and the Jews from Eastern Europe represented the largest groups between 1860 and 1920, though the census of 1920 shows only 13.9 million as foreign-born people in the USA,[8] indicating, perhaps, people coming prior to that date were considered as local.

Canada presents more or less a similar picture, with greater preference for immigrants of European descent and much less reservation for people of non-European origin. Such as, by 1860, Canada had 40,000 black people, as slaves, while immigration from China, Japan and India began in the nineteenth century but Asian immigration was stopped by a regulation from 1886 onwards.

British colonisation of Australia starting in 1788, representing one of the principal sources of 'wool, wheat and gold', got it populated, as mentioned earlier, with transportation of convicts, but shortage of labour from mid-nineteenth century relaxed the policy of keeping it 'white' by way of encouraging cheap labour from 'elsewhere' of British Empire, such as from China, India, and South Pacific islands. But finally, the introduction of White Australian Policy in 1901 turned out to be hostile to the non-Whites and terminated their stay and entry into the country.

On the whole, however, one cannot ignore the fact that Europe turned into the most important epicentre of international migration since 1500 becoming a:

> 'significant exporter of human resources, and transoceanic migration played an important role in economic development. Atlantic Europe played the main role in this regard, with limited contributions from elsewhere. Technological improvements in navigation were a necessary precondition. Consider the first transoceanic voyage ... from Spain to Santo Domingo aboard 32 ships in 1502 ... It was the first true voyage to populate the island with Europeans'.[9]

The role of Europe as the centre-stage for both emigration as well as internal migration taking place side by side is substantiated by facts stated about emigration to the 'New World', beginning from early sixteenth century while the importance of intercontinental movement of people is proved by the fact that 'of the 15 million Italians who migrated between 1876 and 1920, nearly half (6.8 million) went to other European countries, mainly to France, Switzerland and Germany. As a matter of fact, migration of Western Europeans for better future elsewhere, particularly to the empty lands of Americas created a vacuum which was filled by workers from Poland, Ireland and Italy in which Ireland played a major role, and by 1851, 'there were 7,00,000' of them concentrated mainly in the industrial cities, particularly in the textile factories as well as in the building trades in Britain. Jews turning into refugees in Russia between 1875 and 1914 formed the second major group of immigrants into Britain engaged in the textiles. However, the latest groups of immigrants after 1971 were the Bangladeshis.

Among the other West European countries going through the fast paces of industrialisation, such as Germany, the heavy industrial development opened great scopes of employment absorbing no less than 1,64,000 immigrants of Polish origin besides workers from Italy, Belgium, and Netherlands, while in France by 1913 there were 1.2 million immigrants, coming mostly from Italy, Belgium, Germany and Switzerland later joined by immigrants from Spain and Portugal.

However, the period between the inter-war years, that is between the First World War (1914-1919) and the Second World War (1939-1945) witnessed an overall change in the pattern of migration primarily affecting Europe which had been the major venue of the wars. Between 1918 and 1945 migration in the true sense of the term greatly reduced, apart from movements of soldiers brought in by Germany and other European countries pressing many African colonies into forced labour. However, among West European countries France came to be the only exception to experience 'substantial immigration' to balance 'demographic loss' suffered from 1.4 million men killed and another 1.5 million permanently handicapped as war-victims. There were 2.7 million foreigners in France by 1931 composed mostly of Italians, followed by Poles, Spaniards and Belgians.[10]

But following the Second World War, bringing in great changes in the global political scene, the entire situation of immigration went through a revolutionary phase as stated below:

> 'Since the end of World War II, international migrations have changed in character and direction. While for centuries Europeans have been moving outward through conquering, colonising, and settling in lands elsewhere on the globe, these patterns were partly reversed in the second half of the twentieth century. Under the influence of decolonisation, demographic change, rapid economic growth, and the creation of European Union as a free trade and migration zone, Europe emerged as a major global migration destination. While migration of Europeans to the Americas and Oceania rapidly declined in the 1960s and 1970s, Western European countries started to attract increasing numbers of migrants mainly from former colonies and countries located on the European periphery … Immigration rates in many European countries now match or exceed those in the USA or other classical immigration countries'.[11]

According to this report, immigration into Europe consisted of three distinct phases. First, immigrants came into the fast-developing industrial areas of Western Europe from less developed countries in Mediterranean Europe and from Ireland and Finland but ended with the oil crisis in 1973. The second phase happening between mid-1970s and 1990s was characterised by relocation of industries in low-wage developing countries no longer attracted immigrants but 'rapid growth of the service sector' attracted high-skilled workers. 'While the third phase was characterised by rapid economic growth in the southern and eastern Europe zone, particularly in Ireland, Italy and Spain which opened up opportunities for migrants from a wider zone, coming from Eastern Europe, North and West Africa and Latin America.'

The identifying characteristics of migration during the period following the cessation of World War II was migration of workers from the 'European periphery to western Europe and migrants from former colonies' to metropolitan countries (which gave rise to ethnicity disputes). Rapid industrial expansion in the Western European countries, such as Britain immediately after World War II brought in 90,000 male workers from refugee camps with another 1,00,000 European workers between 1946 and 1951 on work-permits. In this respect, France provides a better example, housing 2 million foreign workers by 1970 with 6,90,000 dependents residing in France. Belgium also followed the same policy recruiting foreign workers coming mainly from Italy 'changing the ethnic composition of the industrial areas' while Switzerland becoming highly dependent on migrants comprising almost a third of the total labour force. Similar examples are also provided by the Netherlands bringing in 'guest workers' from Turkey, Morocco, Luxemburg, Sweden. Italy attracted workers from the underdeveloped south. Germany provides a remarkable case of bringing in foreign workers since mid-1950s, the number of foreign workers recruited by the Federal Republic of Germany rose from 95,000 in 1956 to 2.6 million in 1973 resulting from rapid industrialisation but stopped thereafter due to immigrants permanently settling down providing necessary labour[12] (Table 5.1).

Table 5.1: Immigrants as per cent of the Total Population of Western European Countries (1950-1975)

(*In thousands*)

Country	1950	1960	1970	1975	Per cent of Total Population
Belgium	354	444	716	885	8.5
France	2,128	2,663	3,339	4,196	7.9
Germany (FRG)	548	686	2,977	4,090	6.6
Netherlands	77	101	236	370	2.6
Sweden	124	191	411	410	5.0
Switzerland	269	585	983	1,012	16.0
UK	1,573	2,205	3,968	4,153	7.8

Note: Figures for all countries except the UK are foreign residents.
Source: Castle, Haas, Miller. *Migration in Europe since 1945* (5th Edition). 2014 : 108 Table 5.1.

According to Castle, Haas and Miller (2014: 5th Edition), migration from colonies took a very important role in industry and construction in Britain coming mainly from Ireland with their families, many of them settling down permanently enjoying similar privileges as local citizens including right to vote. Gradually numbers expanded to include immigrants from Commonwealth including the former Caribbean colonies and those like the Indian Subcontinent and colonies in Africa by 1961 and the number of immigrants from these sources rose to some 1.5 million by 1981. However, semi-skilled workers, the black and Asian workers engaged in manual jobs in industry and services were characterised as suffering from 'a high degree of residential segregation'.

France presents a similar situation of having immigrants from her former colonies of Algeria, Morocco, and Tunisia as well as from Southern Europe along with small numbers from West African colonies of Senegal, Mali, and Mauritania. Racial discrimination was very acute keeping non-European immigrants confined to very low jobs with social segregation in housing and other facilities very acute.

In contrast, however, Netherlands provides a different case where immigrants from the former colony of Indonesia, having 'up to 3,00,000 repatriates between 1945 and early 1960' provides a case of 'assimilation' with little evidence of 'racism or discrimination' for them.

According to the same source mentioned above, Southern Europe having played the role of labour-reserve for Western Europe, North America, South America, and Australia for over a century reversed its role between 1970s and 1980s from emigration to immigration.

> 'Europe rich in labour but short of land, sent migrants to the Americas, which in turn were rich in land and short of labour. This process produced positive effects on both sides of the Atlantic'.[13]

The nineteenth century is characterised by emigration of Europeans to extra European destinations which amounted to 50-60 million, particularly necessitated by European population growing faster than the rest of the world caused probably by the death rate declining faster than the birth-rate. Those overseas emigrants were mainly from Britain and Germany, the former being major source of emigrants or labour representing about 37 per cent of the total outflow from Europe, amounting to almost 22.6 million people leaving Britain during 1815-1914. Among the countries of the British Isles, however, emigration from Ireland was in a critical stage, providing an 'escape route from extreme deprivations', ravaged by famines in 1845-47. Similarly, Germany faced a critical situation of population pressure with crop failures in the 1840s resulting in mass emigration between 1845 and 1858 of about 1.3 million emigrating overseas with another million between 1864 and 1873 culminating at 4.9 per thousand population in 1881. But overseas migration was of greater significance for the Scandinavian countries when during late 1860s 1,20,000 Swedes facing a similar situation to Ireland's in the 1840s and 1850s emigrated overseas followed by 'next big outflow' in the 1880s amounting to about 60 per cent of the 'natural increase'. Similarly, both Norway and Denmark had the experience of large outflows, comprising 'over two-thirds of the natural increase', the largest for any European country except Ireland while for Italy, already 2,70,000 of the nationals were living in foreign countries by 1871.[14]

Emigration of this order obviously played a vital role in the development of the American economy, particularly in building up what the USA and Canada are today. For instance, it is important to note that Western Europe alone 'exported' about 15 million people to North America between 1870 and 1913, sending about 1 million each year before World War I, attracting almost the same number of immigrants today when her total population has increased by three times.

> In 2010, the continent (Russia included) counted 733 million inhabitants. Without immigration, that number is estimated to drop to 700 million by 2030 and includes both far fewer young people and many more old ones. The population between the ages of 20 and 40 would decline from 208 to 154 million (-26%). This age group accounts for both most immigrants and the majority of child bearing, it is also the peak range for innovative work and the acquisition of new knowledge. Instead, the population over 65 would increase from 119 to 163 million (+37 %).[15]

However, the great importance of European emigration to Americas in particular, and to Australia and New Zealand is of historic significance among all global events considering the fact that it was European labour that built up the American economy from scratch, so to say, when considered against the fact that 'three outstanding contributions' consisting of 11,87,000 Irish, 9,19,000 Germans between 1880 and 1885 joined by 17,54,000 Italians between 1898 and 1907[16] provided the major prop for laying the economic foundation of American economy, with the labour involved requiring no 'costs of rearing and training' for tasks they needed to do. The same thing happened as well in Canada, Australia, and New Zealand, the immigrants taking the major share in building up the local economy. Argentina in South America presents the best example of immigrant-based development with foreign-born people, that is the immigrants, which represented 30 per cent of the population in 1914, though no country could beat the United States which received half of the immigrants of European stock that went to the Americas increasing its settled population of about 5 million in 1800 to over 100 million by 1914.[17]

Interestingly, however, large-scale emigration of Europeans had a rather positive effect on the home economy raising real wages, improving living standards and eroding poverty of those who stayed behind obviously because of greater demand for labour in the burgeoning economy with greater momentum for industrialisation and connected activities of construction, transportation etc. As a result of such internal development, there was a growing prospect of immigration from previous colonies besides intra-country immigration within Europe. As a matter of fact, the existing facilities of high-skilled activities offered a very lucrative market for immigrants, particularly from developing countries having a vast reserve of talent looking for opportunities abroad, which in the name of brain-drain has a great future potential of keeping the flow of immigrants alive still for a long time. According to Livi-Bacci (2010), immigrants already comprise one in six working people in France, but six out of ten in Portugal while the entire EU, comprising altogether 26 (after Britain moved out) countries where the total number of legal, that is authorised, immigrants amount to 5 to 10 million but there were no reliable figures for unauthorised immigrants making a foothold in devious ways.

According to the same author estimates of international migration made by the United States based on census counts is not fully reliable as these do not include unauthorised immigration. In any case, according to United Nations estimate there were 214 million migrants in 2010, increasing from 191 million in 2005, representing 3 per cent of global population. It is worthy of note that the developed and the developing worlds present different status in regard to the migrants, such as the volume of migrants increased from 82 million to 128 million in the developed world between 1990 and 2010, comprising from 7.2 to 10.3 per cent of the total population while in the developing world it increased from 73 million to 86 million during the same period representing barely 1.8 to 1.5 per cent of the total population. Thus, it becomes quite clear that on the whole immigration is much more focused on the developed world, in other words, the developed world has greater opportunities for making a livelihood, keeping the door open for outsiders, or rather the immigrants who could be considered as human capital in view of skill they hold for using in various professions[18] (Table 5.2).

Table 5.2: World Stock of Migrants, 1960-2010 (Millions)

Year	World	Developed Countries	Less Developed, or Developing Countries
1960	75.5	32.3	43.1
1965	78.4	35.4	43.0
1970	81.3	38.4	43.0
1975	86.8	42.5	44.3
1980	99.3	47.5	51.8
1985	111.0	53.6	57.4
1990	154.9	82.4	72.6
1995	165.1	94.9	70.2
2000	176.7	105.0	71.8
2005	190.6	115.4	75.2
2010	213.9	127.7	86.2

Source: Livi-Bacci, M. *A Short History of Migration.* Polity Press. 2010:131, Table 6.

It is further observed that the quota of legal immigration has been fulfilled, the flow of immigration in particular cases may not stop altogether and continue further over time and space by iliegal entry as happened in the case of Hispanic migration, largely of Mexican origin, into the United States that has been taking place since World War II, numbering 48 million altogether, making the largest minority migration even exceeding the number of African Americans in the United States today. However, it is not an unusual case. There are 5 to 10 million unauthorised immigrants in European Union and similarly Russia is facing a tremendous pressure of unauthorised immigrants from Central Asia and the Caucasus, once a part of the USSR, the number of them ranging from a 'minimum of 3 to 5 million to a maximum of 10 to 15 million'.[19]

Of late, immigrants in the form of refugees as asylum seekers fleeing countries in great political turmoil in the Middle East, in some of the African countries and Afghanistan are concentrating in some of the Asiatic countries adjoining Middle East, like Turkey, Lebanon and Jordan and going into EU countries through Greece, looking for accommodation as well as rehabilitation. In fact, they represent the largest wave of mass migration arriving across the Mediterranean in small, leaking boats. It is estimated that in 2014 and 2015, about 1.2 million people crossed the Mediterranean while between 2016 and 2018, the situation worsening in Syria and Afghanistan would force out another 3 million.[20]

However, in the context of mass migration in earlier periods involving the pioneers, the following two tables – Table 5.3 and Table 5.4 – seem to be very enlightening since there is a fundamental difference between them, such as Table 5.3 represents migrants who volunteered to find better opportunities in a new setting while Table 5.4 shows migrants who were not wilful but forced to migrate not even knowing where and why they were being taken.

Table 5.3: Net Migration from Europe to America 1500-1760, by Country of Origin

('000s)

Country of Origin	Before 1580	1580-1640	1640-1700	1700-1760	Total
Spain	139	188	158	193	678
Portugal	93	110	50	270	523
France	0	4	45	51	100
Holland	0	2	13	5	20
Great Britain	0	126	248	372	746
Total	**232**	**430**	**514**	**891**	**2,067**

Note: The data for Great Britain include German migrants on British Ships.
Source: Livi-Bacci, M. *A Short History of Migration*. Polity Press. 2010 : p. 127, Table 2.

Looking at the present situation, it can, perhaps be, concluded that the days of massive migration in international perspective are over since reasons such as the opportunity of populating empty spaces (as offered by the two Americas and Australia), colonisation made on an extensive scale as done in Asia or Africa done by the maritime nations of Europe or kidnapping unintended black labour as slaves and employment of indentured labour on a massive scale do not operate in a more civilised world. It also needs to be clarified further that it was the self-willed immigrants who took the initiative of mass migration and not the emigrants during the entire period of past waves of migrations in building up the economies of the countries they went to as well as populate them. On the contrary, what is happening today in the name of migration is invariably emigration and that too on a very modest scale, mostly though not explicitly directed from lower income to higher income countries, or, rather from developing to developed countries, the latter offering better opportunities in terms of earning as well as higher learning . This, however, does not include emigration for mostly semi-skilled jobs on a large scale in the Gulf-oil producing countries coming mostly from the Indian Sub-continent including Indian, Pakistani, and Bangladeshi citizens discussed earlier. However, both emigration and immigration often represent the two sides of the same coin, the former changing subsequently on approaching the country or countries of embarkation. For example, when Indians emigrate to any developed country to avail of better opportunities by using their skill whether in the USA or in any other developed country they turn into immigrants. In any case, the flow of emigrants turn into immigrants for the host country is far from massive exception in the case of Mexican emigrants entering the USA because much of it is illegal.

Table 5.4: Slaves Transported to the Americas and Europe by Destination, 1450-1870

(000s)

Destination	1451-1600	1601-1700	1701-1810	1811-1870	Total
North America	–	–	348	51	399
Hispanic America	75	293	579	606	1,553
British Caribbean	–	264	1,401	–	1,665
French Caribbean	–	156	1,348	96	1,600
Dutch Caribbean	–	40	460	–	500
Danish Caribbean	–	4	24	–	28
Brazil	50	560	1,891	1,145	3,646
Europe	150	25	–	–	175
Total	**275**	**1,342**	**6,051**	**1,898**	**9,566**

Notes: The Spanish Caribbean is included in Hispanic America. After 1810, Hispanic America refers only to Cuba and Puerto Rico. Europe includes the Atlantic Islands and Sao Tome.

Source: Livi-Bacci, M. *A Short History of Migration*. Polity Press. 2010: p.127, Table 3. (Taken from Philip Curtin, *The Atlantic Slave Trade: A Census, Madison*; University of Wisconsin Press, 1969 : p. 268, Table 77).

In modern times, the emigrants maintaining the flow, however small, comparing with those happening during the sixteenth and seventeenth centuries, are considered as a great loss to the countries of origin, such as India, Bangladesh, Sri Lanka, Pakistan or even China on a small scale, since the country of origin is failing to provide proper opportunity for utilising their skill (developed at their own expense) on better economic terms happen to lose the cream of talents to build up their own economy instead of giving the same over to the host countries of the emigrants. Situation like this is likely to continue for a long time yet as long as birth-rate in these countries does not fall appreciably, having been one of the major factors along with high rate of female illiteracy considered as one of the major factors reducing the birth-rate as well as infant-deaths.

> 'The average woman in Africa today has 5.2 children while the average European woman has just 1.4.... Worldwide about 115 million children were denied even basic primary education – most of them in Sub-Saharan Africa and South Asia. On average girls could expect to receive one year less of education than boys in African and Arab States and two years less in South Asia. In the developing world as a whole, only 58 per cent of women were literate, compared to 68 per cent of men'.[21]

On the other hand, highly-skilled emigrants sending money home – their country of origin – amounting to almost US$586 billion a year, as estimated by the World Bank, mentioned earlier, is nothing but a family wise help even trickling finally into the country's coffer through household purchases does in no way contribute to strengthen national economy as such which remains deprived of local talents lost through so-called 'brain-drain'. The latest instance of such great loss is evidenced further by the recipient of Nobel Prize in Economics in 2019 (Abhijit Banerjee) who was born and educated in India (West Bengal) and developed his theory of development through his work in the USA where he emigrated. This again brings to focus the importance of emigration taking a vital role of deprivation for countries unable to create a situation of holding back talents in the absence of which they look for a better pasture. Such a loss is going to be quite long-lasting, putting a severe constraint on the country/countries' future development till the outward flow of talent – emigration could be stemmed effectively.

In this regard, it is expedient to have a clear idea about the role of international immigration consisting of two constituents – emigration and immigration – of which while the former is much more relevant today than the latter which seems to have lost its relevance so to say in a changed situation where it no longer plays any significant role in shaping the life of any country as it did in earlier periods of nation-building happening earlier in unexplored, empty territories in North and South America and Australia offering no resistance to gun-toting Westerners exterminating native population in their gun-less fights against these intruders for their extreme violence, senseless cruelty and depthless torture.

The long-drawn interlude of this hellish development was carried out by the colonisers or the so-called immigrants in the name of development of the hitherto vast stretches of empty land in each of the continents exposing the depth of unquenchable lust in the name of settling down using slave labour till only one humane voice was heard with deep consideration of love and empathy for the slaves as human lives.

The person referred to above is Abraham Lincoln born on February 12, 1809 in Kentucky of an undistinguished family, he was sworn in on March 4, 1861 as the President of the United States, the sixteenth in the line as a Republican Party nominee since George Washington came to be the first President. As a President he had to go through a turbulent time of civil war with the southern states not until then having joined the emerging United States but even before assuming power, his mind and voice was absolutely clear about hating slavery and made this stand clear in opposition to slavery[22] and declared this in very plain as well as emphatic manner, such as,

> '...I intend no modification of my oft-expressed personal wish that all men everywhere could be free'.[23]

This was further made on 1 January, 1863 as part of his Proclamation of Emancipation, that:

> 'all persons held as slaves within any state, or designated part of a state, the people whereof shall then be in rebellion against the United States shall be then, henceforward and for ever free'.[24]

He, however, did not stop at this. In finalising the wording of his Emancipation Proclamation, he added further:

> 'And by virtue of the power, and for the purpose aforesaid, I do order and declare that all persons held as slaves within designated states, and parts of states, are, and henceforth shall

> be free, and that the Executive Government of the United States including the military and naval authorities thereof will recognise and maintain the freedom of the said persons'.[25]

His self-estimate comes out on April 4, 1864, in more and more convincing, unfaltering trust,

> 'I am generally anti-slavery. If slavery is not wrong, nothing is wrong. I cannot remember when I did not so think and feel'.[26]

After his re-election as the President of the United States he was determined to 'pass an amendment that would abolish slavery for all time' and reminded everyone once for all that,

> 'the stain of slavery was enmeshed in the fabric of American history from its beginning'.[27]

Thus, after almost two long centuries of lifeless existence surviving (those who did not perish) through depthless brutal and physical torture and humiliation for no wrong done by them the slaves for the first time heard this most humane voice recognising them as human beings not different from anybody around them. Since then, they started living a free life called African Americans who could not go back even if they wanted to as they do not know where they came from, kidnapped, and forcibly brought as slaves. Needless to say, that the African Americans living as free-citizens face even today many limitations in the form of segregation in housing, eating places, educational facilities, work-restrictions in general keeping a visible hiatus between them and the 'Whites'. As a result, this clear identification remains a societal hierarchy.

What, however, is clearly recognised in all such developments is that immigration as such is no longer a powerful instrument in affecting human history while emigration still remains very much relevant, particularly having a one-way flow from the developing to the developed world, or, rather, from 'South' to 'North' though instances of emigration exist inside many of these countries. The former, from less affluent to more affluent countries, however, is never on a massive scale, and probably will never become so as the less developed countries meanwhile are putting efforts at improving their own situations. Yet the international character of emigration is quite evident in the present day with fast improvement in the Information System making people knowledgeable about the availability of situations in the talent market all over the world, or, rather in the developed world, enticing the opportune seekers, or the emigrants. Hence, the flow, never a massive one, nevertheless continues.

It, however, needs to be pointed out that still now colour consciousness plays a strong role among the 'Whites', clouding their views on making a correct assessment of people having dark skins which is very dominant in 'White' dominated countries. As long as prejudice against skin-colour is not overcome, an overall justice cannot be achieved, thus keeping the hiatus between the two worlds – the 'White' and 'Non-White' wider. One cannot ignore the fact that according to the UN World Urbanisation Prospects 2014 Revision, of the total global population of 8,42,49,37,000 in 2030 the coloured population living in Asia and Africa amounting to 4,88,68,46,300 against 1,88,99,52,200 white population living in the developed countries of Europe, two Americas, Australia, and New Zealand. But while people in Asia and Africa represent a mosaic of skin-colours ranging from black, brown, yellow, and highly fair (no less than 'Whites'), those in Europe as well as other countries are not seamless 'White' as they also include people of darker skins. Hence, coloured people amount to nearly two-and-a-half times pitted against 'white' people should avoid living in a contesting situation. Like seven rays of the sun to whom we all owe our life we should live in an atmosphere of understanding and respective goodwill assuring peace and harmony.

II. International Migration in the Context of Indian Experience

International migration has played a great, decisive role in building up present-day Indian Society which is a complex mixture of people belonging to a very wide range of cultures and upbringing clearly reflected in the physique, complexion, language, and many other life-practices including its cuisine. It is pointed out by Chinmay Tumbe (2018) that genetic evidence in India today clearly points:

> "to two divergent population ancestral to the majority of the present-day population, providing clues to the colour gradient and much more … the 'Ancestral North Indians' (ANI), are genetically close to Middle Eastern Central Asians and Europeans, whereas the other, the 'Ancestral South Indians' (ASI), are as distinct from the ANI and East Asians as they are from each other … The difference between ANI and ASI … reveals a broad north-south divide in Indian culture and language, running roughly through central India, with word 'Indo-European' used for the north and 'Dravidians' used for the south".[28]

According to the same source, the difference in origin of the present-day population of India indicates signs of migration of people – usually referred to as the Aryans – who came from north-west. The Harappan Civilisation (2500-1500 B.C.)[29] thriving along the Indus Valley shows evidence of a mixture of different racial types, indicating 'different streams of migrations'. This is further substantiated by evidence established by mercantile links with other countries ultimately contributing to racial variations. In this context, one may refer to the networks of foreign trade built-up by the Harappan Civilisation.

> 'It is increasingly clear that a major component of this international commerce was *via* the Persian Gulf sea lanes ... The volume of individual shipments indicated in the Sumerian economic documents recounting this trade is considerable. For example, tons of copper'[30]

were taken by the Harappan traders to distant lands.

Apart from that, there are instances of migration in ancient India 'from the middle of the first millennium BCE to circa 1300 CE', a period of almost 2,000 years during which, as claimed by Chinway Tumbe (2018), immigration mainly from Central Asia took place to India through the north-western passes. The idea is further strengthened by the fact of Buddhism spreading far and wide following the Silk Road to Far East, providing very valid instances of emigration on an international scale from India rather than other instances provided in those cases of, 'other faiths such as Christianity, Judaism, Zoroastrianism, and Islam coming in'.[31]

A further direct instance of migration, though may be on small-scale, is provided involving *Brahmans* across most parts of the subcontinent that took place in ancient India during the 'second half of the first millennium BCE'. Particular words used in India from early times like *Yona* or *Javana*, to denote the presence of ancient Greeks, Parthians, Shakas, Kushanas and Huns between 'second century BCE to third century CE', followed by Turko-Afghans later from the north-west and Mahmud Ghazni in the early 11th century CE followed by Muhammad Ghori in the 12th century CE provide ample instances of migration of people from distant countries visiting India with various motives.

Evidence of migration to and from India in the form of either immigration or emigration find further strength from the fact that the west coast of India, particularly the southern part of Kerala was in close contact with West Asia from ancient times, even stretching further to the Roman Empire. The presence of Syrian Christians and the Jews in Cochin are evidence of such close contact going back a thousand years or so while even Islam, emerging as a faith in the seventh century had found a way into India 'by way of trade' in the 'early 8th century' in Kerala.

In the reverse, Indian cultural intrusion overseas, originating from present Tamil Nadu region since the 4th century had a strong impact on South-East Asia, adopting many of Indian cultural practices as evidenced even now in the life of these people as well as in temple architecture. This is further evidenced in the raids of the Chola Empire (circa 850 CE-1250 CE) on Sri Lanka and in the Straits of Malacca in the 11th century CE. According to Tumbe (2018) following Alexander's invasion of India in 326 B.C. he took back some Indians and a Hindu settlement of about 12,000 persons has been found in Armenia thriving for centuries (from 2nd century BCE to early 4th Century CE). Migrations from India may also be traced in Thailand, Vietnam, and the Malaya Peninsula while a particular case of emigration of 12,000 Indian musicians at the court of the Persian King brought under his request in the 5th century A.D. makes a very interesting case of migration. Even European Gypsies according to some authors, find a link with the 'low-ranking castes and indigenous tribes of north-west India'.[33]

The great improvement in transportation systems during the 19th century and afterwards triggered mass migration, such as between 1834 and 1937, 30 million people emigrated from India to Burma, Malaysia and Sri Lanka of which nearly 24 million returned ultimately, thus making the whole process circulatory. Almost the same thing happened, giving rise to another instance of circulatory migration during the two World Wars when millions of Indians were involved providing the necessary labour force (to be taken up in greater details later in this chapter).[34]

In this context, a review of Indian migration dominated by colonial interest makes a very important revelation. Prabir Bhattacharya (2019) quoting Adam Smith (Adam Smith, Book V, Chapter I, Part III) refers to his comment that the East India Company was appointed by the British Government as the 'plunderers of India' which Bhattacharya (2019) puts at £11.8 million averaging £1.3 million a year (at current prices) between 1783-92 while it was £100 million between 1757 and 1815 according to an estimate enabling Britain to 'liquidate its foreign debts and thus turning it from a 'debtor to a creditor country when imports from India were obtained more or less free'.[35]

What is, however of equally great interest, the use of the Indian army sent long distances for Britain's war paid by 'Indian taxpayers money' to save Britain's commercial interests and extend further British trade. Indian soldiers were sent to Egypt in 1789, to the Cape of Good Hope in South Africa in 1795 and 1806, to Burma in 1824, 1826 and 1852, for taking control of a lucrative timber trade and to

> 'China in 1839, 1856, 1859 and 1909 … to gain ease of access of Britain into Far Eastern markets … to Persia in 1856, to Ethiopia and Singapore in 1867, to Hongkong in 1868, to Malaya in 1875, to Malta in 1878, to Afghanistan in 1838, and then again in 1878, to Egypt in 1899 and Tibet in 1903. Indian taxpayers paid not only the expenses of both Indian and British Troops in India, but also some fractions of the cost of Indian and British troops used in these imperial adventures'.[36]

At the same time, as Bhattacharya (2019) points out, substantiated by statistics, India acted as the 'captive' market for British goods, holding the top place for British exports between 1870 and 1913 while India's exports to Britain fell to about 10 per cent by the 'turn of the century'.

On the other hand, emigration from India took quite an important role in the history of Indian migration particularly in the modern times which took, first of all in the form of indentured labour beginning with the end of slavery in British colonies, as mentioned earlier in Chapter 3, with the first group of them sent to Mauritius in 1834 to work mostly in sugar plantations. Later Indians were sent to Jamaica, British Guiana, Trinidad, Grenada, St. Lucia, Natal, Fiji, Ceylon and Burma. Labour emigration in this form amounted to about 6.5 million between 1834 and 1924 of whom 1.4 million was indentured while the remaining 5.1 million were free of indenture. Here Bhattacharya (2019) gives us very interesting information about large scale emigration focusing on the fact that the number of British persons in overseas emigration was much higher, amounting to 22.6 million persons between 1815 and 1914.[37]

But what is of greater significance is that Indian emigrant labour took a vital role in developing and sustaining the economy of the countries they went to, as in West Indies plantations bringing prosperity to them.

> 'Indian immigrant labour was vital in helping to make Burma the rice bowl of the Southeast Asia, with greater part of the immigrants to Burma being employed in the rice mills. In Ceylon, Indian labour was equally vital in coffee and tea plantations. Coffee exports from Ceylon to Great Britain increased sevenfold between 1845 and 1870.… Similarly, Indian emigration to the Straits Settlements was critical to its development. Malaya bordered on the shortest sea route

> between India and China and was to become important strategic and economic assets for the British overtime.... The Indian labour became indispensable for plantation agriculture in Malaya. Indian labour also constituted an overwhelming number of workers in rubber stations. Furthermore, Indians played a prominent often dominant, role in almost every phase of development of the modern transport and communication system, particularly the railroad and telecommunication networks'.[38]

Tumbe (2018) in this context refers to internal migration in India and according to him currently over '200 million Indians' make one of the 'largest and longest migration streams for work outside their place of birth. As such most of it is characterised by movement from one region to another region within the country depending necessarily on the availability of opportunities. For example, Ratnagiri district in Konkan Maharashtra is one such region wherefrom emigration became a well-established tradition by the middle of the 19th century because of unbalanced sex ratio, the number of females 'never fell below 1100 per 1000 males' from where men have been migrating for work elsewhere and thus tilting the balance in sex-ratio. Udupi in Karnataka is another such region wherefrom men particularly from lower caste migrate on a large scale to coffee plantations in Coorg and Mysore returning home after coffee is harvested. It is, however, interesting to note that the Brahmins in large numbers have been migrating to Chennai, Mysore, and Bangalore to run Udupi food-outlets sprouting up in different cities.

Saran district in Bihar, located west of Patna, makes another region of mass migration started originally as indentured labour taken for sugar plantations in Mauritius and the Caribbean Islands which by the late 19th century involved 'hundreds of thousands', giving rise to distorted sex-ratio with 1200 females to 1000 males, the menfolk seeking opportunities available in a wide range of activities available in different parts of undivided Bengal offering wages five times higher than what they could earn in Saran. Of late, however, Punjab enjoying the benefits of Green Revolution and Delhi's development into multifarious activities, have come to be of greater attraction for migrants from Saran.

Ganjam district of Orissa coast provides another case of out-migration triggered by frequent visits of strong cyclones destroying homes and means of livelihood. The migrants' major choice was Rangoon (Yangon in present Myanmar), half of them working in the transport sector, in the rice-processing industries and earthwork. However, change in the political situation in Myanmar in the mid-twentieth century had an effect on the destination of migrants from Ganjam who henceforth made Gujarat the place of choice.

A surge in specifically male migration happened with oil crisis in 1973 with a hike in oil prices, creating a great demand for labour in West Asia. Kerala took up this challenge sending labour to Saudi Arabia and the United Arab Emirates. It is recorded that by 2008, there were more than 3 million Keralites working in the Gulf countries engaged in a wide range of activities comprising construction to commercial plazas. According to Tumbe (2018), it had been the same for the entire west coast below Ratnagiri from where labour is participating in 'internal and international migration streams'.

This also happens to be the story of Tamil Nadu sending migrants to South-west Asia over a long period and by early 20th century it involved about 1,00,000 people migrating annually, for whom Sri Lanka, Malaysia, Singapore and Burma (Myanmar) had been the main destinations. In fact, the coffee plantations in Sri Lanka happened to be a major destination for migrants from other places in the east-coastal region, such as Tanjore, Trunelveli, Madura and Ramnad[39] (See Appendix I).

It may not be out of place here to refer to emigration of a particular group of people from India to the United Kingdom. Having traditional ties with the British for a long time particularly for the Sikhs working in the British Army, many of them later mainly from the rural areas started migrating to the United Kingdom 'in response to demand for semi-skilled workers during the 1960s' followed by another group consisting of the sons of rich peasants arriving in the late 1970s and 1980s to marry the female members of Sikh families already resident in Great Britain. Those migrants were followed by another group consisting of Sikhs seeking asylum after the operation of Blue Star in 1984 in India. As analysed by K.S. Dhindsa (1998), majority of the migrants arriving at different times were unskilled barring a small number having higher education. As such they are primarily employed in unskilled manual jobs—

> 'in factories, foundries, warehouses, airports, construction premises etc. Only fifteen per cent are doing skilled jobs like working as welders, fitters, plumbers, painters, technicians, laboratory technicians and drivers etc. A very small minority (5%) are doing professional jobs such as doctors, engineers, chartered accountants, lawyers, computer programmers, managers etc. About one-fifth of the immigrants are running their own businesses.'[40]

NOTES

*United Nations. World Migration Report. 2018 : p.15.

'The United Nations Recommendations on Statistics of International Migrations defines an *international migrant* as any person who has changed his or her country of usual residence, distinguishing between *short-term migrants* (those who have changed their country of usual residence for at least three months, but less than one year) and *long-term migrants* (those who have done so for at least one year)'.

1. Livi-Bacci, M. *A Short History of Migration*. 2010. Trans. Carl Ipsen. Cambridge: Polity Press, 2012, p. vii.
2. *Ibid.*
3. *Ibid.*, pp. 4-7.
4. *Ibid.*, pp. 7-8.
5. *Ibid.*, pp. 10-11.
6. Castles, S., Hass, H.D., Miller, M.J. *The Age of Migration: International Migration Before 1945*. 4th ed. Basingstoke: Macmillan, 2014, p. 88.
7. *Ibid.*, p. 90.
8. *Ibid.*
9. Livi-Bacci, M. *A Short History of Migration*. 2010. Trans. Carl Ipsen. Cambridge: Polity Press, 2012, p. 43.
10. Castles, S., Hass, H.D., Miller, M.J. *The Age of Migration: International Migration Before 1945*. 4th ed. Basingstoke: Macmillan, 2014, pp. 96-98.
11. *Ibid.*, p. 102.
12. *Ibid.*, pp. 103-107.
13. Livi-Bacci, M. *A Short History of Migration*. 2010. Trans. Carl Ipsen. Cambridge: Polity Press, 2012, p. 90.
14. Bhattacharya, P. "India in the Rise of Britain and Europe: A Contribution to the Convergence and Great Divergence Debates." *Journal of Interdisciplinary Economics* 33.1 (2019): pp. 17-19.
15. Livi-Bacci, M. *A Short History of Migration*. 2010. Trans. Carl Ipsen. Cambridge: Polity Press, 2012, pp. 95-96.
16. Bhattacharya, P. "India in the Rise of Britain and Europe: A Contribution to the Convergence and Great Divergence Debates." *Journal of Interdisciplinary Economics* 33.1 (2019): pp. 19-20.
17. *Ibid.*
18. Livi-Bacci, M. *A Short History of Migration*. 2010. Trans. Carl Ipsen. Cambridge: Polity Press, 2012, pp. 109-110.
19. *Ibid.*, pp. 114-117.
20. Kingsley, P. *The New Odyssey: The Story of Europe's Refugee Crisis*. London: Guardian Books, 2016, p. 4.
21. Koser, K. *International Migration: A Very Short Introduction*. 2nd ed. U.K.: Oxford University Press, 2016, p. 26.

22. White, Jr. R. C. *A. Lincoln: A Biography*. New York: Random House Trade Paperbacks, 2010, pp. 306-307, 619, 664-665.
23. *Ibid.*, p. 586.
24. *Ibid.*, p. 518.
25. *Ibid.*, pp. 531-532.
26. *Ibid.*, p. 619.
27. *Ibid.*, pp. 664-665.
28. Tumbe, C. *India Moving: A History of Migration*. India: Penguin Random House, 2018, pp. 4-5.
29. Sjoberg, G. *The Pre-Industrial City: Past and Present*. Illinois: The Free Press of Glencoe, 1960, p. 40.
30. Possehl, G.L. *The Harappan Civilisation: A Contemporary Perspective*. 2nd ed. India: Oxford & LBH Publishing Co. Pub. Ltd, 1993, p. 17.
31. Tumbe, C. *India Moving: A History of Migration*. India: Penguin Random House, 2018, p. 11.
32. *Ibid.*, pp. 15-19.
33. *Ibid.*, p. 32.
34. *Ibid.*, pp. 39-59.
35. Bhattacharya, P. "India in the Rise of Britain and Europe: A Contribution to the Convergence and Great Divergence Debates." *Journal of Interdisciplinary Economics* 33.1 (2019): pp. 5, 7.
36. *Ibid.*, p. 9.
37. *Ibid.*, p. 15.
38. *Ibid.*, p. 16.
39. Tumbe, C. *India Moving: A History of Migration*. India: Vikings Penguin Random House, 2018, pp. 39-59.
40. Dhindsa, K. S. *Indian Immigrants in United Kingdom*. New Delhi: Concept Publishing House, 1998, p. 28.

6
Migration by Refugees

I. Refugees: Victims of Political Unrest

Since the end of the Second World War (1939-1945), the world has remained in a very disturbed situation with more than 65 million people made homeless, uprooted from their homelands with over 20 million of them seeking rehabilitation away from home to avoid persecution, thus turning into the most humiliated 'set of human beings, or Refugees'. These people fleeing from political unrest, often threatened by instant death, along with all family members, represent a different type of mass-migration seeking asylum in countries, which are preferably close to the country left behind. Though such cases are not new, as mentioned earlier, having been associated with a very large-scale exodus of people from their homeland following the Russian Revolution, the Hitler regime in Germany, the Partition of the Indian Subcontinent in 1947 on gaining independence from British rule, the dissolution of Yugoslavia into several independent states, and the latest one associated with countries in the Middle East, Africa and Afghanistan uprooting people who are rushing to adjoining countries while the desperate ones are seeking asylum in European countries with which they had no link apart from being the nearest destination for homeless people.

However, the majority of the refugees have taken refuge in countries close to their places of origin, most often speaking the same language and belonging to the same religion, and as such 90 per cent of them are in the developing world, with ten countries accommodating almost 60 per cent of the worlds' refugees. Despite such an alarming situation, the world did not wake up to the realities of such a formidable problem until April 2015 when, for the first time, refugees started spontaneously to move to European countries and in 2015 alone over a million of them sought asylum from countries where internal violence since 2011 had dislodged about 10 million people, while others came from equally disrupting political upheavals in Afghanistan, Iraq, as well as some sub-Saharan countries.[1]

People turned into refugees by internal political strife in their country of origin represent 'the biggest waves of mass migration since the Second World War'. At first, they came across the central Mediterranean in small leaky, overloaded boats landing on the Italian island of Lampedusa but later crossing the Mediterranean from Turkey to the Greek island of Lesbos came to be more popular for its short distance, made mostly by Syrians, Afghans and Iraqis, altogether 1.2 million of them making it from Turkey to Greece between 2014 and 2015 while another 3 million made it between 2016 and 2018.[2]

However, on making a meticulous checking of the origin of the refugees, it emerged that between October 2014 and October 2015, 2,50,000 of them arrived from Syria, 1,10,000 from Afghanistan, 80,000 from Kosovo (not across the Mediterranean), 70,000 from Iraq and 30,000 from Eritrea. Of the over 1 million who arrived by crossing the Mediterranean *via* the relatively short route from Turkey to Greece, over 800 died while crossing the sea though a much larger toll of over 3,770 perished taking the longer route across the Mediterranean to Italy. It is very important to note that each of the migrants availing of this extreme perilous journey had to depend on smugglers paying them more than $2000 each[3], since regular boats and planes refuse passage without proper travelling documents.*

The European Union, after lots of debates, agreed in 2015 to quotas for relocation of refugees arriving by crossing the Mediterranean Sea in rickety, leaking, extremely crowded small boats by way of Greece and Italy allocated to different countries in the following order: Germany 28,000; France 20,000; Spain 9,000; Poland 6,000; Netherlands 6,000; (UK and Denmark did not take any part).

However, the most humane consideration in regard to these rootless people hounded out from their own country is shown by some of the European countries in accepting them for relocation. Thus, applications for asylum were approved by these countries in 2014 in the following order: Germany: 44,555; Sweden: 33,025; France: 20,640; Italy: 20,630, Switzerland: 15,575; UK: 14,065. Majority of the asylum seekers were from Syria, Eritrea, Afghanistan, Iran, and Iraq. It is, however, very important to note that most of the Syrians given asylum were not in Europe, but in neighbouring West Asian countries, 2.3 million were accommodated in Turkey, 1 million in Lebanon and 60,000 in Jordan.

But one feels very sorry to notice the lack of any sympathy on the part of the UNHCR or any other global organisations to offer any financial help towards maintenance of these refugees taking refuge in the developing world and thus making an unbearable financial strain on the host countries while depriving the refugees of a bearable lifestyle. As such, though escaping immediate death in the country they fled from they remained:

> 'the most vulnerable, with no means (money to pay the smugglers to get out of the situation) or desire to travel to Europe, remained in an utterly dysfunctional system. For every $135 of public money spent on an asylum seeker in Europe, just $1 is spent on a refugee in the developing world. Fewer than one in ten of the Syrian refugees in Turkey, Lebanon and Jordan receive any material support from the United Nations or its implementing partners'.[4]

Looking back, it may be interesting to know as well as get a real feel of the situation faced by the refugees getting smuggled into Europe. As mentioned earlier, the money spent per head of each refugee on being transported by a smuggler was $2000 in 2015 for a person of sub-Saharan origin but rose to something around $2500 for a Syrian refugee considered to be financially solvent. In general, though 300 passengers were considered to be the limit for a 17-metre-long boat, quite often the number varied from 350 to 700 or 800 per boat, making it extremely over-loaded, no doubt, and when Africans were there as refugees they were often 'shoved below decks' while other refugees, in general, prior to getting place on a boat had to spend nearly four months in a 'mazara' – heavily-guarded, extremely crowded hiding place – used by smugglers to outwit the local authorities before the refugees could embark on a boat for sailing to Italy.

Libyan smugglers used three kinds of boats for transporting the refugees, 'steel-hulled ships', capable of accommodating about a thousand which, however, happened to be the rarest type scarcely available, followed by 'wooden fishing boats', handling nearly a third of the smuggling operations crammed with from 300 to 700 persons per boat, and, lastly, the Zodiac inflatables representing about two-thirds of the boats carrying refugees across the Mediterranean to Italy, each taking 100 to 150 passengers which ordinarily were designed for taking not more than 20 to 30 persons and that too meant for short trips.[5]

It is extremely discouraging to note that a larger number of people, more than in 2014, crossed the Mediterranean in 2015 and almost 18 times 'as many' died on the way from Libya to Italy more than 1800 compared with 96 the year before. This route finally became more popular as well as less hazardous involving the movement of 'roughly 40,000 people' in 2014, growing to over 7,50,000, having overtaken the other route from Libya in the volume of traffic besides a sharp change in the composition of people, over 'two-thirds of the total by Syrians'. According to the UN, 66 per cent of the 'arrivals in Greece in the first ten months of 2015' were Syrians.

The question here may arise about why the Syrians instead of settling down in the Middle East – such as in Turkey, Lebanon, and Jordan – chose Europe as the destination. The answer is – many of them have tried to settle down in the Middle East, such as, as mentioned before, 2 million in Turkey, nearly 1.2 million in Lebanon, 6,00,000 in Jordan (a tenth of the total population of the country), and 1,40,000 in Egypt. But reduction in food-subsidies provided by the UN from the winter of 2014 made the situation untenable for the refugees and left no choice for the Syrians but to look for a new destination which made Europe as the only alternative almost repeating 'mass exodus of Greeks from Asia' triggered by the Greco-Turkish war in 1922.[6] However, the passage by sea from Turkey to Greece though not long, caused deaths by drowning, running to over 500 in 2015.

> 'The story of humanity is essentially the story of human movement. In the near future, people will move even more, particularly if, as some predict, climate change sparks migration on an unprecedented scale. The sooner we recognise the inevitability of this movement, the sooner we can try to manage it'.[7]

But according to this source (Kingsley, 2016), refugees enjoy a better status in terms of deserving the right to protection, that is, rehabilitation which the migrants do not receive since the refugees are ousted from their home by political circumstances while migrants move out of their own volition. Ultimately, the European Commission in 2015 agreed to resettle 1,20,000 refugees landing in Italy and Greece and take the responsibility of another 40,000 refugees a year continuing for the next five years to 2020.[8] Interestingly, Turkey finally relented in early 2106 to give refugees the right to work though Lebanon and Jordan until then withheld access of the refugees to similar opportunities which, undoubtedly, would have largely stemmed the flow towards Europe.

Perhaps, a more humanitarian approach to the problem is needed to fulfil the policy of the UN's Refugee Agency in facing 'international catastrophe' following the instances of rehabilitation of 12 to 14 million displaced Europeans as a fall-out of the Second World War and the resettlement of another 1.3 million refugees from Indo-China as an aftermath of the Vietnam War in which all the Global-North, consisting of Europe, Canada, the USA, Australia and New Zealand, took interest in their resettlement. If Lebanon, a tiny country with its small population of 4.5 million can manage the problem of 1.2 million refugees, as mentioned above, it is expected that the World's richest continent (with 500 million population) can do the same. In this respect, however, Sweden has shown a highly commendable instance of accommodating 'one in seven' of the refugees, 8,00,000 having arrived in Europe in 2015.[9] In this respect, however, Germany may claim greater credit since 60 per cent of asylum-applicants from Iraq were 'granted' refugee status in Germany as compared with 7 per cent in Sweden.

Refugees and asylum seekers belonging to the same category are considered as forced migrants resulting from:

> violence, armed conflict, human rights violations and repressions, as well as because of natural disasters including the effects of climate change and environmental depression.[10]

According to Alice Bloch and Giorgia Dona (2019), there were 65.2 million forcibly displaced people by the end of 2016, 22.5 million of whom were refugees, 40.3 million internally displaced people and 2.8 million asylum seekers (those who claim refugee status which has not yet been accepted), apart from an unquantifiable number of undocumented migrants who, however, did not make any asylum claim.[11] The same source mentions that 84 per cent of the world's refugees are concentrated in the developing world when half of the refugees originate from Syria, Afghanistan and South Sudan hosted primarily by Turkey, Pakistan, Lebanon, Iran, Uganda, and Ethiopia while the largest number of internal displacements forcing out people as refugees happened in 2016 in the Democratic Republic of Congo (9,22,000), Syria (8,24,000), Iraq (6,59,000), Afghanistan (6,33,000), and Nigeria (5,01,000)[12]. About 86 per cent of these refugees live in the Global South and in 2017 almost two-thirds of them are living in extended exile when in the majority of cases they are living in limbo for over five years,[13] facing a situation like 'permanent temporariness'.

However, asylum seekers constitute a small proportion of the forced migrants about 2.8 million by the end of 2016 and by February 2017, only 3,656 refugees of Syria had been resettled in EU member countries when there were 2.8 million Syrians accommodated in Turkey alone.

Nonetheless, the case of rehabilitation of refugees is found to have been taken more seriously providing permanent accommodation to nearly 2,00,000 in 2016 in which some of the developed countries took greater interest, such as the USA settling 96,900 refugees, Canada taking 46,700 and Australia 27,600 while as mentioned earlier, Britain agreed to resettle 20,000 Syrians under a resettlement programme over a five-year period between 2015-2020. By this time, the most welcome development in the solution of the resettlement of refugees resulting from forced migration primarily caused by political upsurge came in the form of voluntary repatriation of them returning to their countries of origin involving almost 3 per cent of the total refugee population, a total of 5,52,000 of them in 2016 going back to their respective home countries, such as Afghanistan, Somalia and Sudan.[14] This also involves the return of Rohingya refugees, altogether 7,40,000 who fled in 2017 from Rakhine district in Myanmar as victims of religious persecution to the adjoining country of Bangladesh under stress of 'murder, rape and torture',[15] rehabilitated in the Teknaf region of Cox's Bazar district (Bangladesh). To all appearance, the Rohingyas are not very willing to return to Myanmar fearing reprisal, but their prolonged stay in Bangladesh is already proving to be an extremely hard pressure on the Bangladesh-economy which is far from robust.

According to the estimate of UNHCR (United Nations High Commission for Refugees), there were 99.7 million people forcibly displaced by the end of 2016, the highest since the cessation of the Second World War, and the political violence lasting over decades in countries like Somalia since 1990s, in Afghanistan and Columbia since 1980s have almost perpetuated displacement already lasting between three to four decades[16]. According to Voutira (2019) the narrow strip of water, hardly 10 kilometres wide, separating Turkey (Izmir) from Greece (Lesbos), is steeped in history, social memories, and historical significance as no other geographical space reputed, so much so that it even invited a 'visit from the Pope himself' at the height of refugee crisis in July 2015. Incidentally, the Syrian crisis beginning in 2011 came to a boiling point in 2016 when the situation worsened for all time, giving rise to the largest exodus of this century, turning 12 million Syrians into forced migrants the majority of whom, as mentioned earlier, were accommodated by some of the Middle East countries, such as Turkey took nearly 1.5 million of them sheltered in 25 camps in 10 provinces, Lebanon and Jordan also took a large number, as mentioned earlier. On the other hand, the east Mediterranean route from Turkey to Greece came to be a very important route providing passage for refugees into Europe where they sought asylum. This proved to be a much safer route across the Mediterranean in terms of drowning to death for the fleeing people as shown in Table 6.1.

Table 6.1: Arrivals and Fatalities in the Mediterranean Sea, 2014-2017

	2014	2015	2016	2017 (until 03/05)
Arrivals (Europe)	2,19,000	10,04,356	3,63,348	44,209
Deaths (in the Mediterranean)	3,279	3,771	5,079 (incidents that have not been fully accounted for)	1,096 (1,009 of these on Central Mediterranean Route)
Arrivals (Greece)	n/a	8,53,650	1,73,561	5,316
Deaths (Eastern Mediterranean Route)	33	805	434	37

Source: Black, A., Dona, G. *Forced Migration: Current Issues and Debates*. Routledge. 2019 : p.64. (Taken from the Data available with the International Organisation for Migration).

According to data provided in Table 6.1, it is obviously clear that the route between Turkey and Greece, as a short one, proved much safer recording fewer deaths as compared with large number of deaths for the refugees taking other routes, such as the Central-Mediterranean and the West-Mediterranean.

The latest situation in the changing scenario of forced migration is characterised by growing pressure of different host countries – both in the Global South and the Global North persuading the forced migrants, that is the refugees – to go back to their own countries of origin. The practice is officially known as 'forced return or removal'.

> Deportation is forcible rather than voluntary, the decision to deport is in the hands of the state rather than that of individual migrants, the direction of movement is from so-called receiving country to sending country and definitions of origin and membership are disrupted by the act of removal. Indeed, even to refer to deportation as a form of migration challenges common understanding of this term.[17]

The assumption is that refugees, or people forced to migrate from their home country failing to obtain asylum 'return to their country voluntarily or by force' which is not considered as return migration. In this context, it is pointed out by authors, like Nassim Majidi and Liza Schuster (2019) that where the return of the forced migrants cannot be accomplished in view of situation of turmoil in their country of origin having not eased, such as in countries like Sudan, Zaire, Tanzania, Syria and Afghanistan, the Global North could consider resettlement in its own interest for utilising 'a much-needed supplement' to 'post-war depleted national labour force'. Contrarily, mass involuntary repatriation of forced migrants to their neighbouring countries, like Iran and Pakistan for the Afghans, which had hosted 2 million Afghans previously may not be done with deteriorating relationship between them – Afghanistan and Pakistan – and thus leaving the returning Afghans in limbo when they cannot go back to their own country because of continuing hostility.

According to Majidi and Schuster (2019), Kenya provides a similar case which hosted Somali refugees to the tune of half-a-million in 2011 fleeing civil war in their own country, on an understanding with UNHCR providing financial support. But subsequent attacks of Somali militant groups on Kenya changed the entire situation making it obligatory for Kenya to 'push for repatriation' of Somali refugees, but majority of them did not want to return. In Europe, as well the drive for repatriation is increasing in momentum wherefrom 40 per cent of the hapless refugees ordered to go back to their countries of origin had actually left but lack of cooperation between European countries and those from where the refugees were forced out by political upheavals making life highly risky made the situation difficult. Besides, another problem arising in sending back the refugees is identification in terms of their origin. However, EU entered into an agreement with Turkey in 2016, the latter hosting by that time 3 million refugees consisting mainly of Syrians besides some Afghans on a payment of 3 million Euros (later doubled) agreeing to 'take back those who transited Turkey to Greece and to prevent others from doing the same.'

But however defined forcible return is far from a humane process and acts as a 'blunt instrument', and the effects are felt by many more than those physically removed. Involving an element of coercion and force it cannot be considered as a durable solution.[18] EU with its very rich economy and a population of 500 million with its solidarity between twenty-seven states after Britain left, could, on humanitarian grounds afford to absorb another few million, not exceeding 10 or 20 million at the most many of whom possessing higher skill to be treated as *'human capital'* by any host country and rehabilitate them as an asset rather than a burden. In this context, it may be interesting to record that as a whole Europe's population will drop to 700 million which includes 'far fewer young people and many elderly ones'. The population between the ages of 20-48 would decline by 208 to 154 million (–26%). According to Massimo Livi-Bacci (2010), instead the population over 65 years would increase from 119 million to 163 million (+37%).[19]

What EU needs to make this massive need for rehabilitation happen is to get over the strong prejudice for skin-colour. This is, perhaps, the most crucial for EU to weigh very carefully about the source of skilled labour at a very reasonable price in near future in the face of steeply declining birth-rate in many of its constituents along with the growing number of old-age people putting increasing pressure on care-services apart from the requirement of working-age labour keeping up national economy at a sustaining level. This is where the repatriated people may be of gainful use acting as a major prop for an all-round development since the repatriated people with their wide range of skill could provide the necessary services. Hence, a positive outlook for the utilisation based on a policy of dignified understanding between the host and the repatriates may go a long way in future based on a dual partnership.

II. Lack of Mutual Understanding between Host Countries and Refugees

It needs no repetition to say that the issue of refugees is not just a humanitarian one but also is an issue of 'development' since it:

> is not just about indefinitely providing food, clothing, and shelter. It has to be about restoring people's autonomy through jobs and education, particularly in the countries in the developing world that repeatedly host the overwhelming majority of refugees.[20]

In this regard, perhaps, the most significant comment was made by Dag Hammarskjöld, saying that the United Nations 'was not created to take mankind to heaven, but to save humanity from hell'.[21]

As mentioned before, people displaced from their own home country by violence amounting to 65.3 million today, making almost one in every 113 of world population when the number of billionaires has climbed to over 1,800 though the refugees own nothing but just the clothes they wear over their bodies with no food, no home, no future set the sharpest contrast in the world for which they are not responsible. The real fact applying to the status of the refugees, in many cases that they have been the products of power-games between some of the developed countries, such as in Afghanistan, Syria, Iraq, Iran, along with some of the African countries, make it far more obligatory for the rest of the world to take responsibility of their own creation in the form of rehabilitation with all spontaneity to save human life left in such a desperate situation.

Those big powers fighting to gain a foothold in troubled waters are at the back of creating the refugees – all peaceful people living lives of their own never taking any part in those heinous power-games thrown out of their lives without any preamble whatever. For example, the continuing violence in Syria particularly escalated refugees' situation and since 'refugees are defined by flight across a border', the EU removed all border controls in 1999 in the Schengen Area and tried to create 'something approximating a shared asylum and immigration policy'.[22] In practice, however, the adoption of this policy gave rise to serious problems since, states adopted different asylum standards. For example:

> recognition rates of different nationalities, the required duration of residency before asylum seekers would be allowed to work, and social-security entitlements, for example, all varied markedly across Europe. Governments thereby continued to compete with one another to divert, deter and deflect unwanted asylum seekers.[23]

Although it was not an open-arm policy, still Europe being nearer to the internal-strife-ravaged countries of the Middle East particularly Syria, Libya, Tunisia, and Iraq, came to be the main rescue-area for the refugees crossing the Mediterranean with the help of smugglers, mentioned earlier, in small boats to Lampedusa in Italy and later from Turkey to Lesbos in Greece came to be the major escape route for the refugees coming mostly from Libya and Tunisia. However, Italy having experienced the first on-rush of refugees, amounting to nearly 50,000 young male immigrants by August 2011, to accept further refugees was going to be a big burden on the Italian economy where the per capita income having declined by 11 per cent between 2007 and 2015, young Italians were already emigrating in large numbers to North European countries.

The major crisis, however, took a much more serious turn with Syria appearing on the scene between 2011 and 2015 when around 10 million people, half of the entire Syrian population, had fled home to escape violence. Many of them sought safety outside Syria's border, Turkey, Lebanon, and Jordan becoming the most sought-after destinations, while by 2014 half of the 4 million Syrians settled in Turkey, about a million in Jordan and another million in Lebanon. As a matter of fact, both linguistic and religious affinity acted as the binding factor between Syrian refugees and Turkey, Jordan and Lebanon, people in all of them speaking Arabic (though this is not the main language in Turkey), besides Turkey and Jordan were 'best suited' 'both being predominately Sunni' though Lebanon was a 'delicate mix of Shia, Sunni and Christian'.

However, the capabilities of these three countries in providing a haven to the refugees were not the same. Among them Turkey with a 'competent government', a large country being 'heavily integrated into the global economy through trade agreements with the EU and having the same religion was in a better position to take in a large proportion of the displaced persons.[24] In comparison, Jordan was in a weak position depending mostly on 'aid and subsidies from the Arab oil economies' while Lebanon felt the pressure of refugee influx much beyond its capacity to respond to refugee needs requiring help from UNHCR in tackling the problem of having hosted over 1 million of them representing one-fourth of its total population of 4 million. Depressingly, however, UNHCR's role in this respect had been far from praiseworthy. All it did was it:

> limited to the delivery of care relief items and support during winter months. The overwhelming majority of the urban Syrian population have had no contact with UNHCR. Its role has mainly focused on offering targeted support to the most vulnerable 5 per cent through cash assistance.[25]

In other words, being so very little in amount and of such restrictive nature UNHCR's role in helping these countries was scarcely of any importance. The refugees, hence, had to fend for themselves in the host countries, finding means of living in the informal sector. The apparent inactive role of UNHCR was largely due to the uncooperative attitude of the EU countries in providing financial assistance to it, such as the German Government halving its contribution to UNHCR in 2014 which resulted in greater pressure of financial burden on the haven countries. As estimated by experts, the amount needed to provide financial support, even a provision of $1000 per refugee per year, would have meant a drastic reduction in the lifestyle of pre-refugee conditions of the Syrians but even this raised the total requirement to $40 billion which was hard to come by.[26]**

All this, naturally, had a cumulative effect on making the situation untenable for the refugees and seeking a way of finding a living in whatever way they could led to the sole objective of reaching one of the EU countries as the last resort for asylum. By this the 'high profile tragedies' involving deaths of refugees in crossing the Mediterranean to Lampedusa on Italian shore made that route less popular and refugees greatly preferred the other access route across the short distance between Turkey to Lesbos, as mentioned earlier in spite of the fact that, apart from being a member of the EU, the Greek economy was quite weak; weaker than that of Italy, having shrank 25 per cent between 2007 and 2015 compared to that of 11 per cent in Italy.

People, in both Austria and Hungary as well as Germany were welcoming the Syrian refugees including others crossing over to Greece. 'By the end of July 2015 nearly 3,75,000 Syrians' got asylum in Europe. In addition, in the second half of 2015, about 2,00,000 Afghans trekked from their homeland through Iran and Turkey and arrived in the Balkans with an aim to reach Northern Europe. Meanwhile, Germany having turned out to be the major destination for its sympathetic approach to the refugee problem was facing an unmanageable situation with a load of about 3,00,000 refugees by December 2013, and so Chancellor Merkel appealed to the EU Commission for relocation of a part of this huge load among member-countries. As a result of which, the Commission directed to 'relocate 1,60,000 refugees directly from Greece and Italy equitably across EU member states. Following this catastrophic situation, Germany tried to pressurise Turkey requesting for 'tightening controls on refugees to Greece by way of controlling people-smugglers. Turkey's response was very positive in this regard agreeing to accept anyone making the journey to Greece but returned by the latter would be accepted by Turkey as its own responsibility which had a great effect on the Aegean exodus that 'promptly stopped'. At the same time, this eased the situation for Germany releasing her from the onrush of refugees so making it possible for her to keep her borders welcoming anyone reaching Germany. Further, on Chancellor Merkel's initiative an EU-Turkey deal was clinched resettling 72,000 refugees in the EU from Turkey. However, Turkey's major aim to come to such an agreement with Germany putting a check on refugee arrival was to extract money which finally amounted to 6 billion Euro.[27]

However, finally those refugees getting asylum in Germany having high skill or education had better opportunity for employment at higher earnings than others. Although Germany had been selective in resettling Syrians, its contribution, nevertheless was considerable in view of providing home to the dislodged. And the question is very correctly raised if those Syrians comfortably resettled in Germany will ever return to their own country when the conflict over there is over and the war-ravaged country requires them for re-building its devastated land and economy.

At present, the geographical reality of the whole situation looks quite alarming taking in the fact that majority of the refugees representing almost 86 per cent, increasing from 72 per cent a decade ago are concentrated in the developing world, resettled in the neighbouring countries of those in conflict.The total number of refugees in the world today representing barely 0.3 per cent of the world population the problem is not one of 'absolute numbers' but of geographical concentration. For example, as mentioned above, in Lebanon the refugee-population makes up a quarter of its total population, obviously making a great strain on its very limited resources with great deprivation of its own people. Similarly, Kenya and Uganda hosting a million refugees between them, represent almost a similar number of asylum seekers to that shared by twenty-eight EU states in 2015 'at the peak of European refugee crisis' while before Turkey stepped into taking 2.6 million refugees Pakistan had been the most hard-pressed host-country for refugees fleeing from neighbouring war-torn Afghanistan.

These points make the situation quite depressing in view of the stark reality that 'global attention and resources' have so far addressed the requirement of about '0.5 per cent' through resettlement in developed countries or less than 10 per cent of the asylum seekers having moved into the developed world either in Europe or in America when the remaining 90 per cent are left unattended.

Today, the world spends approximately $75 billion a year on the 10 per cent of refugees who moved to developed regions and only around $5 billion a year on the 90 per cent who remain in developing regions … a ratio of about $115 spent on a refugee in the developed world to $1 spent on a refugee in the developing world.[28]

In some cases, some of the developed countries, such as Sweden~~being~~ one of the very generous countries in treating refugees, diverted a part of funds meant for other uses to refugees. As the authors (Betts and Collier, 2018) point out, refugees are not to be treated as costs or burden since they are capable of making an economic contribution to the host country with their experience, skill, talent, and workability. Empowering these people and treating them with dignity as well as trust even the developed countries can expect a meaningful return. In the case of the Syrian refugees, 95 per cent of whom have stayed back in the haven countries may never prove to be a burden when about 'half of the entire university-educated people' among the refugees, along with 'a quarter of the entire stock of people with completed secondary education have gone into Europe. The remaining population do not have ample scope for providing help to the host country's economy in contrast to their loss for Syria in the future (post-conflict Syria) and 'could set the country back for decades'.[29]

It may be pointed out in the context of a humane approach of the host countries to the emerging problems of rehabilitation that what Canada, of late, has adopted as a principle of taking full responsibilities for their (refugees) resettlement and taking a catalytic role in fulfilling their overall requirements stretching from receiving them on arrival, providing accommodation, clothing, household goods, orientation services, enabling them with tackling banking and transportation services, down to enrolling their children in schools. Such an all-pervasive caring system would make them active members contributing to the social and economic progress of the host-country.[30]

It is highly interesting to note that the rush of refugees from the Middle Eastern countries seeking access to European countries has not abated even to this date and referring to the situation in this respect prevailing even in early March 2020, using the shorter route from Turkey to Lesbos in Greece across the Mediterranean. According to a report,[31] more than 1,700 refugees have arrived in Greece over the last week adding to the 38,000 already 'crammed into abysmal and overstretched refugee centres'. All of them are trying to 'cross into the European Union'. It has given rise to a chaotic situation with clashes between refugees and Greek riot police. Further, there are more amounting to tens of thousands of asylum seekers waiting at the Turkey borders to take the same risk.

Looking back to the India-Pakistan situation which took place in and around 1947 as an aftermath of the Partition of India on gaining independence one faces one of the worst and most cruel instances in recent human history involving millions of refugees.

Without going into the justification of the process in dividing India by colonial rules, it can be said with all honesty that India, in fact, suffered from a two-sided blow, the first was inflicted in 1941 when the Japanese army on its march towards India during the Second World War bombed Rangoon (now Yangon), the capital of Burma (Myanmar) on 23 to 25 December, 1941, and set off Indian emigration involving about 4,50,000-5,00,000 people trekking to India on foot across the intervening mountain ranges between India and Burma losing between 10,000-50,000 on the way who never made it.[32] Not much later India was divided (partitioned) into India and Pakistan, the latter having two wings – West Pakistan and East Pakistan – and 26 million displaced people or Hindus migrated into India, mostly into present West Bengal (truncated from Bengal Province) most of them being made destitute for no fault of their own except being born on the other side of the border. Even to any casual observer, the sharp difference in treatment of the refugees coming from West and East Pakistan is not missed.

There is no denying of the fact that refugees from West Pakistan got priority over those from East Pakistan.

> 'Roy (Ranajit Roy, 1971) shows, with figures, how all of them (the West Pakistan Refugees) have been rehabilitated on land and in houses of evacuee Muslims and shops and houses built by the Government of India at its expense and given a compensation to them .... He writes that of the 47.40 lakh (4.740m) of West Pakistan refugees, 37.40 lakh were Punjabis, of whom 27.37 lakh were rehabilitated in Punjab-Haryana and 5 lakh in Delhi and all the land and houses left by evacuee Muslims in Andhra Pradesh, Tamil Nadu, Mysore, Bihar, Orissa, and Himachal Pradesh went to West Pakistan refugees. The refugee figures he gives are: 60 lakh (6m) acres of farmland and 7 lakh (0.7m) houses in Punjab, 3,05,000 shops and houses in urban areas, while the Government built 2,21,000 houses and 19 townships for them; and while loans figured largely in Government aid in the East, it was (gift) aid in the West. He goes on to point out that in Delhi, 73 residential areas and many modern market centres were built in refugee rehabilitation projects incurring a cost of Rs. 60 crore, the Bengali refugee was not given a house or shop from this budget.... A total of 20.02 lakh had found jobs through employment exchanges amongst the West Pakistani refugees, while the Rehabilitation Ministry Report of 1964-65 records that in January 1965, 204 Bengali refugees found employment in the public sector in spite of the registered number of 10,571 migrants'.[33]

The picture of such utter deprivation and neglect of Bengali refugees does not end here. The Government does nowhere express sympathy or even recognition of their utter negligence with even very small instances of positive action towards the rehabilitation of Bengali refugees. As estimated, 26 lakh (2.6 million) of Bengali Hindus migrated as refugees from East Pakistan under the threat to life, killings, rapes, abduction of women, religious conversion, and arson, 25 per cent of whom sought shelter in Government Camps of most temporary nature while the remaining 75 per cent, 'either crowded in with relatives in West Bengal (and Assam and Tripura), or 'struggled on their own'. The Prime Minister of India who had taken such an admirable, open-hearted approach to refugees from West Pakistan was found to be painfully close-fisted in the case of East Pakistan refugees, even suffering from self-made euphoria that the East Pakistan refugees might go back when the political situation eased up. One wonders about the actual source of such an idea in the face of continuing violence in East Pakistan, and this very clear sign of looking the other way is clearly revealed in an utterly miserly amount of Rs. 5 crores (50 million) released to the purpose of 'relief and rehabilitation' in 1948-49 and 1949-50 which actually amounted to 'Rs. 20 per head spread over the two years'.[34] As a matter of fact, according to the Ministry of Rehabilitation, Government of India, the number of refugees from East Pakistan was around a total of 4 million between 1947 and 1958 while another 1 million came before the formation of Bangladesh, between 1964 and 1971.[35] The significance of historical events is evident very prominently in the Indian Subcontinent. The 1947 Partition resulted in the mass displacement of people from India and Pakistan which is evident in 2015 data showing that over 5.2 and 3.6 million foreign-born migrants (respectively) resided in the two countries.[36]

Looking back at the global situation, the total number of refugees was 22.5 million by the end of 2016, 17.2 million of which was under UNHCR's mandate and another 5.3 million were 'registered by the United Nations Relief and Work Agency' for Palestine Refugees in the West Asia. In addition, 2.8 million referred to as asylum seekers awaited international protection. Of about 2 million applicants for asylum in 2016, Germany topped the list of countries receiving applications from 7,20,000 refugees, followed by the United States with 2,62,000 and Italy with 1,23,000.

It is interesting to observe that roughly 51 per cent of the refugee population was under 18 years of age while the proportion of females was between 47 and 49 per cent of the refugees between 2003 and 2016, majority of whom amounting to almost 60 per cent came from an urban background at the end of 2016. The top 10 countries under UNHCR's mandate by the end of 2016 accounted for about 13.5 million refugees or 79 per cent of the total, Turkey with 2.9 million refugees, mainly Syrians, was the largest host country in the world in 2016. Apart from Jordan, Lebanon, Pakistan, and Iran were among the top 10 host countries, and even least developed countries, namely Cameroon, Chad, the Democratic Republic of Congo, Ethiopia, Kenya, Sudan and Uganda as well hosted between them a total of 4.9 million refugees or 28 per cent of global total.[37] However, on the contrary more than 5,50,000 refugees voluntarily returned to their places of origin majority of whom – 3,84,000 – from Pakistan to Afghanistan. Prolonged conflict in the countries of origin has naturally been the greatest deterrent to the urge to go back home while the most creditable response of many host countries numbering 23 in 2016 is undoubtedly a noble gesture in making naturalised citizens, with Canada having made 16,300 in 2016, a little less than done in the previous year when 25,000 received citizenship. At the same time, in the UNHCR's resettlement programmes for refugees, the number of countries taking part has increased from 33 in 2015 to 37 in 2016 with many states in Europe and Latin America having taken an initiative in this, though 'traditional' resettlement countries, such as Australia, Canada and the United States still bear the major share. A total of about 1,90,000 refugees were resettled globally in 2016 with refugees of Syrian, Congolese, Iraq and Somali origin becoming major beneficiaries.[38]

However, the strangest of all facts related to refugees is the scale of 'Internally Displaced Persons' (IDPs) a staggering 25.3 million a year since 2008 caused by geographical hazards, climate or weather-related disasters like floods, storms etc., affecting 24.2 million people, with an average of 25 million displaced persons annually since 2009. Among people affected and made IDPs in 2016, China (74,34,000), the Philippines (59,30,000) and India (24,00,000) take the lead, and altogether 24.2 million getting displaced in 2016 'far outnumbers' people displaced by conflict or violence.[39]

III. The Plight of Bengali Hindu Refugees from East Pakistan for the Andamans, Dandakaranya and other Places

Perhaps, nothing compares with the situation faced by the hapless migrants/refugees who arrived from East Pakistan under the threat of life consisting of 1.9 million Hindus by the end of April 1949, 0.97 million of whom came to Calcutta (Kolkata) and its neighbourhood of whom at least 10,000 refugees 'were squatting at the Sealdah Railway Station Complex itself in March/April 1950' (Anwesha Sengupta, 2017). Usually, the refugees arriving on foot at the Ranaghat Railway Station close to the border of India (West Bengal) with East Pakistan were initially taken to the transit camp, known as 'Coopers Camp', for the time being, wherefrom they were taken as soon as possible by trains to the neighbouring states of Orissa and Bihar and dumped mercilessly in camps hastily built by the respective governments.

We will come to this later as there are two entirely different sides of the story involving the Bengali Hindu Refugees displaced by communal riots in East Pakistan from late 1940s to early 1950s, later continuing till 1970. Indian leaders in power directly involved in truncating the subcontinent into three distinctive parts based on religious differences later preferred looking away from acknowledging the dreadful situation it led to, involving the migration of Bengali Hindus from East Pakistan under the threat of life and honour – may be the largest flow of people in human history – requires to assess the reasons of this great exodus as given in Table 6.2.

It is, rather, interesting to note, as Joya Chatterjee (2017) observes that in the earlier period, as The Census of 1951 reports, 'most of the 13,07,000 or a third of the refugees from East Bengal amounting to a total of 29,99,000 till then ended up in just three districts of West Bengal, the 24 Parganas (undivided), Calcutta (Kolkata) and Nadia while four other districts – West Dinajpur, Cooch Behar, Jalpaiguri and Burdwan (undivided) absorbed 'much of the remaining'. Strangely enough for ten years later, The Census of 1961 showed the same pattern. Interestingly, the spatial distribution remained almost the same even in 1973 when the total number of refugees exceeded 6 million.[40] In order to understand refugees preferring to concentrate in West Bengal than go to other places, Joya Chatterjee (2017) gives a very reasonable explanation.

> 'These remarkably stable patterns can be understood once it is recognised, as government signally failed to do, that the refugees were not pawns or passive victims, but rather active and thinking agents in their own rehabilitation. Their decision to take shelter in particular parts of West Bengal was determined by considered calculations. Very simply, the refugees went to places where they had kin and where they thought they could find work. In this they behaved in much the same way as other economic migrants, and for good reason. Refugees too had to start from scratch to build a new life for themselves in new places. Their search for a new means to sustain themselves was quite as urgent for the refugees as it was for economic migrants. Inevitably, refugees, like economic migrants, went to places where they knew people who were ready to give them a helping hand until they found their feet, and to places where they judged they had the best chance of finding appropriate work.

Considerations such as these attracted educated middle-class refugees to Calcutta and the large towns and industrial centres of Hooghly, the 24 Parganas and Burdwan.... As a hub of business (Calcutta) houses many

Table 6.2: Reasons Why Refugees Fled from East Bengal (East Pakistan) 1946-1970

(Figures in Lakhs/100,000s)

Year	Reasons for Influx	Totals	Into West Bengal	Into Other States
1946	Noakhali Riots	0.19	0.14	0.05
1947	Partition	3.44	2.58	0.86
1948	'Police Action' by India in Hyderabad	7.86	5.90	1.96
1949	Communal Riots in Khulna and Barisal	2.13	1.82	0.31
1950	Ditto	15.75	11.82	3.93
1951	Kashmir Agitation	1.87	1.40	0.47
1952	Worsening Economic Conditions, persecution of minorities, passport scare	2.27	1.52	0.75
1953	–	0.76	0.61	0.15
1954	–	1.18	1.04	0.14
1955	Unrest Over Declaration of Urdu as *lingua franca*	2.40	2.12	0.28
1956	Adoption of Islamic Constitution of Pakistan	3.20	2.47	0.73
1957	–	0.11	0.09	0.02
1958	–	0.01	0.01	–
1959	–	0.10	0.09	0.01
1960	–	0.10	0.09	0.01
1961	–	0.11	0.10	0.01
1962	–	0.14	0.13	0.01
1963	–	0.16	0.14	0.02
1964	Riots over Hazratbal Incident	6.93	4.19	2.74
1965	–	1.08	0.81	0.27
1966	–	0.08	0.04	0.04
1967	–	0.24	0.05	0.19
1968	–	0.12	0.04	0.08
1969	–	0.10	0.04	0.06
1970	Economic Distress & Coming Elections	2.50	2.32	0.18
Totals		**52.83**	**39.56**	**13.27**

Source: Chatterjee, J. *The Spoils of Partition: Bengal and India, 1947-1967*. Cambridge University Press (Reprint of 2007). 2017 : 112 Table 3.1. (Taken from Luther, P.N. *Rehabilitation*. Publication Division, New Delhi. 1972 : pp. 18-19).

large corporations as well as smaller companies, where educated persons could hope to find some work.... A study of Titagarh dominated by jute mills, discovered that many refugees 'engaged in artisanal production, especially making bangles from conch shells, their caste work ... the unorganised informal sector of Calcutta's complex economy revealed that many tailors were Hindu refugees from the east.... after partition several thousand Nath Weavers settled in the town of Nabadwip.[41]

The information given by Joya Chatterjee (2017) leads us further to have a clear idea about the resettlement of the refugees in the earlier part of their exodus from East Bengal (East Pakistan) as shown in Table 6.3.

Table 6.3: Refugees in West Bengal in and outside Government Camps and Colonies (1958)

Districts	No. of Camps and Homes	Population in Camps & Homes	No. of Government Colonies	Population in Government Colonies	Refugees Outside Camps & Colonies	Total Refugee Population
Burdwan	30	43,127	8	6,895	1,08,481	1,58,503
Birbhum	17	17,400	6	1,775	4,375	23,550
Bankura	7	11,165	2	50	4,796	16,011
Midnapur	11	16,838	38	4,390	22,654	43,882
Hooghly	11	18,013	38	21,580	65,017	1,04,610
Howrah	7	7,779	16	7,575	75,781	91,135
24 Parganas	45	43,284	209	1,05,345	7,14,161	8,62,790
Calcutta	–	5,059	–	–	5,71,555	5,76,614
Nadia	7	53,160	32	61,640	5,39,730	6,64,530
Murshidabad	8	12,709	21	9,945	53,443	76,097
Malda	–	–	12	2,939	69,004	72,924
West Dinajpur	1	989	11	3,865	1,58,035	1,62,949
Jalpaiguri	–	–	9	7,850	1,42,306	1,50,156
Darjeeling	–	–	2	3,375	26,668	30,043
Cooch Behar	1	1,159	12	6,550	2,22,118	2,27,827
Purulia	–	–	–	–	1,332	1,332
Total	**152**	**2,40,682**	**389**	**2,43,765**	**27,78,506**	**32,62,952**

Source: Chatterjee, J. *The Spoils of Partition: Bengal and India*, 1947-1967. Cambridge University Press (Reprint of 2007). 2017 : p. 134, Table 3.4. (Taken from Relief and Rehabilitation of Displaced Persons in West Bengal – Statement Issued by the Government of West Bengal, 15 December, 1958 – cited in P. Chaudhuri, *Refugees in West Bengal, A Study of the growth and distribution of refugee resettlement in CMD*, Occasional paper No. 55 Centre for Studies in Social Sciences, Calcutta, 1983).

In this connection, it is important to note that, as Joya Chatterjee (2017, Reprint) points out:

> 'the great majority of the refugees who settled in West Bengal between 1947 and 1970 thus did so largely or solely through their own efforts.... From 1948 onwards groups of refugees poured on to unoccupied plots in and around Calcutta and built their shacks upon it. Most of this land was 'in the industrial belt around Calcutta'. Some of it was privately owned and some belonged to the government – or more frequently has been requisitioned by the government from private landlords during the Second World War. Other land captured in this way belonged to Muslims who had fled from their homes during the riots. By the end of 1950, about 150 such 'squatter colonies' had sprung up, mainly in and around Calcutta, spread over several thousand acres'.[42]

Meanwhile, we have almost forgotten the cases of the 'Bhadraloks (gentlefolks), representing refugees from East Pakistan who started leaving their ancestral homes soon after the Partition of the Indian Subcontinent in August 1947. Most of them were highly educated and held different responsible positions in East Bengal before the Partition and most of them, one can presume, could afford to bring back some money or a bit of jewellery, which came to be of great value later in settling down to a new life in or around the city wherever stretches of empty land was available, such as in the South Jadavpur area known today as Ganguli Bagan, Bijoygarh, Baghajatin and most prominent of them being known now as 'Jodhpur Park along with the stretch of land extending up to present Dakshinapan etc.', opposite Dhakuria, presenting the most remarkable of overall physical change. I have personally seen that area as one extensive green, grassy land sloping away from the road westward. I used to travel everyday by 8B Bus, a government bus in the early 1950s from Dhakuria lying east of this road, a thinly populated area where I used to live when on the west road lay the grassy area sloping away into the golf-course containing some waterbodies.

I clearly remember all this happening in front of my eyes when as a college student, from 1948-49 onwards, almost overnight houses made of bamboo-matting, roofs thatched with straw and mud-floors came up one after another in thousands obviously under political backing (Congress as well as Communist parties) though I had no way of knowing anything beyond visiting some families personally known through acquaintances.

But as far as I know there were no shady deals between the new settlers and the landlords. On the other hand, many of this class settled down with their relatives and because of education and work experience did gradually find a way of living and got assimilated with the city population while some of them in course of time, came to hold high and responsible positions in the society though earning a new name, *'Bangals'* a disparaging expression, no doubt, distinguished from the local people who came to be called '*Ghotis*', though both spoke the same language with different intonations and having some cultural traits of their own. But these differences have already mostly disappeared as both groups went through similar situations.

Nevertheless, the process of assimilation for the refugee population, even of the 'gentleman' class has been far from easy or smooth, involving a lot of harassment and suffering besides the great pain felt for the lost property back in the original home-country, the memory of the life of luxury and pride for many of them which they had to leave without any mental or physical preparations, the trauma faced by innocent people fleeing marauding chasers. Strangely enough, people in power never acknowledged in their deeds or words even an iota of sympathy for the sufferings of these people fleeing their own country with families consisting of women, children in arms, old and unsteady ones which obviously did not touch people in power on this side of Bengal (or India) busy in their own lives of unfettered ambition.

It, therefore, may not be surprising to know that the hard struggle for survival even on the part of the gentleman class of refugees has taken almost four generations for them to get over the sufferance and heal the wounds received by Partition turning most of them destitute (many, in fact dying unknown and uncared for in some of the Refugee Camps in West Bengal like the Coopers Camp).

Here lies the difference between the refugees from East Pakistan and those from European, Middle East and even African countries of origin, while the former (from East Pakistan) belonging to the same country crossing the boundary suddenly imposed by Partition in contrast to all the others mentioned above who moved from their own country to another.

Now, coming back to the episode of Dandakaranya, as described by Anwesha Sengupta (2017) mentioned earlier is firmly corroborated by Joya Chatterjee (2007, Reprint) as follows:

> By far the largest, most ambitious and most controversial of these schemes was the Dandakaranya Project. Under the aegis of government agencies specially set up for this purpose, the Dandakaranya Project was given a huge swathe of territory

> of about 30,000 square miles. The use of these barren wastes of shrub and forest was regarded as the expenditure of the expendable by the state governments of Bihar, Orissa, and Madhya Pradesh which had title of them. Spread over much of Koraput and Kalahandi districts of Orissa and Bihar and the Bastar district of Madhya Pradesh, Dandakaranya lay in a low plateau where the soil was arid and infertile and where previously there had been no settled population at all. Its inhabitants were nomads, mainly Gond forest peoples.... The project aimed to resettle East Bengali peasants, in the main from the lowest castes.... now cajoled, browbeaten or forced to go to distant Dandakaranya.... Most of the plots did not produce enough food to keep the families who farmed them alive. In this bleak and barren terrain, there was no other work by which the refugees could earn a few rupees. Such industries as the authorities tried to run, in a hopelessly amateur fashion, were disorganised, unprofitable, mismanaged and usually closed down soon after they were set-up. For the brief periods that they were open, they paid their workers scandalously low wages. Nor could refugees supplement their meagre diets with fish, as had been their work back in riverine Bengal. Unlike Bengal, with its numerous rivers, ponds, tanks and *bils* where freshwater fish was plentiful, the rocky plateau of Dandakaranya could hardly have been less suitable for the pisciculture the refugees knew so well. There was not enough drinking water, let alone fresh water in which fish could reproduce. Medical facilities were virtually non-existent. Dandakaranya was a place where the hungry, the thirsty, the lame and the sick hopelessly waited for the merciful release of death or tried, with their last twitches of fading energy, to get up and stumble away.[43]

As a matter of fact, there were two distinct destinations as decided by political authorities for the rehabilitation of the Bengali Hindu refugees and very surprisingly one involved some sort of self-imposed choice while the other, to all appearance, coercion.

The first concerned those who volunteered to take the risk of going to the Andaman Islands taking a part in the Refugee Rehabilitation Programme sponsored by both the State and the Central Governments in close cooperation with an idea of expanding agricultural land by clearing forests and to set up new villages peopled by willing settlers from the mainland (Uditi Sen, 2017). The Andaman Islands, located at the south-eastern edge of the Bay of Bengal consisting of over 300 islands of varying sizes forming a great arc almost 620 miles long taken possession by the British in 1858. In reality, the idea for taking refugees to these remote islands came from Administrators of the Andaman Islands whose plans of developing the islands were blocked by unavailability of labour. 'An integral scheme of colonisation and development for the Andamans was launched in 1952' (Uditi Sen, 2017) consisting of basic plans 'to expand agricultural land clearing forests and to set up new villages peopled by willing settlers from the mainland'.

It is interesting to record that on 14 March, 1949, 495 East Bengali refugees consisting of 132 families, 50 of whom were agriculturists, 22 were weavers and 34 carpenters comprising the first batch of refugees opted to go to the Andaman Islands for resettlement, as the then Chief Minister of West Bengal explained on their behalf, it was not forced dispersal. As to their social status in East Bengal (East Pakistan) they were primarily 'Namasudras', a largely rural depressed Hindu caste mostly following the 'heterodox Matua Sect', representing illiterate peasants, the last to leave East Pakistan.

Thus, between 1952 and 1961, over 85 per cent of the agriculturists and between 1965 and 1970 not less than 52 new villages came up at the initiative of the refugees in the Andaman Islands. According to Uditi Sen (2017), there were 'three clear phases of refugee resettlement in the Andamans'. The first phase beginning in 1949 continued till 1951 when they were settled entirely in the South Andamans in villages located further away from Port Blair. But it was the second phase, between 1952 and 1962 which witnessed the best days for them obtaining 'attractive package of loans from the government along with grants of land to agriculturists when 2,413 families from East Pakistan were resettled which meant Bengali refugees were the main force driving forward the Colonisation of Development Scheme in the Andaman Islands that permanently and radically transformed the demography and ecological balance of these islands' (Uditi Sen, 2017). This was followed by the third phase from 1962 bringing a distinctive change in the entire scheme so far because of the 'discontinuation of the Colonisation and Development Scheme' so that agricultural colonisation went out of favour. In spite of that nearly 700 refugee families settled down during this period, families who had to pass scrutiny for acceptance of their eligibility to gain access to land and loans. The vast majority of the refugees came from the districts of Barisal, Jessore and Khulna districts of East Pakistan.

On the whole, after their arrival in the Andamans for resettlement, the Bengali Hindu refugees from East Pakistan had a tough time in getting proper accommodation and apart from the first batch having been allotted 'abandoned fields largely ready for cultivation, the later batches were put in hastily built camps consisting of:

> 'large two storied barracks built of bamboo, cane and leaves, divided into ten rooms. The vast majority of refugee families, who were resettled under the Colonisation and Development Scheme lived in such camps for months – waiting for local authorities to disburse the lands promised to them. Years of struggle followed, against the jungle, wild animals, and the isolation of the remote settlements to carve out sedentary agrarian life. It is this struggle that the refugees resettled in the Andaman Islands spoke of most often when interviewed'.[44]

Incidentally, anybody concerned with the rehabilitation of the Bengali Hindu refugees displaced by communal disturbance in East Pakistan were presented with 'agricultural implements, utensils and even musical instruments by the Government of West Bengal' on occasions as gestures of human-touch before they left the mainland for an unknown destination.

Contrastingly, however such human-touch was very much lacking in the other case, as Anwesha Sengupta (2017) observes about the 'dispersal of refugees (displaced from East Pakistan) taken to Bihar and Orissa in 1950 which was a different kind as compared to resettling Bengali Hindu refugees from East Pakistan in the Andaman and Nicobar Islands and the total number of the former was much higher. According to Anwesha Sengupta (2017), the decision to send Bengali Refugees to Bihar and Orissa was taken before 1950, decided in October 1948, that the Government of Orissa would take responsibility for 25,000 refugees, by the end of March 1950 and refugees started reaching 'Orissa and Bihar in thousands'. On reaching Orissa, they were accommodated in hastily built transit camps while in Bihar temporary refugee camps were opened in places like Ranchi, Gaya, Patna, Mokamah and Hathidali to accommodate 19,000 refugees, reaching by the end of April 1950 (Anwesha Sengupta, 2017). But in sharp contrast to refugees sent to the Andamans on plans for development of the islands mainly as agriculturalists, there was no precise plan for the future role of the refugees taken to these areas in Orissa and Bihar besides easing congestion in Calcutta (Kolkata). On the contrary, in a meeting held in March 1950 between members of the Central and State Governments (West Bengal) it was expressed that some of these refugees would return to East Pakistan 'once things settled down here'! Such wishful thinking was nothing short of virtually ignoring the situation of the sufferings the Bengali refugees were going through.***

In Amanda Camp in Orissa, for example, '50 per cent of refugees were agriculturalists, some 25 per cent belonged to various occupational groups like weavers, carpenters, fishermen etc., and the rest were mostly small traders'. Only a very small percentage of the camp dwellers were educated middle class. Hence, only a few of them could be provided with 'temporary jobs like thatching the roofs of the camp huts, repairing doors and windows and *bidi* making. Some others opened tea stalls at the camps' Anwesha Sengupta (2017).

The important difference between the two cases, that of the Andamans and those sent to the Koraput and Kalahandi districts of Orissa and Bastar region of Madhya Pradesh, together known as 'Dandakaranya', of which the former, that is the Andamans came to be a success for which the refugees were selected from those who expressed willingness to go, whereas in the other case, refugees sent to Dandakaranya and Bihar, the government was coercive in sending off the refugees. It comes out very clearly from the facts that:

> 'In a high-profile ministerial meeting in the middle of 1958, the following points were noted: (a) there are 45,000 refugee families currently residing in various camps in West Bengal. Of these 45,000 families only 10,000 can be rehabilitated within the state. Rest have to go outside Bengal; (b) the families unwilling to go outside West Bengal will be given financial assistance equivalent to 6 months dole. They will not be entitled to any further government assistance; (c) by July 1959, the government relief camps will be closed down. Thus, the camp refugees had two choices either they could go to Dandakaranya or they could choose to face hunger and abject poverty, look for odd jobs and could try to be on their own with no government assistance. Thus, though it was decided that no one would be forcefully taken to Dandakaranya, the reality was otherwise.[45]

Despite such an open threat coming from the government itself to the refugees who were nothing but direct victims of political games played by political leaders at the highest level to fulfil their own higher interests, many of these hapless people refused to go to Dandakaranya on the instances of severe hostilities from the local residents against settling in their areas, such as in Bettia in Bihar. It is really painful to mention that Nehru (the Prime Minister of India) in the 1950s himself did maintain those refugees, victims of political violence in East Pakistan and the last to leave their motherland 'did not belong to West Bengal and should return to East Bengal' (East Pakistan) as if he was unaware of the communal riots taking place both in India and East Bengal (East Pakistan) since 1946 onwards and his wishful thinking was far from stark reality.

As a matter of fact, unlike the Andaman Settlement Programme, the other one involving Dandakaranya and Bihar failed, consequently giving rise to a large number of deserters where 'the conditions of temporary camps were dreadful', to say the least, for instance 'between end March and end November 1950, 776 refugees had died in various camps in Orissa' (Dandakaranya) (Anwesha Sengupta, 2017). In this connection, we may refer to Table 6.4 to get a clearer picture about East Bengal refugees resettled outside Bengal.

All these pretentions on the part of the people in power appear hollow learning from the experience as expressed by one having stayed in the camps mentioned above that apart from 'camp life as empty, boring, and monotonous, where people had nothing much to do but live on a paltry dole of Rs. 2 per adult *(per week)* and Rs. 1.50 per minor. 'Desertion' was the only way to break away from this monotony in search of a worthier way of living' (Anwesha Sengupta, 2017) depending on their own initiative to rehabilitate themselves.

Is it surprising to know that the rehabilitation programme in Dandakaranya was wrong since according to the refugees in Charbatia Camp in Orissa, non-agriculturalist families 'were being taken to agricultural colonies and *vice versa*'? At the same time, cultivator-refugees were given land much farther away from where they lived, making it impossible to watch crops growing by crossing two rivers while local habitats took the opportunity to graze animals and destroyed their crops out of malice in their absence. As a result of such callous and inhuman treatment on the part of the authorities, desertion became a common practice among the refugees, especially from Dandakaranya and Bihar camps, choosing to return to Kolkata, making desertion a 'pattern between 1952 and 1954' starting first in late 1951.

> 'During the late fifties and early sixties desertion by Bengali refugees resettled in Bihar and Orissa, the squatters' agitation to hold on to their own homes in Calcutta, and the grandiose plans of the Dandakaranya Project occupied centre stage'.[46]

Table 6.4: Statement Showing the Number of East Pakistan Displaced Persons Resettled Outside West Bengal

No.	Name of State	Population	Persons deserted before Rehabilitation	Persons who received Rehabilitation Assistance	Desertion from Rehabilitation Centre	Total Desertion from the State
1.	Bihar	62,500	9,589	21,600 (old) 17,105 (new)	3,198	12,167
2.	Orissa	34,742 (*32,623)	15,145	12,437	5,834	20,979
3.	Assam	3,33,414	++	1,55,300	++	++
4.	Tripura	2,80,075	++	1,58,574	++	++
5.	Manipur	1,783	++	1,783	++	++
6.	U.P.	4,090	Nil	4,090	590	590
7.	Andaman	3,315	Nil	3,315	520	520

Note: *Figure indicates number of sponsored displaced persons.
++Figures not available or maintained.
Old Refugees are those who were displaced prior to the 1950 riots.

Source: Sengupta, A. 'They must have to go therefore, elsewhere: Mapping the Many Displacements of Bengali Hindu Refugees from East Pakistan, 1947 to 1960s. Tata Institute of Social Sciences, Patna Centre. 2017 : p. 15. (Taken from the Report of the Committee of Ministers for the Rehabilitation of Displaced Persons in West Bengal 1954 : p. 46).

To realise this situation, it is important to note that in Dandakaranya:

> 'a plot of 6.5 hectares was given to each family and loans were distributed for building houses and purchasing bullocks and agricultural implements. But it was clear from the start that the refugees had to 'make do with the worst lands, hitherto regarded as uncultivatable'… in Pharasgaon zone, '60% of the plots were basically unfit for agriculture, 32% were poor and sub-marginal, 53% could be of medium quality if their moisture retention could be improved, and only 9% were of good quality … The small trader and businessmen among the refugees also faced 'an uphill task'. They were offered a business loan of a thousand rupees and a house-building loan of 2000 and a maximum of three months dole. Within that time, they had to earn enough, not only to pay off the loans but also to maintain their families. The infrastructure,

promised vociferously by the Indian Government, also failed to materialise. Electricity was not available over large areas and there was often an acute shortage of drinking water. The lack of medical services and the poor living conditions led to frequent epidemics with a high rate of child mortality that unsettled refugees'.[47]

All these unsettling conditions of life made Bengali Hindu refugees to take a determined effort to 'start a new life where they can live with dignity'. (Debjani Sengupta, 2016) which led them to choose the 'estuarine delta of the Sundarbans, Marichjhapi, infested with tigers (a tiger conservation area) and crocodiles in the rivers and covered with deep impregnable forests.

But the incident of the unkindest cut involving the Bengali Hindu refugees came from the local government. In 1978, a large number of people suddenly appeared in Marichjhapi, and where there had been no inhabitants before, there were now thousands almost overnight. Within a matter of weeks, they had cleared the mangrove, built bands (dams) and put up huts. It happened so quickly that in the beginning no one even knew who those people were. But in time it came to be learnt that they were refugees,[48] the deserters confined in the prison-like concentration camps in Dandakaranya 'surrounded by security forces and forbidden to leave' … Then in 1978 some of them organised themselves and broke out of the camp and great hardship decided them to settle down in some uninhabited area of Sundarbans entertaining a (false) hope that the Left government which had come to power a year before would not oppose their programme since the party had always been very openly sympathetic to the refugees. But surprisingly enough this time the government in power – the left – seriously opposed their settling down and it turned to an open confrontation between the refugees and the government forces using arms to oust them from their last foothold and it is anybody's guess that nobody among the luckless refugees survived the onslaughts lasting over a year, the eviction completed by mid-May 1979,[49] perhaps leaving none to tell the story of this limitless savagery.

This is corroborated by Debjani Sengupta (2016), writing on the Partition of Bengal, giving a vivid picture of the trauma faced by the Bengali refugees who, deserters of the hostile lands of Dandakaranya, made a most desperate attempt at settling down in Marichjhapi in the Sundarbans in spite of the fact that:

> 'The estuarine delta of the Sundarbans with its mangrove forests is not easy to cultivate. The forests are thick with tigers and the rivers with crocodiles. Yet nothing can deter these men and women. The administration stops all boats that can carry the refugees, but the men snatch a few and set sail.... The new Left Front government in West Bengal that had come to power with the refugee vote, now urged these people to go back to Dandakaranya, refusing to entertain this demand for settling in West Bengal. Many refugees were sent back, around 10,000 Namasudra refugee families ... set sail and settled in Marichjhapi. Although it was not an island that was strictly under the mangroves, the government was in no mood to relent. It declared Marichjhapi as a reserve forest and the refugees as violating the Forest Acts by destroying the 'existing potential forest wealth and also creating ecological imbalance'. On 26 January, 1979, India's Republic Day, the Left Front Chief Minister Jyoti Basu announced an economic blockade of the island to force the settlers to go back – 30 Police launches surrounded the island; the refugees were tear-gassed, their huts, fisheries and tube wells destroyed. Those who tried to cross the river in makeshift boats were shot at. The refugees, armed with carpentry tools and makeshift bows and arrows were no match for government forces. A conservative estimate gave the dead as several hundreds of men, women and children who died either through starvation or who were shot at and their bodies thrown into the river. Marichjhapi became out of bounds to visiting journalists, opposition politicians and even a Parliamentary Committee who came to investigate Police atrocities faced harassment at the hands of the Forest Department Officials. The silence surrounding the Marichjhapi massacres was to continue for some time except stray efforts that tried to expose the lies, deceit and betrayals that came to signify Marichjhapi'.[50]

Before concluding the episode relating to the situation faced by the Bengali Hindu Refugees hounded out of East Pakistan into the equally cruel and unsympathetic hands of the West Bengal government, one may like to know the number of people coming across the border over the years, that is from the time of Noakhali riots in 1946. According to Ashoka Gupta:

> Starting with the Noakhali riots in October 1946, the influx of refugees from East Pakistan continued in spurts and by the end of 1951, 28 lakh Hindus had crossed the border and entered West Bengal, Assan and Tripura. By the end of 1956, the total figure came up to 39.84 lakh. In addition to this number, a large number of persons, approximately another 30 lakhs had also crossed the border within this period but did not register themselves as refugees. Therefore, the total figure comes up to 69 lakh even on moderate estimation.[51]

Similarly, according to Meghnad Saha, M.P. report:

> The first statistical data of displaced people with earlier occupations is only made in 1951. The data included one lakh families of cultivators (5 lakh people) 2.5 lakh families of about 10 lakh persons whose occupations were in industries or services, about 50,000 families of nearly 2,50,000 persons were in miscellaneous occupations while there were about 50,000 families or nearly 2,50,000 persons, who had no occupation in East Bengal.[52]

Government estimates of refugee influx overtime from East Bengal are[53]:

1946 to 1952	25.18 lakh
1953	0.16 lakh
1954	1.04 lakh
1955	2.12 lakh
1956	2.47 lakh
1957	0.04 lakh
Up to 31 March, 1958	0.01 lakh

In this connection, it is highly interesting to know from a report of Meghnad Saha, M.P. and Renuka Ray in the *Statesman,* January 23, 1958 in which the latter states, 'In West Bengal about 2 million displaced persons have been given assistance to the tune of 40 crore rupees... whereas in Punjab and in the Western Region, the amount is about 350 crores. According to another report, the Government acknowledges that out of a total area of 45,00,000 acres abandoned by Muslims in East Punjab, 33,00,000 acres are cultivatable, of these 12,50,000

> acres have been allotted and over 1,77,000 families have been settled on them by the end of 1947.[54]

On the other hand, Alan Roland writing a 'Foreword' for the book written by Jayanti Basu (2013) mentions that:

> The number affected by [the Bengal] Partition are overwhelming. The estimates of those who died range from a minimal number of 2,00,000 by the British to the official Indian government figures of 10,00,000. More recently, Ashis Nandy (2009, Sarah Kailath Lecture at Berkeley University of California, 13 March, 2009) from his research puts the figure at over 20,00,000 and Jayanti Basu (2013) cites figures as much as 35,00,002. Added to this are the refugees or those uprooted, with estimates by Ashis Nandy of 1,60,00,000 and Jayanti Basu for as much as 1,80,00,000. This is by far the largest refugee flow in world history … Then there were the attacks on women to dishonour their families and communal groups, a figure of 1,00,000 or more rapes and some 30,000 women abducted from their families and taken by the other side, whether Hindu, Muslim or Sikh.[55]

In summing up, one cannot fail to notice that migration has played a decisive/significant role in shaping the human world as we see it today. One deplorable reality has been the transformation of large sections of *bona fide* citizens of various nations into refugees who are deprived of citizenship and social status as victims of religious or ethnic intolerance suffered by them, largely in the developing world. Their subsequent enforced migration leads to a precarious existence which denies them all basic living opportunities, robbing them of human dignity and human rights.

As has been stated in this study, migration has had its wide-ranging variations, starting with our forefathers moving into newer surroundings in search of new pastures. This need for sustenance gradually changed to avarice and greed, which entailed the exploitation of defenceless populations in imperial times through slavery and indentured labour. Empire and settler colonies also opened the way for economic migrants who have formed temporary and permanent diasporas in former colonies. In more recent times people with skills continue to seek better opportunities, moving from the global south to the global north, leading to brain drain in their countries of origin. In the past few decades, climate change has impacted on millions who have become homeless and rootless as a result of natural disasters, while others are driven from their land because of conflict in civil and proxy wars and religious or ethnic persecution. This has created the new and ever increasing flotsam of the world, whom most countries deny entry to, unwilling to accommodate them or offer them asylum. Mankind has migrated since the beginning of human history, but the patterns of migration have changed through time, nevertheless, the inhospitable and hostile situation that climate and conflict refugees face today raises questions of the humanity of humankind.

NOTES

*Kingsley, P. *The New Odyssey: The Story of Europe's Refugee Crisis.* Guardian Books, London. 2016 : 44.

'Dozens of Eritrean exiles I met describe a totalitarian state where many citizens fear arrest at any moment and does not speak to their neighbours, gather in groups or linger longer outside their homes. Eritrea is not at war but its first and only President, Isaias Afwerki, plays up the possibility of a return to conflict with neighbouring Ethiopia, which ruled the country until the early 1990s. This threat is used to justify the absence of a constitution, the destruction of a judiciary system, and the implementation of indefinite national service that allows the government to treat each civilian as a modern-day serf for the duration of his or her life'.

***The Statesman.* Kolkata Issue (India). 15 March, 2020.

At least 3,84,000 died in Syria, including more than 1,16,000 civilians since the war began in March 2011, the Observatory for Human Rights said on Saturday.... The war has destroyed the economy and caused more than 11 million Syrians to flee their homes.... the latest death toll includes about 22,000 children and 13,000 women.... NGOs continue to denounce the human rights abuses by the Syrian Government, including lethal chemical attacks, torture, and arbitrary arrests.

***Fraser, B. *Bengal Partition Stories: An Unclosed Chapter.* Anthem Press, London. 2008 : 51,53-54.

End Note 106: Yet in the Western Zone of India Nehru effected an exchange of property and proceeded immediately to solve the problem of the West Pakistan refugees with such thoroughness that within two years they were resettled and integrated into the body of politic of India. (On the other hand) Nehru told a deputation of Nikhil Vanga Bastuhara Karma Parishad ... that they were aliens and that they should contact AICC Bureau dealing with foreigners.

End Note 125: When Nehru told the deputation from Nikhil Vanga Bastuhara Karma Parishad in 1948 that they were aliens, he based it on the fact that he had a memorandum from P.C. Ghosh West Bengal Congress. The consensus was that 'the refugees were all foreigners'.

End Note 126: On August 1948 (a year after Direct Action Day) Nehru writes a letter to Dr. B.C. Roy, 'I have your letter of August 4th about the influx from East Bengal … I think it was a wrong thing for the Hindu leaders of East Bengal to come to West Bengal' … It is interesting to note that Nehru refers to 'East Bengal' and not East Pakistan and it is obvious that he is determined to discourage the East Bengali minority community of East Pakistan from entering India.

1. Betts, A., Collier, P. *Refugee: Transforming a Broken Refugee System*. U.K.: Penguin Random, 2018, pp. 1-2.
2. Kingsley, P. *The New Odyssey: The Story of Europe's Refugee Crisis*. London: Guardian Books, 2016, p. 4.
3. *Ibid.*
4. Betts, A., Collier, P. *Refugee: Transforming a Broken Refugee System*. U.K.: Penguin Random, 2018, p. 3.
5. Kingsley, P. *The New Odyssey: The Story of Europe's Refugee Crisis*. London: Guardian Books, 2016, pp. 63-75.
6. *Ibid.*, pp. 172, 188-189, 191.
7. *Ibid.*, p. 262.
8. *Ibid.*, pp. 263, 293.
9. *Ibid.*, pp. 294, 311.
10. Zetter, R. "Conceptualising Forced Migration: Praxis, Scholarship and Empirics", in *Forced Migration: Current Issues and Debates*, ed. Alice Bloch and Giorgia Dona. London and New York: Routledge. 2019, p. 19.
11. Bloch, A., Giorgia D. "Forced Migration: Setting the Scene", in *Forced Migration: Current Issues and Debates*, ed. Alice Bloch and Giorgia Dona. London and New York: Routledge. 2019, p. 1.
12. *Ibid.*, p. 2.
13. Hyndman, J., Giles W. "Protracted Displacement: Living on the Edge", in *Forced Migration: Current Issues and Debates*, ed. Alice Bloch and Giorgia Dona. London and New York: Routledge. 2019, pp. 74, 77.
14. *Ibid.*, p. 9.
15. *The Statesman*. Kolkata. 28 August, 2019. *The Statesman*. Kolkata. 18 September, 2019.
16. Zetter, R. "Conceptualising Forced Migration: Praxis, Scholarship and Empirics", in *Forced Migration: Current Issues and Debates*, ed. Alice Bloch and Giorgia Dona. London and New York: Routledge. 2019, pp. 36-37.
17. Majidi, N., Schuster, L. "Deportation and Forced Return", in *Forced Migration: Current Issues and Debates*, ed. Alice Bloch and Giorgia Dona. London and New York: Routledge. 2019, pp. 89-90.
18. *Ibid.*, p. 100.
19. Livi-Bacci, M. *A Short History of Migration*. Cambridge: Polity Press, 2010, p. 90.

20. Betts, A., Collier, P. *Refugee: Transforming a Broken Refugee System*. U.K.: Penguin Random, 2018, p. 10.
21. *Ibid.*, p. 11.
22. *Ibid.*, pp. 62-63.
23. *Ibid.*, p. 63.
24. *Ibid.*, p. 75.
25. *Ibid.*, p. 76.
26. *Ibid.*, p. 77.
27. Betts, A., Collier, P. *Refugee: Transforming a Broken Refugee System*. U.K.: Penguin Random, 2018, pp. 91-92.
28. *Ibid.*, p. 129.
29. *Ibid.*, p. 199.
30. *Ibid.*, p. 215.
31. *The Statesman*. Kolkata. 9 March, 2020.
32. Fraser, B. *Bengal Partition Stories: An Unclosed Chapter*. London: Anthem Press, 2008, p. 14.
33. *Ibid.*, pp. 52 - 53.
34. *Ibid.*, pp. 29, 31.
35. *Ibid.*, p. 54.
36. "Migration and Migrants: A Global Review" in *United Nations World Migration Report*, 2018, p. 56.
37. *Ibid.*, pp. 32-34
38. *Ibid.*, p. 35.
39. *Ibid.*, p. 38.
40. Chatterjee, J. *The Spoils of Partition: Bengal and India 1947-1967*. U.K.: Cambridge University Press, 2017, p. 120.
41. *Ibid.*, pp. 122-123.
42. *Ibid.*, pp. 141-142.
43. *Ibid.*, pp. 136, 138.
44. Sen, U. "Memories of Partition's Forgotten Episodes: Refugee Resettlements in the Andaman Islands." *South Asia Chronicle,* 7 (2017): p. 163.
45. Sengupta, A. *They must have to go therefore elsewhere: Mapping the Many Displacements of Bengali Hindu Refugees from East Pakistan, 1947 to 1960s*. India: Tata Institute of Social Sciences, 2017, pp. 12-13.
46. Sen, U. "Memories of Partition's Forgotten Episodes: Refugee Resettlements in the Andaman Islands." *South Asia Chronicle,* 7 (2017): p. 157.
47. Sengupta, D. *Partition of Bengal: Fragile Borders and New Identities*. Cambridge: Cambridge University Press, 2016, p. 163.
48. Ghosh, A. *The Hungry Tide*. Delhi: Ravi Dayal Publisher, 2004, p. 118.
49. *Ibid.*, p. 119.
50. Sengupta, D. *Partition of Bengal: Fragile Borders and New Identities*. Cambridge: Cambridge University Press, 2016, pp. 176-178.

51. *Ibid.*, End Note No. 13, p. 150.
52. *Ibid.*, End Note No. 15.
53. *Ibid.*, End Note No. 21, p. 151.
54. *Ibid.*, End Note No. 26, pp. 151-152.
55. Basu, J. *Reconstructing the Bengal Partition: The Psyche Under a Different Violence.* Kolkata: Samya, 2013, p. viii.

Appendix I

TABLES ON COLONIAL STATUS OF DIFFERENT REGIONS IN AFRICA SINCE 1900

Table 1:1900

A	**Independent**
1.	Morocco
2.	Transvaal
3.	Liberia
4.	Orange Free State
5.	Abyssinia (Ethiopia)
B	**Coloniser: Britain**
1.	Gambia
2.	Sierra Leone
3.	Gold Coast (Ghana)
4.	Nigeria (Nigeria)
5.	Uganda
6.	Egypt
7.	Anglo-Egyptian Sudan
8.	Rhodesia
9.	Bechuanaland
10.	Cape Colony
11.	Nyasaland
12.	Natal
13.	Kenya
14.	Zanzibar
15.	Somaliland (Somalia)
16.	Walvis Bay
C	**Coloniser: Belgium (1920)**
1.	Congo Free State
D	**Coloniser: France**
1.	Tunisia
2.	Algeria
3.	French West Africa
4.	Equatorial Africa
5.	Somaliland
6.	Madagascar
7.	Comoro Islands
8.	Gabon
9.	Djibouti
E	**Coloniser: Germany**
1.	Togoland (Togo)
2.	Cameroon
3.	Southwest Africa (Namibia)
4.	German East Africa (Zambia)
F	**Coloniser: Italy**
1.	Eritrea
2.	Somaliland
G	**Coloniser: Portugal**
1.	Port Guinea (Guinea Bissau)
2.	Congo
3.	Angola
4.	Mozambique
H	Coloniser: Spain
1.	Rio De Oro (Western Sahara)
2.	Rio Muni (Equatorial Guinea)
I	Coloniser: Turkey
1.	Libya

Source: *Encyclopaedia Americana*. Compiled from the map showing, 'The Changing Face of Africa', in 1973 (Print); 1 : p. 321.

Table 2: 1920

1	**Independent**
1.	Abyssinia (Ethiopia)
2.	Union of South Africa
2	**Coloniser: Britain**
1.	Gambia
2.	Sierra Leone
3.	Gold Coast (Ghana)
4.	Nigeria
5.	Bechuanaland
6.	Swaziland
7.	Basutoland
8.	Rhodesia
9.	Nyasaland
10.	Zanzibar
11.	Tanganyika
12.	Uganda
13.	Kenya
14.	Somaliland
15.	Anglo Egyptian Sudan
16.	Egypt
3	**Coloniser: Belgium (1920)**
1.	Belgian Congo
2.	Ruanda Urundi (Ruanda)
4	**Coloniser: France**
1.	Morocco
2.	Algeria
3.	French West Africa
4.	Togoland
5.	Cameroon
6.	French Equatorial Africa
7.	Madagascar
8.	Comoro Islands
9.	French Somaliland
5	**Coloniser: Italy**
1.	Libya
2.	Eritrea
3.	Somaliland
6	**Coloniser: Portugal**
1.	Port Guinea (Guinea Bissau)
2.	Cabinda
3.	Angola
4.	Mozambique
7	**Coloniser: Spain**
1.	Morocco
2.	Rio De Oro
3.	Rio Muni
8	**Coloniser: Union of South Africa**
1.	South West Africa

Table 3: 1947

1	**Independent**
1.	Egypt
2.	Ethiopia
3.	Union of South Africa
4.	Liberia
2	**Coloniser: Britain**
1.	Gambia
2.	Sierra Leone
3.	Gold Coast (Ghana)
4.	Nigeria
5.	Bechuanaland
6.	North Rhodesia
7.	Swaziland
8.	Basutoland
9.	Nyasaland
10.	Tanganyika
11.	Zanzibar
12.	Kenya
13.	Uganda
14.	Somaliland
15.	Anglo-Egyptian Sudan
16.	Libya
3	**Coloniser: Belgium**
1.	Belgian Congo
2.	Ruanda Urundi (Ruanda)

4	**Coloniser: France**
1.	Tunisia
2.	Algeria
3.	Morocco
4.	Libya
5.	French West Africa
6.	Nigeria
7.	Cameroon (United Nations Territory)
8.	French Equatorial Africa
9.	Madagascar
10.	Comoro Islands
11.	Somaliland
12.	Togoland
5	**Coloniser: Portugal**
1.	Port Guinea
2.	Cabinda
3.	Angola
4.	Mozambique
6	**Coloniser: Spain**
1.	Morocco
2.	Ifni
3.	Sahara
4.	Rio Muni
7	**Coloniser: Union of South Africa**
1.	South West Africa (UN Territory ?)

Table 4: 1970

1	**Independent**
1.	Nearly all
2.	**Coloniser: France**
1.	Comoro Islands
2.	French Territory of Afaps and Issas in Somaliland
3	**Coloniser: Portugal**
1.	Port Guinea
2.	Cabinda
3.	Angola
4.	Mozambique
4.	**Coloniser: Spain**
1.	Sahara
5.	**Coloniser: Republic of South Africa**
1.	Southwest Africa (UN Trust Territory)

Appendix II

INTERNATIONAL MIGRATION OF INDIA: AN OVERVIEW

The phenomenon of population migration and associated redistribution of population leading to interplay and transformation of culture has been a significant matter of concern in the anthropo-geographical history of the world. In today's increasingly interconnected world, international migration has become a reality that touches nearly all corners of the globe, often making distinctions. between countries of origin, transit and destination obsolete.[1] The number of international migrants worldwide has continued to grow rapidly over the past twenty years. The spatial distribution of transnational populations varies greatly.

India was the leading country of origin of international migrants in 2019. According to the International Migrant Stock 2019 report (released by the Population Division of the United Nations Department of Economic and Social Affairs)[2], India with 17.5 million international migrants has emerged as the top source of international migrants, constituting 6.4 per cent of world's total migrant population.[3] 'India's Diaspora, the largest in the world, is distributed across a number of major countries of destination.'[4] India has been recorded as having the largest transnational community in the world in 2020 with 18 million persons from India were living outside of their country of birth.

Between 2000 and 2020, the size of the migrant population abroad grew for nearly all countries and areas of the world which is when India experienced the largest gain during that period (nearly 10 million). The Indian diaspora is distributed across a number of major countries of destination, with the United Arab Emirates (3.5 million), the United States of America (2.7 million) and Saudi Arabia (2.5 million) hosting the largest numbers of migrants from India. Other countries hosting large numbers of migrants from India include Australia, Canada, Kuwait, Oman, Pakistan, Qatar and the United Kingdom of Great Britain and Northern Ireland.

Home away from home: Where Indians go

Rank	Country	No of Indians (in million)	% of total Indian diaspora
1	UAE	3.5	22.4
2	US	2.0	12.8
3	Saudi Arabia	1.9	12.1
4	Kuwait	1.0	6.4
5	Oman	0.7	4.5
6	UK	0.7	4.5
7	Qatar	0.6	3.8

Total 15.6 million

Source: Human%20Migration%20in%20India.html

Migration to the Indian subcontinent has also been considerable, accounting for the population diversity on the subcontinent as India has witnessed the largest episodes of voluntary and involuntary migration in the world, and sustains considerable immigration, internal migration and emigration.

'India is a geographical and economic entity, a cultural unity amidst diversity, a bundle of contradictions held together by strong but invisible threads'[5] (Nehru, 1946, p. 562). The diversity in Indian history and culture is an outcome of the legacy of migration in the country. The 'stunning human diversity' in this country is consequential upon 'successive waves of migration'[6] as pinpointed by Tumbe (2018). The quest of Indian ethno-cultural diversity as a corollary of Indian international migration reveals that this diversity has also been exported outside the subcontinent.

An Overview of Prehistoric Migratory Groups in India

The first migrants came with the Coastal Migration/Southern Dispersal 65,000 years ago, whereafter complex migrations within South and Southeast Asia took place. West Eurasian hunter-gatherers migrated to South Asia after the latest Ice Age, but before the onset of farming. Together with a minor number of ancient South Asian hunter-gatherers, they formed the population of the Indus Valley Civilisation (IVC).

The Toba catastrophe, a volcanic super eruption that took place between 69,000 and 77,000 years ago at the site of present-day Lake Toba in Sumatra. According to Michael Petraglia, stone tools discovered below the layers of ash deposits in India at Jwalapuram, Andhra Pradesh point to pre-Toba dispersal. The population who created these tools is not known as no human remains were found. '.... had *Homo sapiens* colonized India before the eruption? The majority of genetic evidence seems to suggest that the initial colonization of India took place soon after the Toba event. It should be noted, however, that on the basis of this evidence, the hypothesis that modern human populations inhabited India before ~74ka and underwent extinction as a result of Toba cannot be ruled out'.[7] This establishes India as a destination for migrants long before recorded history. A new study provides "incontrovertible evidence" that the volcanic super-eruption of Toba on the island of Sumatra about 73,000 years ago deforested much of central India, some 3,000 miles from the epicenter, researchers report.

During this particular ice age, temperatures dropped by as much as 16 degrees centigrade as stated by Prof. Stanley Ambrose of Anthropology at the University of Illinois, who was a principal investigator in the new study with Prof. Martin A.J. Williams at the University of Adelaide. Williams discovered a layer of Toba ash in central India in 1980. The climate effects of Toba have been a source of controversy for years in the assessment of its impact on human populations.

In 1998, Ambrose proposed in the *Journal of Human Evolution* that the effects of the Toba eruption and the Ice Age that followed, could explain the apparent bottleneck in human populations that geneticists believe occurred between 50,000 and 1,00,000 years ago. The lack of genetic diversity among humans alive today suggests that during this time period, humans came very close to becoming extinct.

The carbon isotope analysis shows that forests covered central India when the eruption occurred, but wooded to open grassland predominated for at least 1,000 years after the eruption. Ambrose asserts, "This is unambiguous evidence that Toba caused deforestation in the tropics for a long time". This disaster may have forced the ancestors of modern humans to adopt new cooperative strategies for survival that eventually permitted them to replace Neanderthals and other primitive human species.[8]

With the decline of the IVC, and the migration of Indo-Europeans, the IVC-people contributed to the formation of both the Ancestral North Indians (ANI), who were closely related to west Eurasians, and the Ancestral South Indians (ASI), who were predominantly descended from ancient South Asian hunter-gatherers (Ancient Ancestral South Indians or AASI), who were distantly related to the Andamanese. These two ancestral populations (ASI and ANI) mixed extensively between 1,900-4,20υ years ago[9] and have created the peoples inhabiting the Indian subcontinent today, while the migrations of the Munda people and the

Tibeto-Burmese speaking people from East Asia have added new elements to the subcontinental demographic composition.

Migration of Indo-Aryan people, an ethno-linguistic group that spoke Indo-Aryan languages into the Indian subcontinent is noted as the Indo-Aryan migration. Indo-Aryan population movements from Central Asia into the region are considered to have started after 2000 BCE, as a slow diffusion after the Late Harappan period, which led to transformation of language in the northern Indian subcontinent. Ecological studies reveal that in the second millennium BCE widespread aridity lead to water shortages and ecological changes in both the Eurasian steppes and the Indian subcontinent causing the collapse of sedentary urban cultures in South Central Asia, Afghanistan, Iran, and India, and triggering large-scale migrations, resulting in the merger of migrating peoples with the post-urban cultures.[10]

A Temporal Analysis of the Contour of Indian Migrations

Ancient Migrations

The history of migration in ancient India from the middle of the first millennium BCE to circa 1300 CE, covering nearly 2000 years, is one of immigration, mainly from Central Asia *via* the north-western passes, with the incidence of emigration to the west and the east. It is a complex story of immigration and emigration of religions. Islam, Christianity, Zudaism and Zoroastrianism emigrated to India, while Buddhism emigrated to large parts outside the country. However, a large influx of population in the form of students and monks attracted by Buddhism took place from China to Nalanda in Bihar. Buddhism travelled in the opposite direction from the Indian subcontinent through monks and merchants along the Silk Road *via* the northern passes to East Asian countries. As Chinmay says, 'Both faiths popularized the wanderlust of asceticism and monastic ways of life, leading to new migratory circuits…'[11] (Tumbe, 2018). Immigrants were given various names, viz. 'Yavanas' for ancient Greeks, 'mlechha' for foreigners and tribals. As Tagore puts forward that:

> 'No one knows from where and on which invitation
> Streams of immigrants gush and ease out onto the ocean.
> Aryans, non-Aryans, Dravidians and Chinese,
> Shaka, Hun, Pathan and the Mughals –
> All merged as a single race'[12]
>
> (*Translated by Anjan Ganguly*)

Apart from religious migration, immigration from Western Asia to the north-west part of India with the appearance of agricultural settlements there, one notes a push factor related various circumstances of their homeland. Professor Bhattacharya has observed that these immigrants, 'having no bond with their country of origin' adopted 'newer traits in the new environment' as their culture 'lost its old flavour in course of time'. Thus, their settlements in the mountainous tracts of north-west India 'became Indianized', still retaining cultural affinity with Western Asia[13] (Bhattacharya, 2006, p. 5).

In ancient India, maritime traders crossed the Arabian Sea to reach the west coast, leading to the connection of Kerala with West Asia and even the Roman Empire. The Syrian Christian and Cochin Jews of Kerala have a legacy of well over thousand years. In the 7th century CE Islam reached the subcontinent through trade in Kerala. Again, Tamil Nadu (known earlier as Madras) on the east coast, had extensive links with South East Asia. The Chola Empire (850 CE-1250 CE) witnessed raids on Sri Lanka and the strait of Malacca. Envoys were dispatched to Chinese court to seek control of East-West trade in the Indian Ocean.

The returning of the armies of Alexander and other invaders were accompanied by many Indians emigrating to Central Asia and Europe. Hindu settlements have been observed in Armenia between 2nd century BCE to 4th century CE. Indian immigrants to Thailand, Vietnam, and Malay Peninsula have also been noted (Tumbe, 2018).

Emigration of 12000 Indian musicians to Iran (5th Century CE), of accountants, artisans, physicians, gunners and cooks in West Asia have also been noted. Indians were found in military establishments of the Byzantine Empire (14th Century). Indigenous tribes and lower caste Indians from north-western India form part of the most famous diasporic Romas and Gypsies who are for mobility can be identified. First, mass immigration of pastoral nomads from the Arid zones (East, Central, West Asia and East Europe), along with warriors consisting of the Rajputs, Marathas and armed peasants took place. The north-western part of India became an important battle-site among competing outside rulers for supremacy over the subcontinent. Influx of refugees from Central Asia has also been observed. 'Almost 4,00,000 cavalry and over 4 million infantry served the Mughal Empire under Akbar in the 16th century, when the total size of his empire was pegged at over a 100 million' (Tumbe, 2018). Afghan traders and warriors emigrated to Rayalseema, South India in the 17th and 18th centuries.

Second, integration of India's roads and seas with the consolidation of Turko-Afghan imperial power in Northern India was patronized by the

Delhi Sultanate which led to the in-march of Portuguese (Vasco Da Gama in south India), English, Dutch, French, Danish merchants. Indian textiles acquired a global market, steering the migration of people goods across Mughal India. Surat, the commercial port in western India developed as one of the largest cities. It accommodated numerous traders like the English, Dutch, Arabs, Persians, Turks, Armenians, Jews. The opposite stream of migration took place from coastal India when sailors and nannies moved to England or again when Tamil teachers left for Germany in the early 18th Century. Foreigners in the Mughal Empire came to be denoted by the Persian term '*firangi*'.

Third, pilgrims associated with trade in South India contributed to temple-generated urbanisation which benefited merchants and artisans. From Surat, new routes to Mecca were established for pilgrim-emigrants. Side by side, immigration of Christian missionaries from Europe to Goa took place. 'Migrations in the medieval period were at the intersection of complex military, commercial and religious networks' (Tumbe, 2018).

Large cities were founded during this period which drew a large number of merchants and artisans to them. Furthermore, immigration of skilled labour from beyond Indus was a significant aspect of medieval migration. The Mughal court attracted Persian painters, calligraphers and artisans. Persian carpet makers settled in the Godavari district of Andhra Pradesh. There was also emigration of Indian carpenters and shipwrights to Iran in the 18th Century with Nadir Shah.

Slavery was another aspect of medieval migration. Major international flow of slaves occurred between south-east Bengal and the Arakan (north Burma), 'the same passageway as that of recent Rohingya refugee crisis'(Tumbe, 2018). In the early 17th century, 18,000 Bengali slaves were observed in two centres of Arakan (Tumbe, 2018).

Modern Migration

Migration in the modern period is markedly different from the earlier periods. On the one hand, the colonial powers restricted the spatial mobility of the nomads (Banzaras of Thar Desert or Lambada of Telengana) (Tumbe, 2018) by transforming them into sedentary peasants and bonded labour respectively for surveillance and for increasing land revenue tax base. On the other hand, internal displacement of population was encouraged by the colonial rulers for endeavours like manufacturing of gunpowder, opium, indigo and construction of canals and roads in keeping with their divide and rule policy. About 3,50,000 boatmen were transformed into migrant labourers (Tumbe, 2018).

In the late 19th century, internal and international migration surged as a consequence of the wave of globalisation and intense famines. Between 1834 and 1937, 30 million people emigrated to Burma, Malaysia and Sri Lanka, of which 24 million returned. This was indeed circulation rather than migration. Circulation of a couple of million labourers also took place to the battlefronts in the early 20th Century during World War I and II.

Contemporary Migration

The main reasons behind contemporary international migration of India is forced or involuntary migration caused by natural disasters, wars, riots, persecutions and development projects. Since independence, more than 40 million Indians have been the victims of involuntary migration. Refugee immigrants from Tibet, Sri Lanka, Afghanistan and Myanmar amount to almost one million. The Partition of India (1947) and the Bangladesh War of Independence (1971) accounted almost 10 million refugee immigrants.

'Forced migration due to political strife is seen in Sri Lanka, where Tamil-Sinhalese conflict during the last two decades resulted in a large number of refugees, many of whom escaped to India. The end of colonial rule and Partition of India into two nation-states – India and Pakistan – in 1947, provoked migration of nearly 18 million people on the basis of religion. Nearly 6.5 million Muslims from India are reported to have emigrated to West Pakistan, while nearly 1 million left India for East Pakistan (the present-day Bangladesh after it got separated and gained independence in 1971). In a counter migration, nearly 10 million Hindus emigrated to India from Pakistan.'[14]

However, the primary reason for voluntary migration of 10 million Indians to West Asia and North America is economic; this fact has made India the world's largest recipient of international migrants' remittances. Again, the same number of an influx of people from Nepal and Bangladesh has been recorded. Thus, the size of the Indian international diaspora has recently crossed 25 million.

In August 2015, India and Bangladesh officially exchanged 162 enclaves, marking the end of a 300-year old anomaly that saw the fragmented territory of one sovereign power located inside another sovereign territory. Enclave residents have lived in virtual statelessness since Partition in 1947, without identity documents or access to essential services. As part of the deal, India and Bangladesh allowed residents to choose their country of citizenship.[15]

To sum up, it may be inferred that the dynamism/vitality ingrained in Indian international migration involves geo-political, economic, cultural, technological, administrative ramification/implication in a positive direction, on the one hand. On the other hand, the forced or involuntary migration portrays the reality of disaster, despair, poverty, deprivation and insecurity that humans face, which leads to migration.

Thus, in congruity with *The Human Development Report* of United Nations Development Programme (2009), it may be concluded that migration – 'an integral process of human development'[16] – plays a very important role in achieving sustainable development goals, thereby preventing migration could even be counterproductive. A forward looking outlook is necessary by formulating migration-centric policies, strategies, and institutional mechanisms in order to ensure inclusive growth and development and reduce distress induced by migration. Such policies may increase India's prospects for poverty reduction and achieving Sustainable Development Goals.

NOTES

1. United Nations, *International Migration Report 2015 Highlights*, Department of Economic and Social Affairs, 2015.
2. United Nations, *International Migration Stock 2019,* Department of Economic and Social Affairs, Population Division, 2019.
3. https://www.drishtiias.com/to-the-points/paper1/human-migration-in-india
4. United Nations, *International Migration 2020 Highlights*, Department of Economic and Social Affairs Population Division, New York, 2020.
5. Nehru, J. *The Discovery of India.* New Delhi: Oxford University Press, 1946, p. 562.
6. Tumbe, C. *India Moving: A History of Migration.* India: Vikings Penguin Random House, 2018.
7. Petraglia, M.D., Allchin, B. *The evolution and history of human populations in South Asia: Interdisciplinary Studies in Archaeology, Biological Anthropology, Linguistics and Genetics*. The Netherlands: Springer, 2007.
8. Science Daily, *Supervolcano eruption — in Sumatra — deforested India 73,000 years ago*, University of Illinois at Urbana-Champaign, 2009. https://www.sciencedaily.com/releases/2009/11/091123142739.htm
9. Peopling of India – Wikipedia https://en.wikipedia.org/wiki/Peopling_of_India#:~:text=Other%20IVC%2Dpeople%20mixed%20with,during%20the%20Hindu%20Gupta%20rule.
10. Joseph, T. *Early Indians: The Story of Our Ancestors and Where They Came From*. New Delhi: Juggernaut Books, 2018. https://www.booksatbahri.com/productdetails.aspx?id =211656&colid=0
11. Tumbe, C. *India Moving: A History of Migration.* India: Vikings Penguin Random House, 2018.

12. http://www.geetabitan.com/lyrics/rs-h/hey-mor-chitto-punyo-english-translation.html
13. Bhattacharya, B. *Urban Development in India since Pre-Historic Times*. New Delhi: Concept Publishing Company, 2006.
14. Hassan, M.I. *Population Geography*. New Delhi: Rawat Publications, 2005.
15. Shewly, H.J. "India and Bangladesh Swap Territory, Citizens in Landmark Enclave Exchange", in *Migration Information* source, Migration Policy Institute 2016.
16. United Nations Development Programme, *Human Development Reports*, 2009.
17. https://en.wikipedia.org/wiki/Indo-Aryan_migrations#cite_note-Kochhar2017-14
18. Joseph W. Eaton, ed. *Migration and Social Welfare*. New York: National Association of Social Workers, 1971.
19. Safa, H.I. and Brian, M. Du T. ed. *Migration and Development: Implications for Ethnic Identity and Political Conflict*. Mouton: De Gruyter, 1975.

Contributed by
Dr. Ballari Bagchi,
Associate Professor,
Post-Graduate Department of Geogrtaphy,
Prabu Jagatbandhu College,
Andul, Haora-711302,
West Bengal

Bibliography

Ananthanaryanan, S. *The Statesman*. Kolkata. 2019.

Baird, V. *The No-Nonsense Guide to World Population*. U.K.: New Internationalist, 2011.

Basu, J. *Reconstructing the Bengal Partition: The Psyche Under a Different Violence*. Kolkata: Samya, 2013.

Berlin, I. *Many Thousands Gone: The First Two Centuries of Slavery in North America*. 4th ed. Cambridge: The Belknap Press of Harvard University Press, 2003.

Betts, A., Collier, P. *Refugee: Transforming a Broken Refugee System*. U.K.: Penguin Random, 2018.

Bhattacharya, P. "India in the Rise of Britain and Europe: A Contribution to the Convergence and Great Divergence Debates." *Journal of Interdisciplinary Economics* 33.1 (2019): 24 – 53.

Bloch, A., Giorgia D. ed. *Forced Migration: Current Issues and Debates*. London and New York: Routledge. 2019.

Castles, S., Miller M.J. and Ammendola, G. *The Age of Migration: International Population Movements in the Modern World*. 3rd ed. New York: The Guilford Press, 2003.

Chatterjee, J. *The Spoils of Partition: Bengal and India 1947-1967*. U.K.: Cambridge University Press, 2017.

Childe, G. *What Happened in History*. U.K.: Penguin Books, 1886.

Childe, G. *Man Makes Himself*. 4th ed. U.K.: Spokesman Books, 2003.

Dalrymple, W. *The Anarchy: The East India Company, Corporate Violence and the Pillage of an Empire*. London, New Delhi: Bloomsbury Publication, 2019.

Dhindsa, K.S. *Indian Immigrants in United Kingdom*. New Delhi: Concept Publishing Co. Pvt. Ltd., 1998.

Editorial Column and News Item. *The Statesman*. Kolkata. 28 October, 2019.

Frankopan, P. *The Silk Roads: A New History of the World*. Great Britain Bloomsbury, 2015.

Fraser, B. *Bengal Partition Stories: An Unclosed Chapter*. London: Anthem Press, 2006, 2008.

Geddes, P. (Sir). *The Life and Work of Sir Jagadish C. Bose*. London: Longmans, Green & Co., 1920.

Ghosh, A. *The Hungry Tide*. Delhi: Ravi Dayal Publisher, 2004.

Gubili, Krishna. *Viriah*. India and Singapore: Notion Press, 2018.

Harari, Y. N. *Sapiens: A Brief History of Humankind*. London: Vintage. 2011.

Hirsch, Afua. *Brit(ish),On Race, Identity and Belonging*. London: Vintage. 2018.

Johnson, W. *Soul by Soul: Life Inside The Antebellum Slave Market*. Cambridge: Harvard University Press, 1999.

Kingsley, P. *The New Odyssey: The Story of Europe's Refugee Crisis*. London: Guardian Books, 2016.

Koser, K. *International Migration: A Very Short Introduction*. 2nd ed. U.K.: Oxford University Press, 2016.

Lahiri, H. *Diaspora: Theory and Transnationalism*. Hyderabad: Orient Black Swan, 2019.

Little, W., Fowler, H. W., Coulson, J. *The Shorter Oxford Dictionary of Historical Principles*. 3rd ed. rev. and ed. C.T. Onions. Oxford and Calcutta: Clarendon Press, Standard Literature Company Private Ltd, 1959-1961.

Livi-Bacci, M. *A Short History of Migration*. 2010. Trans. Carl Ipsen. Cambridge: Polity Press, 2012.

"Migration and Migrants: A Global Review" in *United Nations World Migration Report*, 2018.

Mukherjee, S. Perspective. *The Statesman*. Kolkata. 28 August, 2019.

Perspective. *The Statesman*. Kolkata. 13-16 October, 2019.

Possehl, G.L. *The Harappan Civilisation: A Contemporary Perspective*. 2nd ed. India: Oxford & LBH Publishing Co. Pub. Ltd., 1993.

Pries, L. *Refugees, Civil Society, and the State: European Experiences and Global Challenge*. U.K. and USA: Edward Elgar Publishing, 2018.

Saunders, K. *Indentured Labour in the British Empire 1834-1920*. Oxon and New York: Routledge. 2018.

Sen, U. "Memories of Partition's Forgotten Episodes: Refugee Resettlements in the Andaman Islands." *South Asia Chronicle* 7 (2017), pp. 147-178.

Sengupta, D. *Partition of Bengal: Fragile Borders and New Identities*. Cambridge: Cambridge University Press, 2016.

Sengupta, A. *They must have to go therefore elsewhere: Mapping the Many Displacements of Bengali Hindu Refugees from East Pakistan, 1947 to 1960s*. India: Tata Institute of Social Sciences, 2017.

Sjoberg, G. *The Pre-Industrial City: Past and Present*. Illinois: The Free Press of Glencoe, 1960.

The Encyclopaedia Americana. New York: Americana Corporation, Vols. 1, 2, 19, 25. 1973.

The Statesman. Kolkata. 28 August, 2019.

The Statesman. Kolkata. 18 September, 2019.

The Statesman. Kolkata. 9 March, 2020.

Thiara, R.K. "Indian Indentured Workers in Mauritius, Natal and Fiji", in *The Cambridge Survey of World Migration*, ed. R. Cohen. Cambridge: Cambridge University Press, 1995, pp. 63-68.

Tumbe, C. *India Moving: A History of Migration*. India: Vikings Penguin Random House, 2018.

Vertovec, S. "Indian Indentured Migration to the Caribbean", in *The Cambridge Survey of World Migration*, ed. R. Cohen. Cambridge: Cambridge University Press, 1995, pp. 57-62.

Webster's Seventh New Collegiate Dictionary. 2nd print. India: Scientific Book Agency, 1971.

White, Jr. R.C. *A. Lincoln: A Biography*. New York: Random House Trade Paperbacks, 2010.

Index

Act of Emancipation in 1833, 80
Adventurism, 43
Africa, 7, 54
African-Americans, 115
African Association of British Scientists, 10
Agricultural Revolution, 18, 19
Amanda Camp in Orissa, 154
American Independence, 77
Analysis of migrants, 48
  gender of, 48
  home remittances by, 49
  refugees and asylum seekers, 52
  work of, 48
Ancestral North Indians (ANI), 121
Andaman Islands, 152
Andean area, 33
Anglo-Canadian explorer, 7
Asia, 55
Asian migrants, 35
Assimilation, 112
Australia, 10, 11

Bengali Hindu refugees, 157
  from East Pakistan for the Andamans, Dandakaranya and other places, plight of, 145-164
Bipedalism, 1
Black people, 75
British Caribbean colonies, 84
British immigrants, 11
Bronze Age, 20

Canada, 108
Chinese labour, 94
Civil War of Emancipation, 79
Climate change, 40
Colonial Sugar Refining Company, 89, 91
Colonisation and Development Scheme, 152
Commonwealth, 112
Convicts, 11

Dandakaranya, 150
Declaration of American Independence, 77
Declaration of the Rights of Man, 78
Deportation, 136
Developing countries, 114
Diasporas, 29
Diversification of activities, 20
Dutch East India Company, 22

East African rift valley, 16
East India Company, 123
Emancipation Proclamation, 119
Environmental refugees, 40
Ethnic minority and social problems, 38
EU Commission, 140
European colonizers, 10
European Commission, 132
European Economic Area (EEA), 26
European emigration, 113
European Union, 26
Exporting terrorism, 59

Forced return or removal, 135

Geneva Convention on Refugees, 25

Global Terrorism Index (GTI) 2016, 58
Greek-City States, 65
Gulf Cooperation Council (GCC), 32

Harappan Civilisation, 122
High-income countries, 45
Hispanics, 38
Homo erectus, 16
Homo sapiens, 15, 16, 17, 18, 62
Homo soloensis, 16
Host countries and refugees, lack of mutual understanding between, 137
Hudson Bay Company, 7
Human capital, 136
Human Migration more a necessity than an impulse 15
Human migration, 3, 4
Human-evolutional history, 15

Ice Age, 1, 17
Immigration of foreign workers, 32
Immigration, source of, 36
Inca Empire, 6
Indentured labour,
  another instance of international mass-migration, 80
  cultural impact of, 94
India, 55
Indian urban civilisation, 7
Industrial Revolution, 21
Industrialising Asia, 36
Internal migration, 13
Internal-strife-ravaged countries, 138
International migration and development, theories of, 105
International migration, 21
  and the current trends, 44
  as Global force of development-skills and remittances, 29
  in the Context of Indian experience, 121
  recent growing, 31
International Organisation for Migration, 13
Interregional migration, 57
Iranian Revolution of 1979, 25
Iron Age, 21

Jihadis, 28

Labour migration to Europe, 24
Latin American regions, 31
Levant, Christian minorities in, 59
Libyan smugglers, 131
Lunar migration, 3

Mass migration, 116
  scope for new migration paths, 5
Mediterranean, 26, 27
Mesopotamian Civilisation, 7
Middle Ages, 69
Middle East, 34, 35
Migrant-receiving, 47
Migrants,
  a brief history of, 20
  an analysis of, 48
  and ethnicity, 29
  by refugees, 129
  flows and migration paths, 45
  human and non-human, 1-5
  involving Africa, 7
  of animals, 3
Migrant-sending countries, 47
Migration and development, theories of with special reference to India,105
Migration leading to slavery, changing phases, 64
  earliest phase, 64
  slavery in the medieval period, 67
  slave trade during the modern period, 68
Minimum statutory wage, 90
Movements of invasion and settlement, 106

Native American societies (Red Indians), 38
Natural increase, 113
Neanderthal, 15, 16
New Stone Age (Neolithic), 20, 21

New World, 22
Noakhali riots, 159
North America, 6, 22, 107, 108
Old Stone Age (Palaeolithic), 20
Organisation for Economic Co-operation and Development (OECD), 46
Oriental lands, 5
Outward movement of people, 22

Permanent temporariness, 133
Pithecanthropus, 15
Precolonial Africa, 66
Present study (the),
 introduction, 1
 themes of the, 15

Racism or discrimination, 31, 112
Recent migration, an analysis of, 44
Refugees, 61
 victims of political unrest, 129
Rehabilitation of refugees, 134
Rehabilitation programme in Dandakaranya, 155
Residential segregation, 39
Rohingyas from Myanmar, 38
Russian military intervention in Afghanistan, 37
Russian ventures, 6

Scandinavia, 67
Second World War, 9, 24, 110, 133, 134, 149
Sexual abuse of slave-women, 70
Sinanthropes, 15
Skilled emigration, 37
Slavery, freedom from, 77
Slaves, 66
 life of, 71
Slave-trade, 68, 72
Society of paradox, 93
South America, 6
Stone Age, 20
Sub-Saharan Africa, 33
Syrian and Afghan refugees, 56
Syrian refugees, 25

Trail of victims, 18
Trans-Atlantic slave-trade, 69, 71

UN Report, 49
UN World Migration Report 2018, 58
UN World Urbanisation Prospects 2014 Revision, 121
UN's Refugee Agency, 132
UNDESA (United Nations Department for Economic and Social Affairs), 46, 48
UNDP, 48
UNHCR, 25, 26, 37, 52, 53,131, 139, 145
United Nations Convention, 24
United Nations Resident Coordinator, 59

Vietnam War (1955-1975), 26

West and Central Africa, 54
Western Europe, 107
White Australian Policy, 35, 109
White ego, 98
White-distinctiveness, 99
Whiteness, 97
Women, 31
World Bank, 46
World Migration Report 2018, 58
World War II, 115